r.86

STAR WARRIORS

A PENETRATING LOOK INTO THE LIVES OF THE YOUNG SCIENTISTS BEHIND OUR SPACE AGE WEAPONRY

by

WILLIAM J. BROAD

SIMON AND SCHUSTER
New York

355.8251

7-86   BT   2200

Copyright © 1985 by William J. Broad
All rights reserved
including the right of reproduction
in whole or in part in any form
Published by Simon and Schuster
A Division of Simon & Schuster, Inc.
Simon & Schuster Building
Rockefeller Center
1230 Avenue of the Americas
New York, New York 10020
SIMON AND SCHUSTER and colophon are registered trademarks of
Simon & Schuster, Inc.
Designed by Irving Perkins Associates
Manufactured in the United States of America
1   2   3   4   5   6   7   8   9   10
Library of Congress Cataloging in Publication Data

Broad, William, date.
Star warriors.

Bibliography: p.
1. Lawrence Livermore National Laboratory.
2. Military research—United States. 3. Strategic
Defense Initiative. I. Title.
U394.L58B76   1985   355.8'251'072079465   85–14472
ISBN: 0–671–54566–3

The illustration on page 102 is reprinted courtesy of Harvey E. White, from
Fundamentals of Optics by Francis A. Jenkins and Harvey E. White, 4th ed.
(New York: McGraw-Hill,Inc., 1976), page 616.

CONTENTS

I call upon the scientific community who gave us nuclear weapons to turn their great talents to the cause of mankind and world peace: to give us the means of rendering these nuclear weapons impotent and obsolete.

—President Ronald Reagan
March 23, 1983

TO MY PARENTS

PROLOGUE

The breakdown occurred on our way back from dinner. It was late in the evening. Two cars carrying a dozen of us worked their way up California's Altamont pass, which stands about a thousand feet above sea level. The brand-new BMW had no problem. But the old blue station wagon started to wheeze and cough. It was a gas guzzler, bought for a song after the Arab oil embargo. Many of its dashboard lights were dark, windows frozen open, and doors rusted shut. At the wheel was Lowell Wood, 42, a big, ruddy man with a full beard who founded and led the group of young scientists at the weapons lab.

The station wagon was slowing down, bumping along the side of the road as the engine continued to sputter. Lowell pulled off at the top of the pass, and steam billowed as he lifted the hood. It was clearly a case of overheating compounded by some kind of electrical problem. The engine was dead.

Flashlights in hand, Lowell and two young friends tinkered with the engine as the BMW headed off to the lab for jumper cables and water. Meanwhile, the rest of us, caught in the middle of nowhere with nothing to do, eyed the countryside. The nearby hills were covered with windmills that towered in the moonlight. Here as few other places on earth, I was told, wind could be transformed into a steady flow of electricity.

Four of us set off to inspect the mechanical giants. We climbed a steep hill, working our way carefully through the dense brush at its top. Just ahead of me was Larry West, 28, a physicist who had broken paths for me all week long. A seven-year veteran of the group, Larry was a jovial extrovert, proud to introduce his friends, his firm, and his work, which included the design of super-computers and nuclear weapons.

Our last hurdle was a barbed-wire fence. A short run across a field of fresh-cut hay brought us to the foot of a windmill, which seemed to stretch hundreds of feet into the night. It looked like a huge, inverted eggbeater. Soon the young scientists were climbing all over its support structure, their flannel shirts and jeans flapping in the breeze. They analyzed how its blades caught the wind and what its gear ratios must be and whether or not it was an efficient producer of electricity. Bolted to its concrete base was a generator nearly the size of a phone booth.

"This man can tell you all about its efficiencies," Larry said as he introduced a young scientist with a cherub's face. The cherub, who had sat quietly and quite anonymously in the car, began a detailed explanation of how wind was converted into rotational motion. But before he could finish, one of our comrades high in the windmill got our attention by whistling.

"Hey," he cautioned, "somebody's coming."

The lights of a truck were snaking toward us down a ridge. We jumped off the windmill and rushed down the hill, leaping rows of hay and navigating the thicket. The steep final slope was tricky going in the dark. But we made it. And there was no way the truck could follow.

At the side of the road Lowell was deep in conversation with his young colleagues, having given up on the engine. Soon the cool night breeze forced us all into the station wagon to await the BMW. For nearly an hour we talked of time, space, and stars.

As usual, the discussion was laced with references to the group's resident mystic, Peter Hagelstein, 29, who, in typical fashion, was somewhere off on his own that night. Peter's name was often on people's lips. His young peers liked to joke about his fits of depression, insomnia, and insight. But most of all, they admired him. Peter was the brains behind the group's most dazzling success in the world of nuclear design. His triumph had come at a price, however. In the course of his work Peter's girl friend had denounced him and the whole profession of weapons design. Peter, not just a technologist but a pianist and devotee of French literature, had listened to little but Requiems by Brahms, Verdi, and Mozart after the breakup.

The conversation was cut short by the lights of the rescue party. Out of the passenger side of the BMW stepped Rod Hyde, 31, a math prodigy who had graduated from college at the age of 19 and grown into a scruffy, bearded engineer. Rod loved chess and science fiction. And he hated the Soviets with a passion, fearing they would foil his plans to escape the earth in a starship of his own design. The ultimate Cold Warrior, Rod while still in graduate school had invented a novel nuclear weapon to help deter Soviet aggression. Now, as Lowell's right-hand man, he was in charge of evaluating the technical merits of all sorts of advanced ideas put forward by members of the group.

It was May 1984 and, for me, deep into a week of roaming among the young warriors. They had graduated at the tops of their classes from some of the most competitive universities in America. Now they worked at the Lawrence Livermore National Laboratory, a federal facility for the design of nuclear weapons in a dry valley about 40 miles east of San Francisco. Theirs was a world of blue jeans, Coke bottles, and top-secret research that took place six or seven days a week, often all night long. Their labors had helped inspire the "Star Wars" speech of President Reagan and were now aimed at bringing that vision to life. Their goal was to channel the power of nuclear explosions into deadly beams that would flash through space to destroy enemy missiles. They labored not only on weapons but on supercomputers, communication devices, and other vital links for the creation of a defensive shield. And they talked late into the night about how to use their futuristic inventions.

I had come to the lab with some apprehension. After all, while these scientists were celebrating the energies of youth with nuclear breakthroughs, many young people around the world were calling for a nuclear freeze. But the warriors turned out to be anything but humorless automatons. They played pranks, swapped stories, and relished the fun of a community that resembled an extended family. Many professed concern about the future of their country. At times they seemed almost too wholesome; none of them smoked. Their worst addictions seemed to be the consumption of soft drinks by the case and the ingestion of large amounts of ice cream. Most striking, they were charged with enthusiasm for their common goal of using their technical advances to protect the nation from the horrors of nuclear war.

But their excitement also had a dark side. They could be arrogant. At times they seemed to believe that their labors gave them the power to save or destroy the world. They enjoyed black humor. Mimicking a greeting-card slogan, they liked to say the bombs of Livermore were the way to "send the very best."

Soon the station wagon rumbled to life, its radiator filled and battery boosted. We began our descent. The Livermore valley at its eastern end is mostly vineyards and ranchland. That night it was black velvet. As we came out of the hills, the darkness was cut by the distant lights of the weapons lab. It was a patch of artificial daylight about a mile on each side.

Livermore is one of two federal facilities in the United States for the design of nuclear weapons. It makes no production-line warheads. Instead, the weapons are imagined, sketched on blackboards, and modeled on computers. Months or years can pass before Livermore decides to build a prototype and ship its parts over the Sierra Nevada mountains for assembly at a government-owned patch of desert in the neighboring state of Nevada. There it is exploded deep underground in a carefully monitored test. If the weapon is a success, its blueprints may be distributed to the various factories around the country that make warheads for the nation's bombers, submarines, and silos.

All the weapons labs and production plants are owned by the federal Department of Energy, a civilian agency whose predecessor was the Atomic Energy Commission. Even though the warheads are meant ultimately for the military, their production and design is kept in the hands of civilians, a safeguard established by Congress in the earliest days of the nuclear era. The first weapons lab in the United States was Los Alamos, built high in the mountains of New Mexico during the exigencies of the Second World War. Part of the Manhattan Project, it gave birth to the first nuclear weapon. The second one was Livermore, which was carved out of an abandoned naval air station near the sleepy town of Livermore, California, in 1952. Today the lab employs nearly eight thousand people and has a budget of more than $800 million a year.

These two labs are the start of a big industry. In the United States, the development, production, storage, and planning for the use of nuclear weapons involves well over 200,000 people and an annual budget of more than $35 billion, according to Thomas B. Cochran and the coauthors of the *Nuclear Weapons Databook.* Every working day about eight new warheads roll off the assembly line. Old weapons are also retired, but the overall direction of the so-called "stockpile" is up. There are currently some 26,000 warheads in the American nuclear arsenal. By 1990, 30,000 are expected.

We turned off the road from the Altamont pass and made our way toward the lab, which started to dominate the horizon. The engine rumbled happily as we traveled down the slight grade.

The force behind the founding of Livermore was Edward Teller, a principal developer of the H-bomb. He lobbied passionately in Congress and the Pentagon for a second nuclear lab. The site was named after his good friend and the laboratory's co-founder, Ernest O. Lawrence, a Nobel laureate who ran the radiation laboratory at the University of California at Berkeley.

Despite its distinguished founders, the lab's first nuclear effort was a failure. In 1953 a bomb was placed atop a 300-foot tower at the Nevada test site. There was a small spark of light and swirl of dust as the countdown reached zero. Though mangled, the tower was left standing. Scientists from Los Alamos laughed as they scurried for their cameras.

At Teller's urging, Livermore worked hard over the years to surpass its nuclear rival in New Mexico. In a glossy brochure issued during its silver anniversary, Livermore claimed to have designed nine out of ten of the strategic warheads in the nation's nuclear stockpile.

The young men in the station wagon and their peers were laboring to carry on Teller's legacy of innovation. Their weapons, hailed as a third nuclear generation, are much more specialized and precise than the previous two generations, the atomic and hydrogen bombs. In weaponry the steps from the conventional to the first and second nuclear eras represent a thousand-fold increase in explosive power—a ton for TNT, a kiloton for fission, and a megaton for fusion. Powered by A-bombs and H-bombs, third-generation weapons take the explosive energy at their core and channel much of it toward targets rather than letting it escape in all directions.

The key designs of the young warriors number perhaps a half dozen in all. But the details of only one had slipped through the barrier of government secrecy that surrounds all aspects of nuclear design. This was Peter's invention—the nuclear X-ray laser, which produced powerful beams of radiation. Teller had taken the news of the X-ray breakthrough to President Reagan, who a few months later gave his "Star Wars" speech, calling on the nation's scientists to create an impenetrable defense against enemy missiles.

No shield now exists. The nation is naked. Soviet bombs can drop unimpeded on Milwaukee or Washington or any of the 1,000 missile silos scattered across the nation's heartland. There is no way to stop an enemy warhead as it speeds toward its target.

The young inventors of Livermore are attempting to change all that. They would have their weapons fire radiation over thousands of miles of space at the speed of light to destroy hundreds of enemy missiles. As the bomb at the core of an X-ray battle station exploded, multiple beams would flash out to strike multiple targets before the entire station consumed itself in a ball of nuclear fire. That is the vision. But many of the young scientists say their creations will actually bring about an era of unprecedented peace, because the world will know that the threat of nuclear attack from space has forever been laid to rest.

Their vision has won enthusiastic backing in some circles. After President Reagan's speech, a scientific panel headed by former NASA administrator James C. Fletcher called on the government to spend $1.5 billion over six years for research on third-generation nuclear weapons. The recommendation was taken up with vigor by the Pentagon in its research program for investigating the feasibility of a shield, known officially as SDI or the Strategic Defense Initiative. The program is evaluating not only nuclear-powered devices but also conventional lasers, particle beams, and kinetic-energy weapons.

The young scientists of Livermore want to use third-generation nuclear weapons against enemy missiles in their so-called boost phase, the best and most challenging point to try to destroy them. A shield must also stop objects that slip through this first line of defense, destroying warheads in the midcourse and terminal phases of their flight. In all, the five-year plan to investigate the feasibility of Star Wars is slated to receive $26 billion. If that money materializes, it will make Star Wars one of the biggest programs of research in the history of Western civilization, an effort rivaling the Manhattan Project and the Apollo moon program.

Estimates of the cost of actually building a shield have run between $200 and $1,000 billion. In the worst case (something all military men must consider), the cost per household in America would be about $12,000. Parts of the shield might be in place by the 1990s, with a complete shield coming into play sometime after the turn of the century—if, of course, Star Wars is deemed feasible and gets the go-ahead.

The talk in the station wagon started to quiet down. It was late and the long wait after the breakdown had taken its toll. Someone noted the new floodlights at the back of the lab. Management put them up, Lowell said, in anticipation of the most recent big protest. The idea was to better see demonstrators trying to climb barbed-wire fences at night.

Periodically, the lab has been hit by protests, especially in the 1970s. On the public roads that circle the lab, thousands of marchers would block traffic, hand out leaflets, and chant slogans. The protests eventually grew into an organized effort to sever the lab from the University of California, which runs the lab for the Department of Energy. In 1980, California Governor Edmund G. Brown, Jr., led the unsuccessful drive, telling the regents that "the university is profoundly compromising itself by becoming the intellectual home of nuclear weapons and participating in a runaway arms race."

The young scientists of Livermore have also come under fire; some of their critics are veterans of the earliest atomic projects in the United States. These were the whiz kids of an earlier era. They helped create the current stocks of nuclear weapons and the dogma that goes with them: that war will be deterred because no aggressor will risk the possibility of terrible and swift retaliation. We have missiles. The Soviets have missiles. If they fire, we fire, and vice versa. In short, the superpowers are held hostage to each other. Known as Mutual Assured Destruction, or MAD, this orthodoxy has kept an uneasy peace between the superpowers for more than a third of a century.

The critics see nothing but heresy in the "futuristic schemes" of the young scientists. They say a defensive shield would be futile, costly, and provocative. First, they say defensive weapons would fail to shoot down the 1,500 or so strategic missiles now in the Soviet arsenal. An enemy could outwit a defense by attacking it, by protecting the skin of offensive missiles, or by simply overwhelming it with increased numbers of missiles, decoys, and hard-to-detect cruise missiles. Second, they say the worldwide switch to defense would touch off an expensive round of new American offensive weaponry meant to try to penetrate a Russian shield. There would be an endless spiral of spending. Third, they say defense is bad even if it works because it can be viewed as aggressive. A nation with a shield, they say, might be tempted to launch a first strike against an enemy's missiles, confident it could brush aside any feeble attempts at retaliation. The real issue, the critics insist, is not new technology but whether a new generation of atomic scientists is doomed to repeat the mistakes of the past.*

During the week I spent with them, the young scientists repeatedly chided their critics for being largely uninformed about their work and the merits of defensive systems. Worst of all, they said, the skeptics have simply lost the ability to absorb new ideas.

We turned a corner toward the laboratory's main gate. Bright street lights illuminated nearby signs. "No Trespassing" read one. "Trespassing and Loitering Forbidden by Law" warned another. Beyond them was a fence topped with barbed wire, further still the dim outlines of darkened buildings.

We pulled into the lab's entrance. On our left was a squat wooden building where I had picked up my identification badge earlier in the week. To get it, I had given a secretary my social security number, birthplace and date, home address, and driver's license. A quick FBI check was said to insure that visitors had no

---

* Henry W. Kendall, chairman of the Cambridge-based Union of Concerned Scientists, once sent me a letter listing a dozen "older geniuses" who at one time had been nuclear enthusiasts like the young warriors of Livermore but who had eventually seen the "wisdom" of arms control. Included in Kendall's list: Robert F. Bacher, head of bomb physics at Los Alamos during the Second World War; Hans A. Bethe, head of theoretics at Los Alamos; Richard L. Garwin, early developer of hydrogen bombs; Philip Morrison, Los Alamos physicist who helped assemble the first atom bomb; Norman F. Ramsey, scientist in charge of bombs dropped on Hiroshima and Nagasaki; Theodore B. Taylor, Los Alamos bomb designer; and Herbert F. York, first director of the Livermore weapons lab.

criminal records or warrants out for their arrest. Clipped to a shirt collar, a visitor's badge was to be worn at all times. The permanent badges of the young scientists looked similar except for the addition of a color photograph that helped guards make quick identification checks. Another difference was that permanent badges gave access to top-secret areas and documents.

On our right as we drove toward the checkpoint was a large blue sign. "Prohibited items," it warned, included "guns, explosives, binoculars, telescopes, radio transmitters, recording equipment, and alcoholic beverages."

We stopped at the checkpoint, a small kiosk containing a guard with a gun. We held out our badges for inspection. The guard touched them all, one by one.

"I'll vouch for this man's identity," said Lowell as the guard touched my photoless badge. "Very good," said the guard as he waved us through.

It was long past midnight as we drove up to the group's cluster of small buildings, almost a mile from the entrance. The night was still young for the star warriors. Some of them would pass through doors equipped with combination locks, sit down at their desks, and work until dawn.

RECRUITS

It was morning of the first day. Lowell Wood, the leader of the young scientists, had been kind enough to let me stay at his house for the length of my week-long visit. The structure sat alone on a high ridge overlooking the Livermore valley. A steady wind sang in the tall grass and birdcalls were all about. In the valley below were ranches, small hills, country roads, and occasional trees. It was soothing in the morning light, the contours gentle, the hills smoothed by time. The valley floor was a golden-brown patchwork of grass, barley, alfalfa, and hay, the individual ranches having different shades. Toward the middle lay the town of Livermore, partly hidden by low hills.

Nearby was Teller's nuclear laboratory. Its site was, in effect, a fortress surrounded by mountains—the Diablo Range of the California coastal system. To the lab's south and east was a subsidiary range, the Hamilton, and to its west the Bay Hills. North of the lab were the Diablo Hills and Mount Diablo itself, a huge mass of rock topped with dark green vegetation.

A few tall structures stood out at the lab. But mostly it was a blur of hundreds of low buildings, trees, roads, and parking lots—nearly eight thousand people practicing their high-technology arts in the middle of nowhere.

The young scientists and their predecessors at Livermore had overcome not only geographical isolation but also a historic prejudice against the lab among the nation's scientists. Livermore was a child of the Cold War. The nation was divided and so was opinion on whether another weapons lab was needed. After it was founded, Teller's stormy career heightened its intellectual isolation. Many of the nation's scientists felt that Teller had betrayed and brought about the downfall of J. Robert Oppenheimer, the most famous scientist of his day. For a long time top graduates of the nation's best universities shunned both Teller and his Livermore lab.

The Hungarian-born Teller told his biographers, Stanley A. Blumberg and Gwinn Owens: "If a person leaves his country, leaves his continent, leaves his relatives, leaves his friends, the only people he knows are his professional colleagues. If more than ninety percent of these then come around to consider him an enemy, an outcast, it is bound to have an effect. The truth is it had a profound effect."

Though only 42 years old, Lowell had known Teller for almost a quarter century. As Teller's main protégé, Lowell now labored mightily in a very personal fashion to carry on the nuclear heritage.

Lowell's house, nestled in the gentle hills overlooking the lab, was a rambling, two-story structure made of logs—rugged yet modern, with large windows, skylights, and porches. Lowell said he designed it himself from modular units. It was still half-finished. He occasionally worked on it weekends and often had the help of young scientists from the lab.

A bachelor, Lowell spent little time at home. The house was big enough to easily accommodate visitors, and young scientists coming to work at the laboratory for a summer would sometimes stay several weeks. Yet it did not seem to be the focus of a lively social life. Lowell was wedded to his work and to the development of a cadre of young scientists. It was a calling that consumed him.

Lowell had a curious love of mechanical things that was evident in the area around his house. There was an old Thunderbird that had sat long undriven, a large bin of old car parts, and a huge solar panel for heating water. In general, it was not an area of neat walkways and well-trimmed grass but simply the top of the hill, covered with gravel and long, dry grass. Behind the house, near a road that curled down the back of the ridge, was a lone tree that had been sculpted by the steady wind, its branches swept back. Lowell called his home "Windy Ridge."

That morning I drove my rented car down to the city of Livermore, telling Lowell I would meet him later at the lab. I wanted to see what kind of diversions the area offered a group of young scientists and engineers who had recently attended college in such places as Pasadena, Palo Alto, Berkeley, Ithaca, and Cambridge.

The seven-mile drive to the heart of Livermore highlighted the area's rural nature. I passed a red farmhouse, a giant semitrailer loaded with hundreds of bales of hay, and wide fields dotted with cows. The town itself, incorporated in 1876, had a population of about 50,000. Its center was marked by a flagpole at the intersection of First Street and Livermore Avenue. Nearby was one of the town's oldest structures, the two-story Masonic Building, dedicated in 1905. Across the street was the American Bakery, painted red, white, and blue. Surrounding the intersection were storefronts that bespoke small-town California and the West. There was the Livermore Saloon Casino. There was the Tri-Valley Cobbler & Boot Shop, containing row upon row of cowboy boots in a striking assortment of colors. "America's most wanted boots at discount prices," read a sign in the window. Across the street was the California Gun Works, and in another direction the Hideaway Restaurant ("Dance & Cocktails").

Scientists from the lab probably lived all over the place, but their impact was not particularly evident. The first restaurant I passed after leaving city center was Señor Taco ("Burritos 49 cents"), followed by Mountain Mike's Pizza. On the streets, along with all the compact Japanese imports, were a number of souped-up cars, hot rods, and pickup trucks.

Livermore was not very far from the nation's hub of high technology, Silicon Valley. But its only real high-tech development was a facility on the outskirts of town that made integrated circuits out of silicon wafers. It employed about 300 women, mostly homemakers, to perform delicate assembly work.

The town had a two-year community college that offered an Associate of Arts degree. According to a brochure handed out by

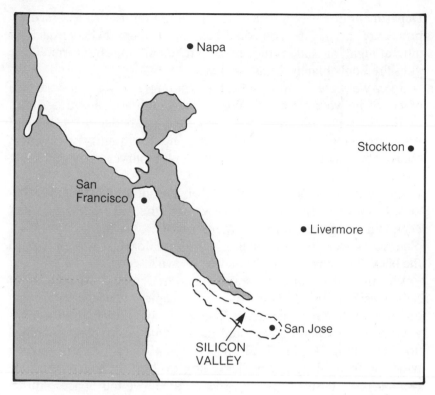

an amiable lady at the Chamber of Commerce, the city's other "cultural" resources included "one library, three newspapers, one radio station, seven TV channels, one cable TV system, twenty-six parks and playgrounds, and one theater."

In short, as might be expected, Livermore was the sort of place that might wear thin after a few weeks. Nevertheless, in one respect it was quite special. The official seal of the city depicted a cowboy on horseback, a cluster of grapes, and, in the very center, an atom, the symbol of the nuclear era, its electrons whirling about the letter *L*.

I met Lowell in one of the lab's cafeterias, where we had a late lunch. It was located outside the barbed-wire fence. The large, modern room was empty except for a small group of men in battle fatigues and camouflage hats who had knives and guns strapped to their belts. Lowell said they were working under the aegis of the

Department of Energy, which was holding exercises to test security procedures at the lab. You could hear bursts from their submachine guns at night, he said, as they tried to take buildings by storm. Their guns fired only blanks, he assured me.

Soon we were driving the lab's winding roadways toward the offices of his young recruits. We passed buildings, pine trees, piles of girders, something that looked like a huge boiler or an ancient submarine, a fire station, radio towers, and, to my surprise, a fitness course courtesy of the Perrier company, the purveyors of sparkling water.

We pulled up to a cluster of four or five squat, flat-roofed buildings. Lowell said they were actually prefabricated trailers that had been joined together to form larger structures. On the grounds were pine trees—not groves of them, just a few dozen scattered toward the back. The surrounding grass was brown.

We entered a long hallway and were greeted by strains of rock music from someone's office. "Dreamer, you always were a dreamer . . ." went the lyrics. The walls were covered with maps and posters and photographs and plants. One bushy plant stretched floor to ceiling. A philodendron perhaps 40 feet long crisscrossed back and forth along one wall. "Going to Work in Space" read the caption on a poster showing a fiery launch of the Space Shuttle. Another held an inspirational saying attributed to Victor Hugo: "There is nothing more powerful than an idea whose time has come."

I peeked inside a bright office with a sunny window. Here was a continuation of the plant motif, huge ferns and philodendrons and avocado plants taking up half the space. There were two computer terminals on the cluttered desk. A poster showed Earth suspended in space, "Love Your Mother" cut in bold letters across its top. The numerous bookshelves were only half filled with books and binders. The rest of the space was taken up with magnetic tapes for a large computer, stacks of records, and a stereo component system, including turntable, amplifier, and headphones.

The offices and hallways were alive with young men. Women were nowhere to be seen. Jeans, checked shirts, and running shoes were common. In general, members of Lowell's group looked as if they would fit into the engineering or physics department of any major university in America. The only visible difference was that each person had a green badge clipped to his collar.

Amid such casualness it was easy to miss the potential power of this dedicated group of young men. At Los Alamos during the Second World War, the average age of the technical personnel had been 27, and the people in the hallway looked about the same age. The overall impression was one of activity. Individuals came and went, huddled for a few minutes, and then moved on. In one office three young men were locked in conversation, one standing, one straddling a chair, and one sitting on the floor, his back to the wall. A paging system came alive every so often with the voice of a woman calling one of the young scientists: "Bruce McWilliams, com line"—meaning McWilliams was to pick up one of the nearby telephones.

In the military, such a group is sometimes known as a "skunk works," an elite band of scientists and engineers that labor in secrecy on important projects. The outside world, if it knows about them at all, has no idea what such individuals do. One skunk works that eventually became well known built the U-2 and SR-71 spy planes. Military labs around the nation have a number of these secret groups, which often go under the innocuous title of "Special Projects Offices." The one at Livermore was unusual in the breadth and depth of its endeavors.

Lowell's group was not universally admired at the lab. Some researchers dismissed it as a clique of brash young scientists who were spoiled and snobbish. Hugh DeWitt, a critic within Livermore who opposes the construction of new weapons, had told me its members were "bright young hot shots who are socially maladjusted. All their time and energy is spent on science. There are no women, no outside interests. They focus on far-out technical projects and extreme defense ideology."

On the other hand, a high Livermore official praised both them and Lowell. "They're a unique group, eccentric and extraordinarily bright," Roy D. Woodruff, head of the lab's weapons programs, told me. "Lowell is the leader and, if you will, the guru-advisor to these guys. He has been extraordinarily gifted in finding talent, and in bringing it into the laboratory to work on scientific programs that are second to none."

Whether praised or ridiculed, the young scientists by their very presence represented a critical victory. A lab brochure by Bruce M. Boatman, *Institutional Plan 1983–1988,* described how recruiting for the lab was being inhibited by such factors as "nuclear-freeze ballot initiatives, an increasing number of public demonstrations, some resurgence of anti-weapons groups on college campuses, the media accounts of litigation arising out of early weapons-test programs, and the general public concern over radiation effects." Some of these factors would pass, the brochure noted, barring further incidents and publicity. Even so, "the competition for high-technology personnel will remain strong, and the recruiting for weapons programs will be particularly difficult."

As we wandered the halls, Lowell took me into a room that served as a kitchen. It had a microwave oven, a refrigerator, and an upright freezer. Along one wall, stacked floor to ceiling, were dozens of cases of Coke and Diet Coke in 16-ounce bottles. On the table with the microwave were a telephone, a popcorn popper, and a cluster of condiments. Along another wall was a shelf filled with empty tubs—for ice cream, it turned out. The upright freezer was filled with huge tubs of ice cream. A list on the door kept track of how much Coke and ice cream each person consumed.

Lowell was putting ice cubes into plastic glasses when he discovered that the ice maker was jammed. Out of his pocket came a jumbo Swiss Army knife, the kind that seems to have at least a dozen blades. He immediately fixed the balky device.

Cokes in hand, we walked to a small library. With a large round table at its center, it also served as a conference room.

Lowell was a big, powerfully built man, heavy set and well over six feet tall. His reddish-brown beard gave way to light brown hair that spilled over his collar. Overall he was rough in appearance, with a crease in his nose, perhaps from a fall. His eyes were very direct and quick. And he had a quick smile, too, one that could turn into a smirk. When he talked his whole body could become animated, his frame becoming electrified, his eyebrows arching up, his shoulders hunching forward, his voice taking on an edge. Unlike scientists who wallowed in technical jargon, Lowell was a gifted speaker. He loved word play.

Lowell was the kind of person who inspired either love or hate in those who knew him. I heard both. He had been called rude, crude, sarcastic, arrogant, cocky, crazy, irresponsible, and abrasive. He also had been called clever, smart, loyal, witty, patriotic, creative, sensitive, and deft. From my limited experience, he clearly had a lot of energy. He talked incessantly.

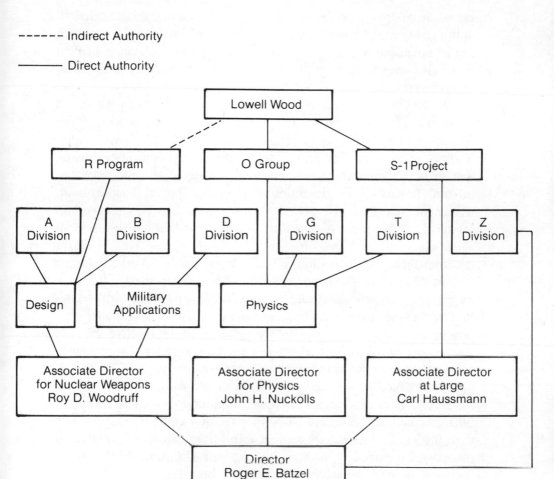

I wanted to know what the group did. The Laboratory's literature on the subject had been extremely unhelpful, amounting to
disinformation. A booklet issued on the occasion of the lab's thirtieth
anniversary said Lowell's group was "engaged primarily in research
on an advanced digital computer." I knew there was such a project
but I also knew that the group had been midwife to some of the most
controversial advances in the history of nuclear weaponry.

During the next three hours, Lowell answered all my questions
in detail. First he outlined the bureaucracy. In the world of the
lab—which included large programs for weapon design, weapon
testing, military applications, lasers, magnetic fusion, laser fusion,
chemistry, computation, engineering, biomedicine, and environ-
mental research—his dominion was in the physics department,
which in total had just over 300 employees. Lowell belonged to
none of the department's regular divisions but had his own special
turf.

His primary organization was O Group, which worked on the
design of nuclear weapons and other advanced projects. It had a
dozen full-time members and another dozen known as "indeterminates." These were part-time graduate students and people no
longer actively associated with the group who kept active security
clearances so they could return at a moment's notice.

His second organization was a spinoff known as the S-1 Project.
It was devoted to the design and construction of a series of ever
more powerful and compact supercomputers. The final computer
in the sequence was meant to be the size of a cocktail coaster. The
S-1 Project had about three dozen full-time members, indeterminates, and technicians. As was the case with O Group, all S-1 members had to have top-secret clearances.

Security at the lab differed from building to building, Lowell
explained. There were three levels. The lowest was a "red" area.
Here workers had "P clearances" that gave access to secret materials. We sat in a red-area building that was the headquarters of
the S-1 Project. Like all buildings at the lab, it had a number, this
one being 1877. The next level of security was a "green" area,
where "Q clearances" gave access to special top-secret materials related to the design of nuclear weapons. The buildings and offices of
Lowell's groups were a mix of red and green areas. At the lab the
most closely guarded sites of all were green ones known as "exclu-

sion" areas, home to such activities as the fabrication of nuclear weapons. Besides the fences that ran around the lab's mile-long perimeters, exclusion areas were surrounded by an extra set of fences topped with barbed wire.

Next, Lowell explained what brought young scientists to his groups and what kept them there. One factor, he said, was that he was an interviewer for the Hertz Foundation, an organization that gave fellowships to graduate students in the applied sciences. John D. Hertz—a poor boy made rich by his many business ventures, including Yellow Cab and Hertz rental cars—started the foundation in the 1940s as a way to challenge what he saw as threatening advances by the Soviets. Both Lowell and Teller were now on the board. The foundation's address was a post office box in the city of Livermore. It supported some 120 graduate students every year with the income from assets of about $14 million. The weapons laboratory, with 29 of them, was the largest single employer of Hertz fellows and alumni. According to a Hertz brochure, the foundation has an "express interest in fostering the technological strength of America" and "requires all fellows to morally commit themselves to make their skills and abilities available for the common defense, in the event of national emergency."

Sometimes in the course of Hertz interviews, Lowell said, an extremely talented individual would appear whom he would try to recruit for Livermore. One of the brightest was Rod Hyde. Lowell met Rod in the spring of 1972, when the young engineer was getting ready to graduate with straight A's from the Massachusetts Institute of Technology, in Cambridge, Massachusetts, at the age of 19 The teenager came to the weapons lab that summer, mainly to work on the design of a starship. Later he became a Hertz fellow. After joining the lab full time he rose through the ranks, and now analyzed the feasibility of new ideas in O Group, including those relating to nuclear weapons.

Lowell said Rod was eager to come to the weapons lab because his alternatives had been so dismal. "Kids usually get treated extremely poorly until they get their bachelor's degree," he said. "They are considered subprofessionals, not preprofessionals. So they usually are unemployable except in minimum-wage jobs serving hamburgers across the counter. In the summers Rod had been doing agricultural work—stoop labor. The previous summer he had graduated to working at a cannery in rural Oregon—strawberries and beets. After he came here I asked why he had accepted the position. He said, 'It was a choice between your bomb factory and a beet cannery'!

"And that's the case with a lot of other bachelor's-degree holders, ones just out of school. Their employment history has been bleak. The prospect of coming to a laboratory—any laboratory—and doing research is extremely appealing."

I asked if he was ever accused of attracting young students with promises of peaceful research and turning them into bomb makers.

"They're free, white, and twenty-one when they come here, with one or two exceptions," Lowell answered. "My ability to turn them into bomb builders and hold them here is obviously almost non-existent. They don't have to turn if they don't want to. They don't have to stay here if they don't want to. There're lots of people who do nothing but basic research in O Group, who never set their hands to bomb design or defense work."

In contrast to Lowell, lab administrator Roy D. Woodruff had put the situation this way during an earlier interview: "By and large, many of these people eventually work on weapons applications. When they first come a lot of them don't have that in mind. But it turns out that they feel a lot more comfortable with the overall ethics after they start looking at the question of where the lab is going and why we're doing what we do, questions of world stability and that sort of thing. Some of the best and most intellectually sound debates on issues of weapons development and deployment occur right here. These people are well informed. It's not that they see the future any clearer than anybody else, but they've really thought about it. Sometimes I think that people opposed to these activities have not."

As we talked, Lowell, sipping Coke, described several people who had left his realm, not because they had qualms about the work but because they decided to test their talents in the marketplace. Several had become millionaires. Most of these entrepreneurs still kept a connection to the lab (as indeterminates) or as part-time consultants. Lowell was clearly proud of their achievements. Their story also suggested the diverse types of research projects that started in the group—and where some of the unclassified ones could go.

"People that come to O Group tend to be unusually capable, in my judgment," Lowell said. "And people who stay here for a while tend to become very hard working if they weren't before they arrived. The combination is almost unbeatable."

Two alumni who had achieved superstar status were Thomas M. McWilliams and L. Curtis Widdoes, Jr. Curt and Tom came to O Group in 1975, Curt a graduate student in the Department of Computer Science at Stanford University and Tom just before starting graduate work there. Both were Hertz fellows. At school they had the same thesis advisor, and at Livermore Lowell asked the graduate students to team up and give some thought to designing a supercomputer from scratch.

Supercomputers are the fastest computers of all, some performing billions of operations per second, whereas most home computers do thousands. They are used for extremely complex problems, such as forecasting the weather, exploring for oil, designing aircraft, modeling nuclear weapons, and breaking secret codes. Because of their cost ($5 million or more) and complexity, by the early 1980s there were still only about seventy supercomputers in the world. There were fewer still at the time Lowell handed out the assignment to Curt and Tom.

Undaunted, the students sat for excruciatingly long hours at their terminals, writing programs that told a computer how to design and build another computer. Surprisingly, they made quick headway. "It was clear at the end of four years that they were going to win in a startlingly large fashion," said Lowell. "What Curt and Tom realized, to their everlasting credit, was that the things that people usually do by hand could be done better by computer. They were the first people to have a computer design a computer. Their software did the design, tested it to make sure it was done right, and checked to see that it worked at the specified speed. Computer companies used to have squads of people to do those kinds of things."

Using their program, they designed the S-1, a computer meant to be roughly comparable to the Cray-1, at the time the fastest supercomputer in the world. By automating the tedious and time-consuming aspects of the job, they had been freed to concentrate on the creative elements of design.

Their advance was named SCALD—for Structured Computer-

Aided Logic Design—and it soon played an important role in the birth of an industry known as computer-aided engineering. After designing the first S-1 computer, Tom and Curt took their program and founded a company, Valid Logic Systems, Inc., in the heart of Silicon Valley. Since their program had been developed at a federal laboratory with public funds, it was in the public domain, and other people founded companies to sell and develop the innovative tool at about the same time.

"The market value of these firms is now somewhere near a billion dollars," said Lowell. "Last fall when they took Valid public, it had a market value of about $150 million. And the stock's been generally going up since then."

Other O Group alumni had founded companies that also prospered, Lowell continued. One was Lumicon, a firm that makes innovative filters and films for amateur astronomy. Another was Symbolics, which markets programs and computers in the field of artificial intelligence. Lowell said their founders are all millionaires.

The door of the small conference room popped open and in walked Larry West. "Hi," he said and plopped into a chair. Larry, 28, was a senior O Grouper pursuing his Ph.D. at Stanford while working at the weapons lab. He too was a Hertz fellow. Tall and mustachioed, Larry had so much energy and earnestness that his words spilled out in a torrent. "Curt and Tom were considered off-the-wall crazy because it was well known that the big computer companies would have done it if it had been possible," he said. "The fact that it hadn't been done meant it was foredoomed—they were absolutely wasting their time. They got an enormous amount of ridicule. Just because people say you're crazy doesn't mean you're going to win, but sometimes it sure looks like a necessary condition for success."

Lowell explained that Larry was facing his own challenge in trying to create a new generation of supercomputers that ran on light instead of electricity. Such a goal, he said, was something many professionals in the computer world had ridiculed. Lowell then shooed Larry out of the room.

As the door closed, I asked if Larry's goal was indeed a dream.

"No," Lowell answered, "it cannot be proven to be impossible. It's a challenge. One of the more interesting ways we proceed around here is to try and write a proof that something is impossible.

It's a good way to spot the chinks in the armor, so to speak. A lot of things can neither be proven nor disproven. Physical theory is mainly just silent. It doesn't say anything."

An example of an "impossible" problem that was solved recently by one of the young scientists, said Lowell, was the theory behind the construction of a gamma-ray laser pumped by a nuclear bomb. All lasers produce concentrated beams of energy. A gamma-ray laser would be the most powerful of all, having higher energy and shorter wavelength than even an X-ray laser. A decade ago, Lowell explained, he and another physicist at Livermore had written a paper saying construction of a bomb-pumped gamma-ray laser was all but unattainable. "Unfortunately it sort of finished off the field," Lowell said. "In the preceding half dozen years there had been lots of papers on the subject. But this one was too successful. It killed things off. It didn't leave enough loose ends to build on or to tie subsequent work to."

Then unexpectedly a young O Group scientist popped into Lowell's office late one night and asked how hard it was to create a gamma-ray laser. After Lowell explained the formidable obstacles, the young scientist suggested a way to overcome them.

A Hertz fellow, David B. Tuckerman was typical of the bright, ambitious scientists that populated Lowell's group. Boasting straight A's, he had graduated with simultaneous B.S. and M.S. degrees from the Massachusetts Institute of Technology in 1980 at the age of 22. Recently the young scientist had been awarded a Ph.D. from Stanford University after writing a thesis on methods of extracting large amounts of heat from small objects, such as integrated circuits the size of an aspirin tablet.

Late that night in Lowell's office, Dave suggested that his heat-extraction technology could be applied to the problem of creating a gamma-ray laser. "With the right kind of cooling," said Lowell, "we decided you could probably pump it with a bomb. It looks very promising. The reason I mention it is that it's an interesting scientific experiment. It would never be a weapon. You have to do absolutely crazy things, which means it has exactly zero military potential. But it's a very interesting physics experiment. It would create a type of electromagnetic radiation that is almost impossible in principle to get any other way. It would also have a frequency purity roughly a million times greater than anything else."

The atmosphere in which the impossible was pursued, in which young men were challenged with problems that older individuals had relinquished, was clearly one of the things that kept the bright young scientists of O Group from running off on their own. Instead, the recruits signed up for extended tours. They seemed to be hooked on the challenge.

Lowell said another attraction of the place was its spirit of co-operation. Last year he posed the group a "national security" problem—often a euphemism for the design of a nuclear-pumped weapon. "I called them together and said we were going to have evening meetings because there was this important problem to be solved. By the end of the second meeting, the outline of the solution had been obtained and after a couple more meetings it had been fleshed out in adequate detail to do a design for detailed computer simulation and so forth. It was genuinely a group effort. People remember that it wasn't any single person's idea—including the ones that didn't bother to show up and subsequently told me to insist that they come to such meetings in the future. Those sort of recollections can be compelling—that we're strong individually but even stronger as a group."

These two episodes—Dave Tuckerman's idea for the gamma-ray laser and the group's session of collective weapon design—showed how easy it was for the young scientists to lend their talents to nuclear issues. As Lowell said, many people in O Group probably never have anything to do with bombs or military matters. Yet the spirit of the place was such that nuclear problems were often addressed, a situation quite different from the one described in the laboratory's booklet.

The episodes also hinted at the variety of the place, which was undoubtedly an attraction. There seemed to be no single, all-encompassing project. By contrast, a good part of Silicon Valley was created by teams of young workaholics who slaved on pet projects. According to Lowell's description, O Group maintained that kind of drive despite its diversity. There seemed to be lots of cross-fertilization. People would tinker on the projects of the guy across the hall as well as on their own. The lure of the place was becoming evident. The young scientists were engaged in a high-tech free-for-all.

It was a remarkable creation, and it traced its roots to Teller. I asked if the elderly physicist was currently at the weapons lab. Lowell said he was getting ready to go on a trip, but with luck we might slip into his office for a quick visit.

Two phone calls and a short drive later, I was ushered into Teller's office atop Livermore's tallest building. Though a prime force in the lab's founding and once its director, he was now retired and served as a high-level consultant. The back wall of his large office was covered with documents and pictures, including a photo of Lowell and more than one mushroom cloud. Teller was sitting at his desk. To his left was a large safe for top-secret documents. Above his desk was a chart of the periodic table of the elements and their radioactive isotopes. In front of him on a shelf were a number of books, *Real Peace* by Richard M. Nixon standing out. On his desk were African violets and a picture of his wife, Mici. Out his window was a tiny dot on the horizon that appeared to be Lowell's house on Windy Ridge.

Teller turned as I sat down. He was 76 years old and had recently had a serious heart operation. "Well," he said in his famous, slow Hungarian drawl, "what can I do for you?"

It was easy to understand the dark portraits that had been painted of this man. He seemed almost a caricature of himself. His huge, bushy eyebrows came together and the melancholy gray eyes bored into you. The voice could easily be called doom-laden, especially when he set out the words one by one, like great blocks of granite.

I asked whether a defensive shield was possible and to what extent its development depended on the efforts of O Group.

"I can tell you that the ideas with which we are now working are greatly superior to what we had ten or more years ago," he answered. "But, on the other hand, defense is *not* easy."

"The fact that a great many American scientists, perhaps the majority, are against it puzzles me, disturbs me," Teller continued. "I believe that my young friend, Lowell Wood, is a first-rate scientist. And I know that he has an extraordinary knack for getting talented young people interested in the topic and making them work hard and willingly on it—not like a chain gang but like a football team. Still, this is a small fraction of the talent there is in America. And almost necessarily it is much less than the talent the Soviets can deploy in the same field. If we had worked during the Second World War in the same way, Hitler would have won."

Lowell came into the office and quietly sat down.

"A lot of ingenuity is needed," Teller continued. "And we just don't have enough talent. Lowell and his friends are doing an incredible amount of work. But the number of people on our side who could make contributions but who instead exhaust themselves in fabricating objections is legion. The majority of these people opposed the H-bomb because it was too terrible. Now they are opposing defense because it is apt to make a nuclear war less terrible and therefore more probable. Somehow I don't feel that they can be right both times."

I mentioned that his old colleague Hans A. Bethe, a Nobel laureate, seemed firmly opposed to the notion of defense when I had spoken with him before coming to the lab.

"Bethe sees the future and I don't," Teller replied. "Bethe sees the future in a too easy manner. He was there at the birth of quantum mechanics and he was there when we constructed the first atomic bomb. Yet he now says there won't be anything new under the sun. Hasn't he seen enough new things?"

The interview over, a secretary escorted me to an area outside the building and the barbed wire where I was to wait for Lowell. I sat on a bench under a tree and enjoyed the shade.

During our conversation, Teller had twice mentioned the H-bomb and its critics. And twice he questioned their judgment, pointing to the reality of the H-bomb and suggesting that now, in a similar manner, they would be proved wrong about the feasibility of a defensive shield.

The comparison was not quite fair, since the H-bomb was a single device whereas strategic defense would require the construction and coordinated operation of perhaps thousands of devices, many of them working autonomously in space. Several critics had remarked favorably about the physics of the X-ray laser yet still voiced doubts about the feasibility and desirability of defense.

And who would create the shield? Remarkably, Teller had mentioned no one except Lowell and O Group. They alone were to fight the Soviets. It was a stark vision. Here was the man who had been the driving force behind the development of the H-bomb, an invention meant to put the Soviets on the defensive once and for all. But paradoxically, like so much else in the arms race, it had come back to haunt the United States. Now Teller's intellectual heirs were to make breakthroughs of similar magnitude and use them to create a new, safer world where Soviet H-bombs would no longer be a menace. It was a demanding job, and Teller clearly felt his devotees were up to it. If nothing else, the existence of O Group— including its talented young Hertz fellows and alumni—seemed to suggest that the intellectual isolation long ago imposed on Teller and his laboratory had been overcome.

The seeds of that isolation had been planted before the lab was built, the key factor being Teller's obsession to build a hydrogen bomb. In 1942, Teller forcefully discussed his plans for the so-called "super" with scientists laying foundations for the Manhattan Project at the Los Alamos laboratory in New Mexico. Impatient with his endless advocacy, they argued instead that work had to focus on the atom bomb.

After the war and the atomic destruction of Hiroshima, Teller again urged a crash program to develop the H-bomb. But he felt the scientists at Los Alamos were dragging their feet. Moreover, the scientific advisors to the Atomic Energy Commission, headed by J. Robert Oppenheimer, who had been the scientific director of the Manhattan Project, disparaged the idea. "We all hope that by one means or another the development of these weapons can be avoided," wrote the AEC's General Advisory Committee in 1949. Frustrated, Teller in 1951 lobbied the Air Force and the Atomic Energy Commission for the creation of a second weapons lab where research on the novel device could forge ahead. Livermore was founded the next year.

The world's first superbomb was exploded in 1952. The 10 megaton blast caused the Pacific isle of Elugelab, one mile in diameter, to disappear. Its power was roughly a thousand times that of the Hiroshima bomb.

Teller had been right about the technology, although every element of the H-bomb's design had been worked out at Los Alamos, not the fledgling Livermore lab. The explosion nonetheless proved that the superbomb was much more than Teller's personal obsession. However, the cost of his triumph was high. The founding of Livermore and the backlash from the creation of the H-bomb drove a wedge through the ranks of American scientists as they divided for and against Teller.

The schism reached its apex after the security hearing of Oppenheimer. In 1954, at the height of the McCarthy era, he was accused of being a Soviet agent. Indeed, his brother Frank had been a member of the Communist Party, and so had his former wife, Jackie. Oppenheimer himself, sympathetic to the Communists in the 1930s, always stopped short of becoming a party member. In fact, no evidence was presented at the hearing that showed he had given secrets to the Soviets. Instead, a new charge took shape: that Oppenheimer had argued against a crash H-bomb program for reasons of politics. His friends were aghast. This was a matter of policy, not security. They were intellectuals who took delight in their disagreements. Now all of a sudden divergent opinions were being treated as a matter of high treason. Oppenheimer's peers rushed to his defense at the hearing, arguing that there had been good technical grounds for a slow approach—that no one during the postwar era had any idea how to build a superbomb. In fact, Teller's own role in the H-bomb breakthrough had not come until 1951, rather late in the game. But amid the fanaticism of the McCarthy era such arguments carried little weight. Teller testified that Oppenheimer's judgment had been colored and that his security clearance should be withdrawn. Said Teller: "If it is a question of wisdom and judgment, as demonstrated by actions since 1945, then I would say one would be wiser not to grant clearance." Soon it was revoked. And Oppenheimer, the most famous of all the wartime scientists, fell from power.

Afterward, Oppenheimer was widely seen as a scientific martyr and Teller as his persecutor. The newly created Livermore weapons lab had been physically isolated in rural California. Now the isolation extended to Teller personally as he was cut off from the intellectual mainstream of American science. Colleagues avoided him. Contacts dried up. Teller one day thrust out his hand to greet an old friend, but the man shot back an icy glance and walked away.

One of the greatest losses for Teller was the friendship of Bethe, who had directed the theoretical division of Los Alamos during the war, advised the weapons lab afterward, and later won a Nobel Prize for describing the nuclear reactions that power the sun and the stars. Bethe and Teller had founded their friendship in the 1930s. The Oppenheimer affair ended it. In 1954 Bethe wrote a long article charging that Teller, not Oppenheimer, had hindered the nation's pursuit of the superbomb between 1946 and 1950 due to a series of mathematical errors. It was only after the magnitude of Teller's mistakes became apparent, Bethe wrote, that Teller and a mathematician, Stanislaw Ulam, were forced in 1951 to find the right way to go about building the super.

Scorned by scientific colleagues, Teller in the 1950s started to consort with generals, financiers, industrialists, and politicians. The military looked on him as a prophet. Richard M. Nixon, then Vice-President and second only to McCarthy as a fervent anticommunist, sought his advice. Nelson Rockefeller became a fast friend. In the 1960s, at Teller's invitation Ronald Reagan became the first governor of California to visit the Livermore weapons lab.

During this critical realignment in Teller's career, a key issue for his weapons lab became where to find young researchers—the driving force behind so much scientific innovation. The nation's campuses tended to be dominated by pro-Oppenheimer liberals. It was in the 1950s, however, that Teller forged a link to the Hertz Foundation. Teller, a board member and interviewer for the fellowship program, made sure that some Hertz fellows ended up at the weapons lab.

On the Hertz board Teller worked with a remarkable group of men who reflected his broadened interests in the wake of the Oppenheimer affair. There was Robert Lehman, head of Lehman Brothers investment banking firm; Floyd B. Odlum, the financier who single-handed backed development of the Atlas missile, the first meant to drop warheads on Russia; and J. Edgar Hoover, director of the Federal Bureau of Investigation.

Over the years the Hertz board was joined by other luminaries of the military and industrial world. There was General Curtis E. LeMay, head of the Strategic Air Command and chief of staff of the Strategic Air Forces when the first atom bombs were dropped on Hiroshima and Nagasaki. There was Arthur R. Kantrowitz, a physicist who helped develop the first reentry vehicles for the nation's ballistic missiles. There was Charles S. Draper, a pioneer of inertial guidance for missiles and founder of the 2,000-person laboratory in Cambridge, Mass., that bears his name. There was Hans Mark, former Air Force secretary. In addition to these men, there were a number of New York financiers on the board.

Its president was Wilson K. Talley, chairman of the Pentagon's Army Science Board and one of the few board members who was actually associated with a university. The institution he worked for was unique—a little-known division of the University of California that Teller, in his quest for a place to train young recruits, established at the weapons lab in 1963. Located just inside the barbed wire, it was known as "Teller Tech," or, more formally, as the Department of Applied Science. Its official connection with the University of California was through the campus at Davis. According to a lab article by Frederick Wooten, the Department of Applied Science now consists of one large building, Hertz Hall, a $1 million facility made possible through a matching grant from the Hertz Foundation.

By the 1970s Teller's role as recruiter had been largely taken over by Lowell, who not only interviewed applicants for fellowships but joined the foundation's board with the title "Coordinator, Fellowship Project." According to a recent income tax return for the foundation, Lowell received some $8,000 a year for his services.

At universities across the country, a Hertz fellowship was considered something of a plum, although not as much as it had been in the past. The annual stipend for an unmarried graduate student was $10,000 in addition to a tuition allowance of up to $5,500. There was a unique condition connected with the award. Unlike most other fellowship programs, which evaluated candidates on academic performance and financial need, a Hertz candidate in addition underwent close scrutiny during one and sometimes two personal interviews.

Except for giving an occasional cash prize to a fellow or a school, the foundation's sole purpose was to award fellowships. Thus, Teller and Lowell were the key points of control for a bequest of many millions of dollars.

My thoughts under the tree were interrupted as Lowell himself approached. We headed to building 1877.

Back in the small conference room, Lowell told me that about two-thirds of O Group was made up of Hertz fellows or alumni. In his own case, Lowell explained, he had not applied for a Hertz fellowship while in graduate school because his interests at that time tended to pure rather than applied physical science. However, he had met Teller while in college, and began to interview for the foundation soon after receiving his Ph.D.

"It sounded as dry as chips going around on Saturdays and Sundays interviewing people," Lowell recalled. "But Teller was a reasonable guy and didn't suggest insane things and was spending time doing it. So I thought, well, it's worth a try. It turns out that most of the interviews are incredibly tedious. The rare ones are exceedingly interesting, and they make up for all the rest. There are enormous gradations in people's capabilities at the age of 21 years old or thereabouts. It's very striking. What you really look for is an outstanding capability that has been developed and exercised in some direction. Most people don't have that even though they have straight A's."

Some of the best and the brightest, Lowell said, were invited to work at the weapons lab for a summer in an intern program. "It's by no means the case that you have to be a Hertz fellow to get in here," said Lowell. "It doesn't even particularly help. It's just that someone pays for the initial meeting. People that get Hertz fellowships all tend to be very good. Some of them are very, very good, but they just lack that spark."

Some Hertz fellows worked in O Group as they pursued their Ph.D.'s, and did so with a dedication that only a graduate student could muster. "The best graduate students tend to do very marvelous work because it's a win-or-die situation for them," said Lowell. "There's no graceful second place. If somebody else publishes the definitive results in the area, they go back to zero and start over. So you literally have to win or else. There's one other thing which is an advantage from their point of view. They don't realize how extremely challenging these problems are. So they aren't dismayed or demoralized at first. By the time they begin to sense how difficult the problems are, they've got their teeth into them and made sufficient progress so that they tend to keep going. Most of them win. They occasionally lose, which is very sad to see."

It was getting late in the afternoon, and Lowell suggested it was time for dinner. He picked up a nearby phone and barked over the paging system: "Achtung! All to the parking lot for dinner at Burger King or else." Rather than scaring up dozens of volunteers, this order produced three—a sign, it seemed, that Lowell could talk tough while his young lieutenants felt free to ignore his orders. The dinner group was made up of Rod Hyde, the bearded head of O Group evaluation, Larry West, the gregarious graduate student working on light-powered supercomputers, and Hon Wah Chin, a member of the S-1 supercomputer project. They drove off in one car while Lowell and I went in his Volkswagen diesel Rabbit—his day-to-day vehicle. (The big blue gas guzzler was saved for large group outings.) Its license plate read: "S-1 BUCKS."

Lowell explained that a dozen or more people often went to dinner together, but that night there were fewer because we were leaving so early. He had to give a talk on space weapons at a nearby community college that evening. At the Burger King, Lowell tried, unsuccessfully, to make Hon Wah and Rod show him their Livermore badges. He was looking for a tiny "AE," which meant they could be Administrative Escorts for visitors. I was not to be left unattended at the lab. The responsibility for keeping an eye on me fell to Larry, who was more easygoing than the others.

I was indeed a responsibility. If I managed to smuggle a secret document or two out of the lab, Larry could go on trial. According to provisions of the Atomic Energy Act, the penalty for such a breach of security, depending on the nature of the secrets and the party that got them, could range from loss of clearance to imprisonment or death.

Hon Wah, a native of New York City, drove quite fast on our way back to the lab, his tires squealing as we rounded corners, his stereo belting out Beethoven's *Fifth* in counterpoint.

When Lowell returned from his talk, we prepared to go on a tour of the main O Group building, 1878, where Lowell and Larry had their offices. In terms of security, we were going from a county jail to Fort Knox. The 1877 building in which I had spent the day was a red area, whereas 1878 was green.

We walked into the dry night air, the stars overhead. The door of 1877 was wooden and equipped with a small combination lock built into its doorknob. As we approached 1878 I could see it had an outer door of metal and glass. Behind that was a tiny, well-lit booth followed by a metal door protected by a large circular combination lock.

One by one we went through. Last of the group, I opened the glass door and went into the booth. There were fluorescent lights around what looked like a bathroom mirror. I took off my badge and placed it in front of a tiny slot below the mirror. After a few seconds, the inner door buzzed and I was able to enter the building. Inside 1878, Larry explained that there was a TV camera behind the mirror and that a guard at a remote site checked the badges of all who entered, making sure the face matched the picture on the badge. A microphone in the booth had been used to tell the guard that a visitor was coming through.

Lowell went ahead of us, moving quickly through the building to hide any classified documents or materials and to alert occupants that an uncleared guest was in the area. It was after midnight and few people were about. The hallways in Building 1878 were austere and serious. They had little of the other building's clutter of plants and posters. This was appropriate. The other building was home to a supercomputer project, whereas this building was the site of some of the most advanced work in the world on new kinds of nuclear weapons.

Lowell rejoined us as we walked into Rod's office, which had a look of comfortable disarray, the floor covered with technical journals. He was not there, but all his personal paraphernalia was, including a stereo and a large stack of records with some by Tanya Tucker on top. There was also a huge assortment of different kinds of teas, because, Lowell said, Rod felt he was packing away too many calories in Coke. With a grin, Larry disagreed and said it was because Rod was too cheap.

The next office we looked into was equipped for round-the-clock service. On chairs and bookshelves were stacks of underwear, socks, and towels. On the floor was a Japanese cushion that could fold down into a bed. Lowell said the office was used by a visiting scientist who often slept there. The nearby men's room had a shower.

There seemed to be at least two computer terminals in every office. Lowell explained that one was for classified work and the other for routine jobs and interoffice electronic mail. The classified ones were bigger and were covered with more metal and shielding, he explained, to block out electromagnetic clues that might radiate and be picked up by distant spies equipped with sophisticated antennas. It was a government regulation. All computer terminals used for secret work had to be shielded in that fashion.

The terminals were all connected to the laboratory's huge central supercomputers, as fast as any in the world. The whole classified system was called the Octopus. It ran day and night, seven days a week, Lowell said. With a sneer he added that their rival in the business of weapons design, Los Alamos, rented out some of its supercomputers at nights and on weekends.

On the door of one office was a color photograph of a bright cluster of warheads streaking through the earth's stratosphere at night. It was obviously a missile test with dummy warheads. Yet this was exactly how it would look seconds before the end.

It was rumored that images of extinction and nuclear humor

were not uncommon in the corridors of 1878. One story, perhaps apocryphal, was that the door of Lowell's office held two pictures, one labeled "before Lowell," the other "after Lowell." The first was a map of the Soviet Union. The other was a similar-sized map of the heavily cratered far side of the moon.

We came to Lowell's office. Its door was bare. His room was the picture of creative disorganization, his desk covered with a mass of paper and books. On the floor next to it was a well-worn leather briefcase fat with papers and reports. While Lowell was rummaging around in the back of his office Larry confided that they had once slipped a 20-pound lead brick into the briefcase. Lowell, unknowing, lugged it around the country for months until they let him in on the joke.

Lowell came forward with two sections of heavy-gauge electrical cable, each about an inch in diameter and a yard long. He said the cables had once been part of two long lines that connected a trailer full of instruments at the Nevada test site to a bomb buried deep beneath the earth. They had helped take measurements during a nuclear test. "The electrons in the cable jerked for about a thousandth of a second," he said with a smile. "And that's all that cable did for its entire existence. It would have lain on the desert floor and been buried and forgotten, but I decided to go out and retrieve sections of it because the electrons had jerked in a particularly meaningful fashion. The cables are souvenirs of a particularly happy time."

I suggested we call it a night, the need for sleep overtaking my interest in the group's inner sanctum. Lowell agreed but said he first wanted to introduce me to Peter Hagelstein, a key member of the group. Peter, a former Hertz fellow, had worked harder and achieved more over the years than any of Lowell's recruits. Peter was the young inventor of the nuclear X-ray laser.

But Peter's office in 1878 was empty. Lowell said Peter had a couple of other offices around the lab and several hiding places where he worked when he didn't want to be disturbed. Lowell could tell Peter was at the lab because an organizational directory on the Octopus showed Peter was running a program on one of the supercomputers.

We said good night to Larry and drove across the laboratory in Lowell's Volkswagen, heading for the seven-story main administration building where I had talked to Teller. But Peter wasn't there.

Lowell looked miffed. He was at a loss for where Peter could be when such a high-priority program was running on the super-computer.

We took the elevator back down to the ground floor and Lowell showed me a display of several framed letters in the lobby of the building. They were from various presidents, and most were marked SECRET (having subsequently been declassified). Lowell said they had been classified because correspondence with the lab could be politically embarrassing. The shortest was from President Carter, who campaigned actively for a Comprehensive Test Ban Treaty that would have put an end to the lab's business of designing new nuclear weapons. Without a series of tests beneath the Nevada desert, no physicist could ever be sure a bomb would behave as designed. Carter's letter consisted of a few terse lines congratulating the lab on its twenty-fifth anniversary.

On the other side of the lobby was a display of strange-looking cylinders covered with paper and wavy lines. Lowell said they were seismographs connected to a series of motion-sensitive devices located throughout the Southwest. When a bomb was detonated in Nevada, he said, the lines would jump all over. He said experts at Livermore could watch the wiggles and tell the approximate size of a nuclear blast faster than most scientists in Nevada.

It had been a long day. We drove past the fences on the outskirts of the lab, across the Livermore valley, and up through the hills to Lowell's house on Windy Ridge. Before going in we gazed across the valley.

I had known dry generalizations about the history of the nuclear era—the birth of the H-bomb, the Oppenheimer affair, the ostracism of Teller. Now the past was coming alive. Teller's lab, born an outcast, had managed to prosper and grow. Hertz had played no small role, helping to recruit whiz kids and to further the education of those already at the lab. Now, with the birth of the nuclear X-ray laser, the lab was poised to try to achieve a vision that had consumed Teller for decades—defense of the nation against enemy missiles and their deadly H-bombs. Perhaps Teller was right and this ambitious goal could be achieved. As he said, maybe it is just a question of manpower, of getting enough talented young scientists to devote their energies to the job. On the other hand, maybe it was just the fantasy of an old man who desperately wanted to be loved and remembered for doing something good in the world. The

H-bomb, after all, had come back to haunt Teller, and this was nearly his last chance to do something about it.

The night air was cool, the scent of fresh-cut hay on the breeze. There were more stars than I had seen in years. The Milky Way stood out in the jet-black sky. In the valley below was a galaxy less familiar, the weapons lab, its lights shining in the dark.

LAWRENCE LIVERMORE NATIONAL LABORATORY

The young warriors work in a dry California valley some forty miles east of San Francisco at the Lawrence Livermore National Laboratory, one of two facilities in the United States for the design of nuclear weapons. Here they labor six and seven days a week, often all night long. Their goal, which helped inspire President Reagan's "Star Wars" speech, is to channel the power of nuclear explosions into beams that would flash through space at the speed of light to destroy enemy missiles.

CORNELL UNIVERSITY

ROGER RESSMEYER / WHEELER PICTURES

AIP NEILS BOHR LIBRARY

LAWRENCE LIVERMORE NATIONAL LABORATORY

The leader of the young warriors is Lowell Wood (lower right). While still a teenager, Wood came under the influence of Edward Teller (upper right), a principal developer of the H-bomb and a founder of the Livermore weapons lab, as well as Willard F. Libby (lower left), a cold warrior with impeccable scientific credentials. Opposed to the goals of Wood and his cadre of young scientists is Hans Bethe (upper left), a nuclear enthusiast during the Second World War who later turned to the cause of arms control.

Peter Hagelstein came to the weapons lab at the age of twenty and went on to invent the nuclear X-ray laser, the most dazzling success of the young scientists. He did so despite strong reservations and the protestations of his girl friend, Josie Stein, who disparaged his work on nuclear weapons and marched in demonstrations outside the lab's barbed-wire fences.

LAWRENCE LIVERMORE NATIONAL LABORATORY

LAWRENCE LIVERMORE NATIONAL LABORATORY

LAWRENCE LIVERMORE NATIONAL LABORATORY

Tom Weaver (upper left) was named first director of a large team formed to develop the nuclear X-ray laser from a promising idea into a powerful weapon. Rod Hyde (upper right) leads the group's search for other innovative weapons ideas. Boasting straight "A's" Dave Tuckerman (left) came to the lab from MIT and promptly came up with an idea for a gamma ray laser.

Larry West (left) designs both supercomputers and nuclear weapons. "We're working on weapons of life, ones that will save people from the weapons of death," said Larry. Bruce McWilliams (right) heads an ambitious project to design compact and extremely fast supercomputers that could be the "brains" behind a national system of defense. Offices in Building 1877 (below) are sometimes the scene of creative disarray. Nearby is the group's stockpile of Coke.

VALID LOGIC SYSTEMS INCORPORATED

The Pleasure of Your Company
is Requested at the

Billion
Bit
Bash

· Celebrating The Very First Billion Bit High-Speed
  Memory System on a Supercomputer, and
· Honoring Its Creators:

Ted Anderson
Bill Bryson
Steve Correll
Mike Farmwald
Harry Lindsey & Co.
Tom McWilliams
Jeff Rubin
Joe Simpson
John Zugel

LAWRENCE LIVERMORE NATIONAL LABORATORY

Breakthroughs are usually celebrated at parties, such as the one referred to in this invitation. Two alumni of the group who achieved superstar status are Tom McWilliams (above left) and Curt Widdoes (above right). Their innovative program, which helps computers design computers, is a guiding force behind the group's supercomputer efforts and has been commercialized by a firm they founded, Valid Logic Systems. Valid's products (lower right) are used widely in the computer industry.

VALID LOGIC SYSTEMS INCORPORATED

Nuclear weapons developed by the group are exploded at the government's underground test site in Nevada. Bombs and detectors to measure explosive output are either placed in horizontal tunnels beneath the desert (above) or in deep vertical shafts. (right) Cables that run from buried experiment to instrument trailers (below) carry electrical pulses generated during the fiery detonation of a weapon.

At first Peter Hagelstein was firmly opposed to working on nuclear weapons, his original goal being the creation of a peaceful laser for biomedical research. The site of his quest was the lab's huge Novette laser (right). Eventually, however, he lent his talents to weapon design, creating the nuclear X-ray laser. Livermore artist's conception (below) of a nuclear pump X-ray laser firing at a group of Soviet missiles.

LAWRENCE LIVERMORE NATIONAL LABORATORY

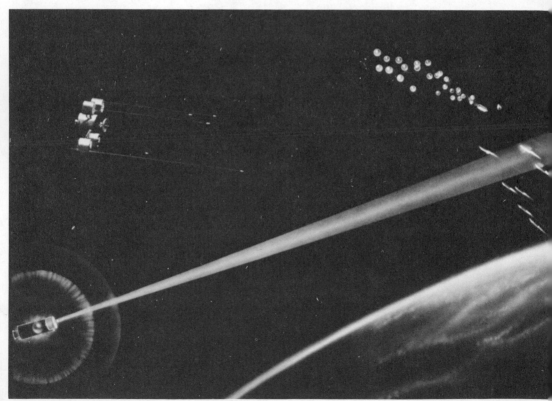

LAWRENCE LIVERMORE NATIONAL LABORATORY

WEAPONS OF LIFE
★

I asked Larry West what he thought of the appeal by Pope John Paul II urging scientists around the world to give up their "laboratories and factories of death" and to reject research on the machinery of war.

"I don't think I fall in that category, of working on weapons of death," Larry responded. "We're working on weapons of life, ones that will save people from the weapons of death. It's a moral decision and I believe in it very strongly. I can't understand why everybody in the world isn't working on finding ways to eliminate nuclear war. Obviously the decision to build bombs has been there for forty years and we keep getting more of them. Why not find technical solutions to a technical problem?"

It was the second day. Larry sat across from me in the small conference room, talking about his past, his current work, and his vision of the future. Larry's first love was his optical computer, a device neither good nor bad in itself. It might be used to guide missiles or print welfare checks. He also had applied himself to weapon design, and expressed confidence that the group's new generation of nuclear weapons would be used exclusively for good, that they would escape the moral neutrality of much technology and remain "weapons of life."

Larry smiled easily and dressed neatly. "I didn't want to be known as a weapon designer," he said. "I still don't. I want to be known for doing something much more significant for society. On the other hand, I'm very interested in designing weapons because I believe in being able to defend the country. Also, I find the problems fascinating. When I first came here, I was against devoting 100 percent of my time to weapons. Nowadays I suspect, when I finish my optical logic, I would be quite willing to work on weapons full time because I see the vast possibilities. A tremendous amount of creativity is needed and there are very few scientists willing to do it."

Larry was born on July 4, 1955, and grew up in the southern California city of La Habra. Once surrounded by groves of oranges, lemons, walnuts, and avocados, La Habra over the years was caught in the urban sprawl of Los Angeles. In the course of Larry's childhood the town became one long stretch of homes, apartments, shipping docks, shopping centers, and used car lots.

Larry's parents were divorced when he was young and he ended up living with his mother. Those were bad times. He did have aspects of a normal childhood—going to Episcopalian services on Sunday and to Boy Scout meetings during the week. But there also was much poverty and little stability. Evictions kept Larry and his mother and older brother moving from apartment to apartment. In elementary school he started working odd jobs in order to bring home some money. In junior high school, he frequently worked from six until midnight in a bowling alley.

An escape from the traumas of childhood came in high school when he immersed himself in science. "I loved it," Larry recalled. "It was a treat. I had emotional problems at home with my family life and my mother. Science was a world that was pure and no longer had emotions. It would never go away and would never leave you. And it was always correct. There was always a right answer. So it had a strong attraction for me emotionally. On top of that I had a knack for it."

His high school teachers were not impressed with Larry's work, partially because his older brother had done so much better. Then happenstance gave Larry a chance to shine. Los Angeles County held a math contest, and an entrant from Larry's school got sick at the last minute. Larry filled in and the competitive atmosphere brought out his best. "I pretty much aced it," he recalled.

By his senior year, Larry was getting recognition at school for his achievements in math and the sciences. But not the humanities. "If it wasn't sciences, I wasn't interested, because everything else was imperfect and arbitrary. I wasn't about to listen to a teacher's opinion just because he was going to give me a grade."

Larry was a rebel. He went to high school in the early 1970s and took up the trappings of the counterculture, wearing hair down to his shoulders and driving recklessly. "We couldn't afford brakes for the car, so I always had to down shift," he said. "One time I got cut off by a truck while speeding down a street, so I locked up my wheels and started spinning and wrapped it sideways on a telephone pole. The motor still ran. So I managed to wrench it off the pole and get away before the police came."

Despite time on the streets, Larry's knack for science and his steady application during high school landed him a scholarship to the California Institute of Technology, one of the country's toughest schools. It was there that Larry really started to shine. In 1977, after four years of study, he graduated from Caltech with simultaneous bachelor's and master's degrees. He ranked at the top of his class.

This was no mean feat. Located in Pasadena, Caltech has academic pressures unmatched by any other school in the country. Indeed, it has one of the nation's highest rates of suicide, almost every class losing several members over the course of four years. Its reputation for academic excellence is based in part on the intimacy of the education. The student-faculty ratio is 3 to 1. The professors include twenty Nobel laureates. Each entering class is small, just over two hundred students, and they have the highest SAT scores of any group of freshmen in the country.

In national rankings, Caltech comes out on top in physics, chemistry, engineering, and just about everything except the humanities and social sciences, where students grudgingly take a fifth of their credits. Because of the high-tech atmosphere and reputation, older students tend to be quite sensitive to being labeled "nerds" and encourage newcomers to avoid such habits as wearing calculators on their belts. The vast majority of the students are white males.

The school is widely known for the pranks of its students, which on occasion are officially sanctioned. In a course called "Experimental Projects in Electrical Circuits," two students with an interest in computers got credit for electronically invading and rearranging a scoreboard during a Rose Bowl game.

In general, the school excels in high technology and its attendant skills. "Caltech students tend as a group to be more the people who solve the problems than those who raise them," the school's president once remarked to Edward B. Fiske, Education Editor of *The New York Times.*

This was the environment in which Larry thrived, and which he considered leaving for the weapons lab. In the course of a Hertz interview, he had been encouraged by Lowell to become a summer intern. But professors at Caltech warned Larry that the lab was a bad place—not for reasons of ethics but because of its poor scientific reputation. "At the time it was not known for outstanding physics," Larry recalled. "The professors did not know about O Group so in general I think their assessment was correct. It was as if people at the lab were designing Chrysler Caravans instead of Cordovas. There was no group to do outstanding innovation and breakthroughs in the weapons field."

In contrast to faculty wariness, Larry's peers were enthusiastic about the lab. "There were two other students at Caltech who had worked here," Larry said. "They told me about their wonderful experiences and how the resources were as exciting as the projects."

Skeptical, Larry joined as a summer intern and found a group of kindred spirits who spoke the same language. "When I got here I thought it would be another eight to five job," said Larry. "But I found out totally differently. The people were the top from many universities. It was very exciting. Even at Caltech, with all its great people, they still didn't have the caliber of individual they had here. I could talk to most people and have them understand me very rapidly, which was absolutely astounding. I just loved it."

Despite the attractions of the place, Larry did have hesitations about work on weapons, as did some of his friends. Their apprehension showed when they spoke of bomb designers as having "dirty hands." Rod and Lowell fell into that category. But there proved to be a way around the problem. Most of O Group dealt with "off the shelf" bombs that were used merely as power sources in the creation of third-generation weapons. That work was seen by Larry and his friends as challenging and elegant. It pushed the limits of pure science. In fact, most members of the group who dabbled in the nuclear arts did not consider themselves "bomb makers," a pejorative term, but "weapon designers."

With his new-found friends, Larry hesitantly set to work on the group's nuclear research as well as a spectrum of other projects. Seven years passed. And Larry's attitude became that of an enthusiast. "There are almost an infinite number of issues to be pursued," he said. "The number of new weapons designs is limited only by one's creativity. Most of them have not been developed beyond the stage of thinking one afternoon, 'Gee, I suppose you can do so and so.' There are a tremendous number of ways one might defend the country.

"We can try to negotiate treaties and things like that. But one thing I can do personally, without having to wait for arms control, is to develop the technology to eliminate them myself, to eliminate offensive nuclear weapons."

Larry's optimistic view of third-generation technology, neatly summed up in the phrase "weapons of life," was very individualistic. Larry believed that special types of bombs could save the world. But other observers saw it differently. One view was that tools, whether bombs or hammers, were ethically neutral. This school of thought held that man transformed tools into agents of good and evil. A more pessimistic approach held that nuclear technologies were inherently evil because of their unprecedented power. According to this view, nuclear weapons would always remain tools of mass destruction.

Teller, like his young devotee Larry, fell into the class of nuclear optimists, having long tried to harness the atom for something other than blowing up cities. Throughout his career Teller had called on scientists to develop nuclear reactors for electrical power, nuclear weapons for shooting down enemy missiles, and nuclear explosives for construction projects. But skeptics had questioned his vision of a beneficent atom.

"So you want to beat your old atomic bombs into plowshares," remarked I. I. Rabi, a Nobel laureate, when first told of plans for digging ditches with nuclear bombs. He had doubts. So did the nation, which eventually turned its back on the so-called Plowshare program. It had been founded by Teller and the Eisenhower administration to develop nuclear explosives for peaceful uses.

Not easily put off, Teller vigorously promoted the goal closest to his heart—using nuclear weapons to free the West from the threat of enemy missiles. His crusade to build nuclear-tipped interceptors went on for decades. But it was a lonely one. He never fully got the backing of the nation or the majority of his scientific peers. In 1972 his vision was formally spurned by the superpowers when they signed a ban on the construction of large antimissile defenses. Nonetheless, Teller continued to pursue his goal with fervor. That the nation is again considering the issue of defense is a tribute to his persistence, if nothing else.

The quest for strategic defense began long before the launching of the first American or Soviet intercontinental ballistic missiles. On both sides, military planners in the early 1950s began to think about how to thwart nuclear weapons that traveled over great distances.

Sputnik, the Soviet artificial satellite that first circled the earth, quickened Teller's quest. He once wrote that the sight of it silently moving across the night sky in 1957 chilled him to the bone. After all, Sputnik signaled the advent of something entirely new in the world of military strategy—bombs from space. If the Soviet Union could use missiles to loft satellites, they could launch nuclear warheads as well and have them land anywhere on the United States. Bombers could be shot down with conventional weapons. But there was no way to stop what, in effect, would be a speeding bullet from space.

In response, the United States spent billions of dollars on missiles to match those under development in the Soviet Union. The race was on.

Also in response, Teller and other military planners started the formidable job of developing systems of defense against enemy missiles and warheads. Soviet missiles would rise from central Asia and release their payloads in space. The warheads, each about a yard in length, would be accelerated by the force of gravity during their fall back to earth to speeds of several miles a second at the ends of their trajectories. The idea would be for American interceptor rockets to rush to meet them as they zeroed in on targets in the continental United States. If hit head on, the warheads would easily be destroyed. If missed, there would be no second chance.

The problem was that no bullet could be fired accurately enough to hit another bullet. American radars and computers at the time were too primitive to accurately locate and track swarms of fast-moving warheads. One attempt at solution was to tip interceptors with their own nuclear warheads. That way the interceptors only had to get close to their targets, the nuclear fireballs being powerful enough to destroy everything in the immediate vicinity.

In the early 1960s, the feasibility of that idea was tested by detonating nuclear warheads high in the atmosphere. Some were even exploded in the vacuum of space, where a bomb's powerful rays could travel much further than in the earth's atmosphere. The tests were meant to answer scores of technical questions. No one knew what to expect.

"All of a sudden a greenish-white flash lit up all of Hawaii," recalled an eyewitness to one such experiment. "The sky started turning pink, then orange, then red. The heavens were filled with a ghastly light." It occurred in July 1962. The bomb had been launched from Johnston Atoll, a tiny speck in the Pacific about eight hundred miles southwest of Hawaii. The pyrotechnics started a few minutes later, when the nuclear weapon exploded in space. It was the sort of display that might accompany the detonation of third-generation weapons during a nuclear war.

Such tests gave the military increasing confidence in their ability to zap Soviet warheads, but hurdles remained. One was tracking enemy warheads amid the electromagnetic chaos wrought by exploding nuclear bombs. Another was trying to figure out which objects to attack. After all, Soviet missiles would unload decoys as well as real warheads.

In the 1950s and early 1960s, Teller quietly used positions of power within the government to advocate research on systems of defense. From 1958 to 1960 he was director of the Livermore weapons lab. After quitting the directorship, he took his case to the public. In his 1962 book, *The Legacy of Hiroshima,* Teller lauded the quest for defense, saying "it would be wonderful if we could shoot down approaching missiles before they could destroy a target in the United States." But he warned that the Soviet Union might also attempt to create a shield—a possibility fraught with terrible consequences. "If the Communists should become certain that their defenses are reliable and at the same time know that ours are insufficient, Soviet conquest of the world would be inevitable," he wrote. His fear was unstated but clear. An aggressor with a good shield might be tempted to use his sword, confident he could deflect the weapon of his opponent.

Teller's quest was soon frustrated by political impediments. In 1963 the Senate debated whether to ratify a treaty that would prohibit the testing of nuclear warheads in the atmosphere. Teller denounced the treaty, testifying that it would thwart the development of nuclear-tipped interceptors. It was ratified anyway, the 1963 Limited Test Ban Treaty barring all nuclear tests except those underground.

Despite this setback, throughout the 1960s the nation's nuclear labs worked on the design of warheads to be used for defense. The systems under study had such names as Nike-X and Sentinel. Their prototype warheads were detonated in tunnels dug beneath the Nevada desert. Such tests could verify the correct design of a warhead. But unless the test ban treaty was broken, the complex workings of the defensive system and its nuclear-tipped interceptors could only be simulated.

The continuing work on defensive systems widened the split that had already opened among the nation's scientists. One of the most notable and firm critics of all defensive systems was Bethe, Teller's old friend. He had been a driving force behind the test ban treaty. During the 1960s he opposed defense, saying systems of anti–ballistic missiles could be viewed as provocative. "We exist in peace today only because each side knows it cannot win a nuclear war," he told a meeting of the American Association for the Advancement of Science, according to a report by Lee Edson. "Once this balance of terror is broken—as it will be with the ABM since that will let one side think it has an advantage—then we will have a continuing spiral of increasing arms and further instability."

No opinion could have been more different than Teller's. In a long interview with *U.S. News & World Report* in 1969, he pressed his point. "I cannot tell you how much more I would rather shoot at enemy missiles than to suffer attack and then have to shoot at people in return. I want to repeat—with all possible emphasis—that defense is better than retaliation."

The antimissile proposal that sparked such contradictory comments from the two physicists was known as Safeguard. Though vigorously opposed by many of the nation's senior scientists, President Nixon gave it the go-ahead, and Teller's lab labored to bring its nuclear warheads to life. At a cost of $5.7 billion, the Safeguard system was finally erected in the 1970s at the very northern edge of North Dakota. Like so many of its predecessors, however, the system was flawed. Its high-altitude nuclear fireballs would not only have vaporized Soviet warheads but also have bathed the United States with powerful surges of electromagnetism that would have disabled the radars of Safeguard, knocked out communications and computers across the nation, and possibly ended the President's ability to communicate with his troops. The existence of the EMP, or Electromagnetic Pulse, had been known by the military for years but generally ignored.

Safeguard's hidden flaw—and the fact that the system had nonetheless been deployed—hinted at the technical problems with all types of defense. Indeed, in defiance of Teller's vision, the conventional wisdom over the years had so changed that by the early 1970s most experts held that missile defense was too difficult, expensive, and destabilizing to pursue in a serious way. Such reasoning gave birth to the Anti–Ballistic Missile Treaty of 1972, which limits both superpowers to a token force of 100 interceptors. Though it could have been operated under the terms of the treaty, Safeguard was abandoned less than a year after it was switched on.

For advocates of defense, the technical feasibility of their goal increased dramatically in the 1980s with the advent of the nuclear X-ray laser and the other third-generation weapons. Earlier defenses were meant to work just seconds before warheads burst over their targets. But third-generation weapons are meant to direct their energy over vast distances in space to destroy missiles before they have a chance to unload their payloads of warheads.

This is a key aspect of the Star Wars breakthrough. The job becomes much more feasible in space, where "layers" of defense can operate independently, each working to pick off targets that slip through previous layers. There are at least three distinct battle zones: over enemy territory for "boost phase" intercepts of missiles before they have released their warheads; in space for "midcourse" intercepts; and near the ground for "reentry phase" intercepts of warheads.

The advantages of a layered defense are many, especially its boost phase. First, missiles carry many warheads, so whatever success a defender achieves in knocking out missiles drastically reduces the number of warheads to be fought by subsequent layers of defense.

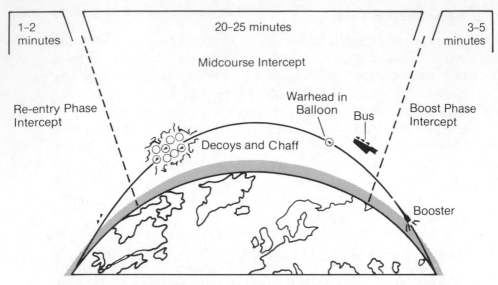

1–2 minutes

20–25 minutes

Midcourse Intercept

3–5 minutes

Re-entry Phase Intercept

Warhead in Balloon

Bus

Boost Phase Intercept

Decoys and Chaff

Booster

"Layers" of defense start over Soviet Union, where missiles rise from silos. The "bus" atop a missile dispenses warheads. Altogether, it takes warheads about 30 minutes to reach targets.

Second, missiles move much more slowly than warheads. Third, boosters have bright flames that make good targets for defenders and ease the task of aiming. Fourth, boosters are much more fragile than hardened warheads. Finally, a missile, once hit, might explode or fall back onto enemy territory.

For Larry West, the real appeal of the high ground is the weapons that can be used in space for boost-phase intercepts. In the past, a single defensive weapon on the ground was meant to blow up a single enemy warhead, tempting an aggressor to try to overwhelm a defense amid the general chaos of nuclear war. That was one of the drawbacks of Safeguard. By contrast, multiple beams from a single third-generation weapon in space might be able to knock out dozens of speeding missiles. This unprecedented rate of destruction would radically shift the odds in favor of the defender.

For Larry, a final allure of defensive nuclear weaponry is its light weight and the relative ease with which it can be placed into battle. Small bombs pack a huge punch. The Pentagon is studying many different types of lasers, nuclear and nonnuclear. But some of the conventional lasers need so much power and their generators are so large that they might never be able to be lifted off the ground.

All these advantages add up to the raw material for a strategic revolution, according to Larry. He is a firm believer in the feasibility of Star Wars, saying he never worries that it might fail. "In general, working or not working can be very critical," he said. "In a human, if you lose a heart, you die. But in these systems, if you lose a component, only a fraction of the system dies. So it's not like work or not work. It is a question of overall performance."

If the system captures 99.9 percent of the warheads, that's fine, but what happens if only 80 percent are knocked out?

"The problem, of course, is that you never want to have to use the defensive system," he answered. "You never want to have to rely on it. You want it to be just enough of a deterrent so that nobody is ever tempted to do anything."

What if the Soviets decided to attack anyway? Wouldn't there be a terrible chance that 200 warheads might slip through our shield?

"Although you reduce the number of their bombs, you really don't know by how much," he said. "So you've not only reduced it, you've also added uncertainty. Uncertainty in a military mind is worth a hell of a lot. No military man can attack something when he has no idea whether he is going to be slaughtered or not—even if he's a madman. So a defensive system has the advantage of both eliminating the nukes and taking away the incentive to attack."

I asked whether the Soviets, despite all logic, might not decide to try to overwhelm a defense by building more offensive missiles.

"If we were spending for defense and the Russians were spending money on building more nuclear warheads, that would be just great—but only if for every dollar they spent we were spending twenty cents," Larry replied. "I'd like to see them try to escalate and spend their entire budget and see their country go to ruin. I only hope it would go that way. On the other hand, if we can't come up with defensive weapons that can cheaply counter their efforts, it shouldn't be done."

Before visiting Livermore, I had tried to find a description of the third-generation weapons. Details were slim. Their designs, their mere existence, are some of the federal government's top secrets. Nonetheless, specifics came to light, as well as some general characteristics of third-generation weapons. The nature of A-bombs and H-bombs imposes certain constraints on the design of third-generation devices. How these older weapons work is therefore an important issue in the design of third-generation devices.

What drives an A-bomb is subatomic particles known as neutrons. When a free neutron strikes an atom of uranium or plutonium, the atom splits into lighter elements, and in the process emits, on average, two or more neutrons and considerable energy—about ten million times as much, atom for atom, as that given off by an ordinary chemical reaction. This is called a fission reaction. If a critical mass of plutonium is packed together in a small space, the fission of one atom will trigger a chain reaction. One secret of the A-bomb is to push enough plutonium together, usually by means of conventional explosives, and hold it there long enough for a sizable part of the dense metal to undergo fission. Another is to inject free neutrons into the critical mass at just the right moment.

Considerable energy is liberated by a fission reaction. The vast majority of it radiates spherically outward in the form of X-rays and gamma rays. (The heat, blast, and light of nuclear explosions in the atmosphere are mainly the result of this radiation interacting with the surrounding air.) These rays can heat nearby objects to incredible temperatures—so hot, in fact, that certain materials will undergo a further nuclear reaction, the one that creates H-bombs.

At temperatures of tens of millions of degrees, isotopes of hydrogen such as deuterium and tritium fuse together to form heavier elements, and in the process release much energy, as evidenced by the sudden disappearance of the island of Elugelab. Bombs that work on this principle are called "thermonuclear" because they are triggered by heat. The challenge of creating an H-bomb is to ignite the fuel before the expanding debris and neutrons from the nearby A-bomb simply destroy it. The solution is to utilize the atom bomb's X-rays and gamma rays, which travel at the speed of light. This was the breakthrough of Teller and Ulam. Their idea was to separate the fission and fusion elements in a tube. The radiation from the A-bomb was reflected along the tube's interior well ahead of the expanding debris, flashing to the fusion fuel and igniting it. The upshot was a spectacular burst of thermonuclear energy.

Third-generation weapons take off from this point. Their interior bombs consist of the two previous generations, A-bombs and H-bombs, known respectively as the "primary" and the "secondary." Their specialty is to focus that explosive energy through the use of various devices, arrays, metals, and other materials. The trick is to use the first wave of radiation—which expands outward at the speed of light—before the ensuing fireball destroys everything. All third-generation weapons are by definition one-shot devices.

The power of third-generation weaponry in some cases is dictated by the size of its nuclear furnace, a big bomb producing more powerful beams than a small one. Since the task of defense calls for all the punch a beam weapon can muster, the criterion of power alone suggests that all third-generation weapons start with an H-bomb. One challenge is to fashion the H-bombs in such a way that their expanding sphere of radiation is paced with that of the triggering A-bomb. The goal is to have as much radiation as possible arrive simultaneously at the delicate arrays of energy converters, target trackers, and all the other associated hardware of third-generation weapons. Since what starts the process is a conventional explosive that slams together the parts of an A-bomb, one might expect that the mechanical shock wave could disable the delicate gear of a third-generation weapon. Not so. The shock wave is said to travel quite slowly, quickly being overtaken by radiation moving outward at the speed of light.

As to the specifics of third-generation weapons, various press accounts and rumors among the community of defense scientists point to four main possibilities out of an untold number that are actually being pursued.

X-RAY LASER. Already referred to, this is the most extensively tested and most formidable of all the third-generation weapons. It is also the only one whose details are known publicly. Around the H-bomb at its core are long, thin metal rods which, when struck by radiation, emit powerful bursts of X-rays. What makes the bursts so special is that they are *coherent;* that is, they are made up of radiation whose waves are all in step with one another. Ordinary radiation, such as that from a light bulb, is made up of waves that are jumbled and quickly dissipate in the dark. By contrast, laser light is concentrated. It can bounce off the moon and return to earth. In the nuclear X-ray laser, individual rods range in length up to a few feet. So far these rods have come to life only in painstakingly crafted tests beneath the Nevada desert. In space their mission would be much more challenging. Rods might be subject to thermal warping (from the heat of the sun) and residual mechanical motion (from trying to point at targets), either one of which might misdirect them. Nonetheless, glowing accounts in the aerospace press, based on much technological optimism, report that as many as fifty laser rods might be assembled around a single H-bomb, meaning that in some scenarios one battle station might be able to hit as many as fifty enemy targets. Since X-rays do not penetrate very far into the earth's atmosphere, these weapons can be used with any effectiveness only in the void of space.

EMP WEAPON. Any nuclear bomb detonated high above the atmosphere bathes the area below in a powerful electromagnetic pulse that is likely to burn out delicate electronic chips, transistors, computers, and power and communication systems. This happens at the speed of light, and can cover an entire continent. Ever since high-altitude EMP was discovered in 1962 (during the blast that lit up the skies of Hawaii), military planners in the United States have struggled to protect critical systems against its crippling effects. Their assumption is that the Soviets do the same. One of the third-generation ideas is to try to enhance this pulse so that it could knock out an enemy's critical communications and electrical systems. Exploded just before or during a Soviet attack, an EMP bomb would sow chaos and generally foul battle plans.

MICROWAVE WEAPON. In the manner of EMP bombs only more so, this weapon concentrates energy into a narrow band of frequencies of the electromagnetic spectrum in order to knock out enemy missiles. If hit by a sufficiently powerful pulse of energy, the delicate electronics in a missile's navigation system might be upset or ruined. The lure of microwave weapons is that they would better penetrate the earth's atmosphere than X-rays, and that a single one might be able to knock out a large group of missiles as they rose from their silos. The problem is that missiles, too, have long been shielded from electromagnetic attack because of fears about EMP, although much uncertainty surrounds how good this shielding may be, both for American and Russian missiles. Another drawback is that microwave weapons cannot produce a "hard kill" in which a missile explodes or drops back to earth. Rather, it might zoom off course.

PARTICLE BEAMS. All the preceding weapons try to exploit different types of electromagnetic waves moving at the speed of light. By contrast, another idea is to use a nuclear explosion to accelerate tiny subatomic particles toward a target. These cannot move as quickly as the output of directed-energy weapons, although in some cases they can approach the speed of light. Candidate particles include electrons, protons, and ions (electrically charged

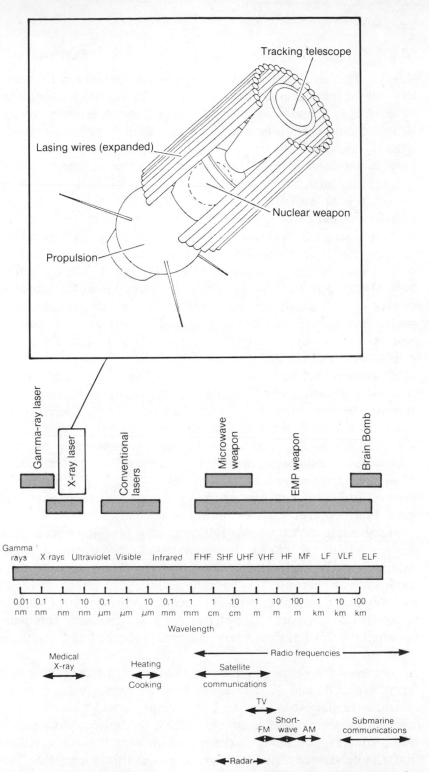

Third-generation nuclear weapons and ideas in relation to electromagnetic spectrum. Wavelength is given in metric units, from nanometers (one billionth of a meter) to kilometers. Only nuclear X-ray laser is known publicly in detail.

atoms). The main problem is getting them to the target. In space, the path of these charged particles is bent in hard-to-predict ways by the earth's magnetic field. The focus of research is thus to create beams of neutral particles with no charge. While very hard to shield against, and thus potentially devastating, such beams would work only in the void of space. Collisions with air molecules would quickly turn them back into charged particles. In short, they would penetrate even less far into the atmosphere than X-ray lasers, and therefore would be of use only to shoot at objects in space.

These four weapon ideas are relatively new, although the concept of using highly specialized nuclear bombs is decades old. During early considerations of missile defense in the late 1950s, the Eisenhower administration set up Project Defender, which included studies of such exotic ideas as directing hot nuclear plasmas and particles at targets (projects Casaba and Howitzer), and speculative work on X-ray and gamma-ray lasers. The project was abandoned in the early 1960s.

At Livermore I had spoken with one of the people behind this early nuclear work, John H. Nuckolls, a short, clean-shaven man in his mid-50s who combined youthful enthusiasm with a sense of urbane sophistication. Nuckolls told me there were several reasons why the speculations of the past were today turning into nuclear realities, including the financial support of the Reagan administration, better computers for simulations, a youthful cadre of enthusiastic designers, and the rise of new administrators at Livermore who supported the notion of weapons innovation.

He also alluded to possible future directions of third-generation research. It is well known that humans suffer confusion and disorientation when subjected to long wavelength radiation of sufficient strength, he said. It is entirely possible that physicists might one day find a way to direct and concentrate the power of nuclear weapons into this part of the electromagnetic spectrum, producing a "brain bomb" that would leave an enemy stunned and unable to wage war.

The quest for strategic defense is clearly not the only thing that keeps Nuckolls and his colleagues hard at work. A brain bomb would have many uses. And an EMP weapon could be used to sow chaos prior to an offensive attack. Indeed, the Soviets had attacked President Reagan's vision of defense, dismissing it as rhetoric that hid a more sinister aim. In a statement issued days after the "Star

Wars" speech, Yuri Andropov said the President's plan for a national shield would seem defensive only to "someone not conversant with these matters." The United States, he said, would continue to build offensive missiles in "a bid to disarm the Soviet Union in the face of the United States' nuclear threat." His fear seemed to be similar to the one expressed by Teller more than two decades earlier—that a warrior with a good shield might be tempted to use his sword, or at least to wield it in a threatening manner.

All such scenarios rest on a complex mix of offensive and defensive weapons and battle plans. But there is also the possibility of pure aggression with the weapons of the young scientists. "There are very few technologies in the history of warfare that have been either totally offensive or totally defensive," Paul L. Chrzanowski, head of military evaluation and planning at Livermore, had told me during an earlier visit. "If you can shoot down boosters, it's equally plausible that you could shoot down satellites."

Larry had defined third-generation devices as "weapons of life." But when pressed, he too could envision other uses for them. He had talked about economic competition with the Soviets and how he hoped their nation would be ruined by a spending race with the United States. In general, he touted all technical achievement because he said it would widen the gap between East and West.

"Anything we do to advance society in the United States will also allow us to make the country more defendable," he said. "If we can pull away from the Soviet Union and leave them in the dust along with Afghanistan and India, technologically, then in essence we've won.

"If nothing else it would prove to the world that democracy works. And I think it would have a stabilizing effect because if we had that much advancement of our society, the Soviets would have no incentive to attack us, because of the fear, and we would have no more incentive to attack them than we would to attack Pakistan right now.

"Let's say we had overwhelming odds over the Soviet Union, like we did after the Second World War. Back then, we could have had the Soviet Union. On the other hand, that was not our desire. We had no reason for disturbing those people. So the United States as a whole decided not to do it. Although I'm sure," he added with a chuckle, "there were a few generals suggesting things along those lines."

Larry found versatility of application not only in "weapons of life" but also in a very different aspect of the group's interests—computers. In fact, they were central to his philosophy of defense. Both his optical logic and fast computers in general, he said, were key to the creation of a defensive shield in space.

"Some of the things I'm doing will be small enough eventually to fit into the nose of a missile. They'll be radiation-hard and impervious to EMP because they're optical." There was always the danger, he explained, that a defensive system in space might suffer an EMP attack by an enemy trying to knock it out. Wires and metal pick up EMP, but glass does not.

"They'd also be faster than regular computers," he added. "During an attack you've got about five minutes for decisions and battle management. It doesn't matter if your computer program is cost effective. What matters is if you've got the computational ability to predict the trajectories fast enough to kill the warheads before they kill you. It is absolutely essential to get that speed. If you don't have it, you lose. You die."

Larry was working on a Ph.D. at Stanford University as a Hertz fellow and pursuing his optical logic at the weapons lab. His goal was dual: to win a degree and to help create a robust defense for the nation. Larry's challenge was to create an optical device analogous to the transistor—the building block of all silicon "chips" and thus of all computers. Transistors in computers do something very simple. They switch electrical currents on and off. The sheer power of computers comes from millions of transistors switching all at once. One of the limits on the swiftness of a computer is the operating speed of its transistors. The best possible transistor can switch in about a billionth of a second. Larry's optical logic promised to be a thousand times faster, making the transition in a trillionth of a second. Instead of electricity, Larry's computer would run on laser light flashing through millions of logic gates at great speed. A problem that took days to solve on a regular computer would be finished on Larry's machine in a few minutes.

I asked if he had anticipated the military applications when he first began.

"I saw it right from the start," he said. "I'm not naive enough to believe that supercomputers are needed by the general population. There are only a few places that need them. The lab uses them for designing warheads.

"Everything in war happens faster these days," he added. "You no longer have guys sitting in airplanes with machine guns. It's totally different now. No human can possibly handle the amount of computation with the amount of needed accuracy. We saw in the Falklands how easy it was for Argentine missiles to come in and attack. Some of the British defensive missiles were in a position to counterattack. But the British didn't have the computers to do that. A British ship could defend itself but it couldn't defend its neighbor. They lost a ship and many lives because they didn't have a certain computational ability. They almost lost the war that way.

"I consider computers to be as much a weapon as nuclear warheads are," Larry said. "They have as much importance to the salvation of society. They can save millions of lives. During the Second World War it was computers that broke the secret German codes. It's probably one of the reasons we're not speaking German today. The importance of computers is not just military but also economic. If our society is able to use computers to make better products, to make more efficient systems everywhere, our country will begin to pull away from the Soviet Union. We will eliminate a lot of the threat."

What about the critics, I asked, who said computers and defensive machinery would always be prone to unexpected failures during the complexities of nuclear war.

"The Space Shuttle is a lot more complex than what we're doing," Larry replied. "An automobile is more complex. Have you ever looked under the hood of an auto? They have no basis for those kinds of criticisms." This type of reasoning did not reassure me. At Cape Canaveral I had covered Space Shuttle missions and had to rewrite stories as one glitch after another called for a complete change of plans.

I asked Larry if he thought the critics are unpatriotic.

"No," he said. "Maybe they're right. Maybe the best way to eliminate arms is just to throw the missiles into the sea, totally disarm, and shake hands with the Russians. I've thought about that. But I don't believe it's a real possibility. Historically it seems that anybody who has tried that approach hasn't gotten very far."

Larry said that the objections of the critics were often based on guilt over their contributions to the start of the nuclear arms race, especially over the bombing of Hiroshima and Nagasaki. "They saw that tens of thousands of people died from their deeds. The only way they can seek salvation is by going out and denouncing weapons entirely. Some of their points are valid. On the other hand, when they start getting so fanatical and denouncing things that can kill nuclear weapons, then you start to wonder. They can say a defensive shield will never work. But that's the oldest argument in the world. You never know until you try."

Larry suggested that we look around the complex of local buildings, which I had yet to visit. As we walked down the plant-lined corridor of Building 1877 I noticed an assortment of tongs and utensils that hung on the wall outside the "kitchen." Larry said the group had a charcoal grill that it sometimes used at noon for barbecues.

We passed out the back of 1877 the same way we did the night before. Directly ahead was 1878, O Group headquarters. To our left was a low, modern structure, 1879, with one continuous bank of windows that spanned its entire length. As we headed in that direction Larry said it held the main S-1 computers.

Inside, rather than corridors and separate rooms, there was one large, low-ceilinged area perhaps a hundred feet on a side that was lit by soft fluorescent lights. At one end were orange and blue racks of electronic gear that ran floor to ceiling. These were the S-1 supercomputers. Distributed around the room were oscilloscopes, other computers, hard-disk drives, spools of wire, neat desks, soldering irons, and miscellaneous tools of the electronics trade. The overall scene was one of extreme order, everything in its place, everything color-coded, everything clean.

The large, colorful racks were known as Mark IIA processors. The S-1 was the overall designation for the supercomputer project, but it included various goals, each stage resulting in computers that were progressively smaller. The smallest of them all was to be the Mark V, which would try to shrink the circuitry of an entire supercomputer onto a five-inch wafer of silicon.

"One attraction of this place is the support to do revolution," Larry said, referring to the sweeping changes wrought by technology. "There's really no one working as hard as we are in these areas, classified or unclassified."

I asked what kept the group together when it worked on such a spectrum of projects.

"I think a lot of it is Lowell," he answered. "He's a very unique person and a very inspiring person. He has a combination of brilliance and a willingness to try things that have never been tried before. Most people would say you're going to die if you take a few steps into the jungle. But Lowell charges right in. A lot of times I debate what he says very vigorously but I usually end up agreeing with him.

"Lowell has a reputation around the lab for being a real bastard, a very rough guy, because he tends to talk tough. But inside he's just the opposite. He's really very self-sacrificing. He doesn't get the privilege of doing the research himself. All he does is push these other people to do it."

The room had several Mark IIAs in a row, each about the size of a truck and looking as if it weighed a ton. On the side of their tall, orange racks were large decals that showed an anchor surrounded by spinning electrons. "Naval Electronic Systems Command," they read.

Moving into a different corner of the large room, Larry showed me the S-1 prototype—the Mark I, which Tom McWilliams and Curt Widdoes designed with their SCALD program. Its racks were mounted on hinges so it could swing open. Inside was a blizzard of bright-colored wires and circuits.

A brochure on a nearby table described some uses of the S-1 supercomputers, which the group was designing for the Navy and for the Office of Military Applications of the Department of Energy. It said, for instance, that they could be hooked up for processing synthetic-aperture radar, a technique that increases a radar's capability many thousands of times. On the Space Shuttle, such a radar has been used to search the earth's surface for sites of anthropological interest, to monitor crops, and to try to find standing water in forests as a means of fighting the malaria mosquito.

As with all tools, there are other uses as well. The S-1 brochure mentioned no potential targets of observation. But in military circles it was generally believed that such radar techniques allowed radar satellites to sort out tiny differences in the size and shape of waves on an ocean's surface so they could detect the almost imperceptible waves raised by deeply submerged submarines. Radars in space might also be able to see tanks parked under trees.

The big obstacle in processing the signals from synthetic-aperture radar was time. It usually took hours to construct one image. The supercomputers envisioned by the S-1 Project might do the job in seconds. If ever achieved, this speedy processing would allow synthetic-aperture radar to be used in fast-moving battles. None of this was mentioned in the brochure. But it did say the S-1 computers "could have a revolutionary impact on warfare."

It was also clear that the computers were having a powerful impact on a small group of very select graduate students. After all, these computers were their creations, tools, and toys. It was a lavish setup compared with what Larry and his peers had at Caltech or Stanford. The opportunity to build such machines comes only a few times in the life of a professional designer, yet these graduate students were cranking out supercomputers like cars on a production line. Moreover, they used their most recent models to help create new ones. The Mark IIA, for instance, was an aid in designing circuitry for the wafer-sized supercomputer.

"At Caltech I worked on esoteric scientific projects that had no impact on society," Larry said as we walked about. "In general most of your research went on a dusty shelf and that's where it stayed. I decided that I'd had enough of that. I wanted to do something that was going to impact society, that was important."

In addition to computers, the graduate students and their older colleagues had other powerful tools. Moving about the room, Larry pointed one of them out—their electronic connection to the military computer network known as Arpanet. Their gateway, a blue and beige cabinet with "BBN Computer" stenciled on the front, was the start of a global electronic pipeline that led to more than 300 computers and 50,000 people in the United States, Europe, and Korea. The Arpanet, named after its creator, the Defense Advanced Research Projects Agency, was the Pentagon's oldest and largest computer network. Connected to it, although sometimes accessible only with secret passwords and codes, were the North American Aerospace Defense Command, the Pentagon, the CIA, the National Security Agency, the weapons laboratories, and various universities that performed research for the military.

We moved out of the building and crossed the courtyard to another squat structure that contained offices, cubicles, and computers. This was Building 1826. Larry moved quickly, saying he had to leave soon. In the building were more Mark IIA's undergoing testing, and a smaller, orange and blue cabinet with a plaque on the front: "S-1 Mark IIA Memory." This, Larry said, was the world's first billion-bit high-speed memory for a supercomputer. Back in the conference room I had seen an invitation to the "Billion Bit Bash," a party in April 1984 which had honored its creators.

We moved past a cubicle that contained only a chair, desk, and blackboard. "Gone fishin" read a message across its top. Further down the blackboard, amid a series of equations and electronic diagrams, was another note: "Starlight, starbright, S-1's on my mind tonight."

Larry dropped me back at the conference room and ran off to a meeting. Hon Wah came in and invited me to a lecture Freeman Dyson was giving at Stanford University that evening.

An advocate of strategic defense, Dyson is a respected physicist at the Institute for Advanced Study in Princeton who has worked on nuclear weapons, consulted for the Defense Department, and written widely on issues of war and peace. He favors the creation of defensive shields but strongly opposes their being built with nuclear weapons, instead favoring "smart," computer-guided projectiles and other nonnuclear means of interception. His rejection of nuclear weapons is so complete that he believes the atom bomb had no military significance during the Second World War, saying even its possession by Germany would have done little to alter the war's outcome.

About a dozen people started to gather at the parking lot. Soon four of us, including Hon Wah, got into a car and headed for Stanford, just south of San Francisco Bay, about an hour's drive away. Sunset fast approaching, we sped through lush valleys and hills, chatting about S-1, Lowell, and strategic defense. We stopped at a Burger King, going to the "drive through" window to pick up Whoppers, Whalers, and fries.

Soon we were in the heart of Silicon Valley, moving past the Moffett Naval Air Station, the NASA Ames Research Center, and the Lockheed space tracking facility, its huge dish-shaped antennas pointing at the sky. I mentioned that the facility was said to control most of the "black" or intelligence-gathering satellites of the U.S. Air Force. With a frown, Hon Wah said he could "neither confirm nor deny" that statement. It was a catch phrase for those in the know. It also represented one of the problems with getting a security clearance. Keeping track of what was secret and what was not was often difficult. The usual practice was to err on the side of caution.

At Stanford Hon Wah led us through the intricate paths of the campus as if he had lived there all his life. The Terman Auditorium was packed with a standing-room only audience. In his talk, Dyson did not dwell on Star Wars. Rather, he talked of "restoring some sense of purpose and honor to the military profession." The problem, he said, was nuclear weapons. They had distorted man's natural impulses so that self-defense was considered evil. Moreover, atom bombs had been given too much luster, he said. One reason was that people incorrectly believed they helped end the Second World War. They didn't, he asserted. Even if Hitler had gotten the atom bomb and used it, Germany would have nonetheless lost the war.

After the formal part of the lecture, a student asked Dyson if it was possible to lessen some of the attractions that scientists might find in the creation of nuclear weapons. Dyson confidently answered that they were going away all by themselves.

"It's still true, of course, that many people have tremendous fun designing weapons," he said. "That's part of the game. If you do the job right, it's always exhilarating. But I don't think that today there's anything close to the feeling at Los Alamos of doing something really epoch-making. People there felt they were going to change the world. Of course, that's not true today."

I thought of Larry—his excitement, his grin, his rush of enthusiasm as he described what he considered the dawn of a new era of nuclear weaponry. Contrary to Dyson's opinion, the spirit of the Manhattan Project seemed to be alive at least in one small corner of the planet.

When reading Dyson's book *Weapons and Hope,* I had been surprised to find passages in which he called the design of nuclear weapons a "scientific backwater" and said that serious scientists were giving it up. His attitude seemed to stem partially from the fact that he could find no constructive use for the bomb. Although he advocated some types of defensive systems, Dyson ruled out nuclear ones as (a) too expensive, (b) unable to be thoroughly tested, (c) requiring a vast proliferation of nuclear warheads that increased the chance of accidents and nuclear theft, and (d) easily turned back into offensive systems.

On the last point, he did not mean that a good defensive shield might allow an aggressor to feel safe in launching a first strike and sweeping aside a feeble retaliation. Rather, he meant it literally. A bomb was a bomb. He said that even in a world free of offensive missiles, the components of a nuclear defense were "still weapons of mass destruction and can too easily be converted into offensive missiles. If the shift of the world from offensive to defensive weaponry is to be permanent, all mass-destruction weapons must be forbidden and any permitted ABM systems must be nonnuclear."

It was a statement in sympathy with the appeal of the Pope. Some things are inherently evil, Dyson seemed to be saying. There *are* factories and laboratories of death. Nuclear bombs would always have the potential to be weapons of mass destruction, no matter how ingenious the attempts to change them into agents of moral excellence. Of course, Dyson was wrong to think weapon designers were going to give up the profession and the "exhilaration" he mentioned. O Group was stark evidence to the contrary. Perhaps he was mistaken as well about the impossibility of extracting good from nuclear weapons. Maybe old bombs really could be beaten into "weapons of life," as Larry insisted. Surely there was a possibility that they might work as part of a defensive shield. But Larry's statement had been too simple. There obviously was a range of applications for the weapons of the young scientists. So much of their world seemed to be at odds with the conventional wisdom. They saw computers as weapons and bombs as the means of attaining a new kind of peace. Was this new or old? Was it bright kids creating a new world or merely a manifestation of Teller's old obsession? Was it man creating innovative tools or had the evolution of technology somehow gotten out of hand?

RUSH TO THE FRONT

Teller's personal contribution to the vision of strategic defense is known as "pop up." Its main requirement is that no weapons orbit the earth. Rather, nuclear X-ray lasers and other third-generation weapons would be kept aboard American submarines and shot into space at the first sign of trouble. Rising above the earth's atmosphere, the battle stations would lock their sensors onto the hot flames of Soviet missiles and explode, sending their beams flashing across the heavens at the speed of light.

The rationale for Teller's strategy is the vulnerability of objects in space. Battle stations in orbit would be relatively easy for an enemy to find, track, and destroy. Space mines could disable them. Lasers and regular nuclear bombs could knock them out.

"We are not talking about battle stations in space," Teller told the House Armed Services Committee. "They are much too vulnerable. We should merely try to have our eyes in space and to maintain them. At the same time, when we notice that there is something amiss, we must be ready with pop-up systems. This involves not putting things in orbit, but putting appropriate objects to high altitudes in a great hurry from the earth's surface. The time available to act, if you take into account how much time you consume in accelerating these objects to high altitude, is counted in seconds—perhaps a hundred seconds."

More than any defensive system proposed in the past three decades, pop up is challenging. It requires a host of new technologies to make it work. Beyond the weapons themselves, it calls for breakthroughs in such fields as rocketry, communications, and computers. Advances are being made on all these fronts—not a few by Teller's young recruits.

"In Livermore we have a magnificent development," Teller told the committee, "the S-1 computer project, which for a total, multiyear cost of perhaps $30 million, is creating the needed computing hardware. By using these upcoming supercomputers, we can make decisions in proper time so that we can orchestrate our defenses, and we can make sure that we do the best possible job in shielding ourselves from any strategic attack."

As with defensive systems of the past, however, pop up has gathered a large, distinguished, and devoted body of critics who hold that technical breakthroughs are not enough. They insist that pop up could be easily foiled by a clever enemy, and that it is intrinsically flawed because of the great speed with which its hardware must be placed in space. There is no way, they say, that its nuclear weapons could remain under Presidential control. The rush to the front would force a war to be fought by computers.

It was the third day. With me was Bruce McWilliams, a slow-talking midwestern physicist who wore his jeans without a belt and smiled a slow, Cheshire grin. He was twenty-eight years old but looked younger and was clean-shaven. He wore a wedding ring, a rarity in O Group.

Bruce was the head of the most ambitious aspect of the S-1 Project—the quest to squeeze the circuitry of a supercomputer onto a thin silicon wafer. His colleagues had already created the large S-1 mainframes. His job was to dramatically shrink them down. A generalist, Bruce had mastered his computer skills while pursuing other projects. He grew up in Webster Groves, Missouri, and went to college at Carnegie-Mellon University in Pittsburgh. There he received a Ph.D. in high-energy physics, a science best known for its atom smashers. He heard about the weapons lab from his older brother, Tom, the O Group luminary who helped found Valid Logic

Systems. Younger brother Bruce came to the lab in 1982 and devoted himself to the wafer challenge, as well as to problems in the design of nuclear weapons.

The reason wafer-scale integration is so important is that, if achieved, it would allow information to be processed with incredible speed—a critical requirement for pop up, as Teller pointed out. A tiny wafer on board a rising X-ray laser could be the battle station's brain—controlling engines and navigation, gathering data from sensors, receiving commands from the ground, pointing laser rods, and triggering the nuclear chain reaction that would result in the battle station blowing up and firing its rays at distant targets. As Teller said, it would all have to happen in seconds.

Hundreds of wafers could also be stacked together to form ground-based computers of almost unimaginable power. These would be quite necessary, especially at military command centers in the United States. Before any nuclear X-ray battle stations could be popped from submarines into space, an awesome number of steps would have to be taken. Signals from early-warning satellites and from radar stations would have to be quickly processed and double-checked to verify that an attack was underway. The "threat cloud" would have to be resolved into individual missiles, whose trajectories would be plotted. At the same time, computers would have to try to discriminate between real missiles and decoys. After acquisition and processing, such data would be assigned to different submarines thousands of miles away from command centers and transmitted to them, so they could divide up the job of trying to shoot down hundreds and perhaps thousands of Soviet missiles, rising ever more rapidly toward the edge of space. Powerful computers on the ground would be especially critical after the first stages of the battle, when thousands of speeding warheads and decoys might have to be attacked by the second and third tiers of a defensive shield.

No existing computer was sufficiently powerful to handle the challenges of pop up. Military machines and their operators were said to be able to process and verify data from early warning satellites in about two minutes. If the computers in Teller's vision were that slow, pop up would fail before it ever got off the ground.

Bruce explained the essence of the group's solution. The key feature of the computer-making technology was to allow the complex circuitry of thousands of silicon chips to be etched onto a single wafer. The result would be speed. Electrical signals would travel from one transistor to another almost instantly. By contrast, large computers, fast as they were, spent most of their time in a holding pattern as they waited for electrical signals to flash back and forth along the hundreds of miles of wires that connected the thousands of separate chips. This waiting period determined the basic "clock" rate of a computer—the pace at which it performed calculations. For a wafer, the clock rate would be far and away the fastest ever.

The secret of turning a simple wafer of silicon into a supercomputer, Bruce said, was to focus a laser down to a point of light nearly a hundred times smaller than the diameter of a human hair. Rapid pulses of this light would shoot through a cloud of metal-bearing gas, heating tiny spots on the wafer and triggering a reaction with the gas at those spots. By moving the wafer back and forth and changing the type of gas, circuit lines with different conductive properties could be drawn on the silicon. By this process a wafer composed of sand that had been chemically purified could be transformed into the ultimate computer.

"Basically what the laser allows you to do is control chemical reactions both in space and time," Bruce said. "You can focus down to a small point on the surface and cause the reaction to happen only there. It's like a tiny blow torch that you can move around at very high speeds, turning it on and off to cause deposition or etching to occur where you want it to. You can also measure the electrical characteristics of the thing you just built without removing it from the reaction chamber."

Bruce and his colleagues had not invented the process from scratch. Its chemistry had been pioneered by a former Hertz fellow, Richard M. Osgood, who taught at Columbia University. But they had enormously extended the process, so far having built single transistors and small circuits composed of transistors. Members of the group were in the process of creating the machinery for etching complete wafers. In a year or so they hoped to have miniature blowtorches making transistors and connecting them on a wafer at the rate of a thousand per second.

Testing while still in the chamber was the key to being able to cover a whole wafer with circuitry. When a flaw was found, it could be corrected on the spot and the process continued, step by step, until the whole wafer was covered with tiny transistors.

COMPUTER MAKING

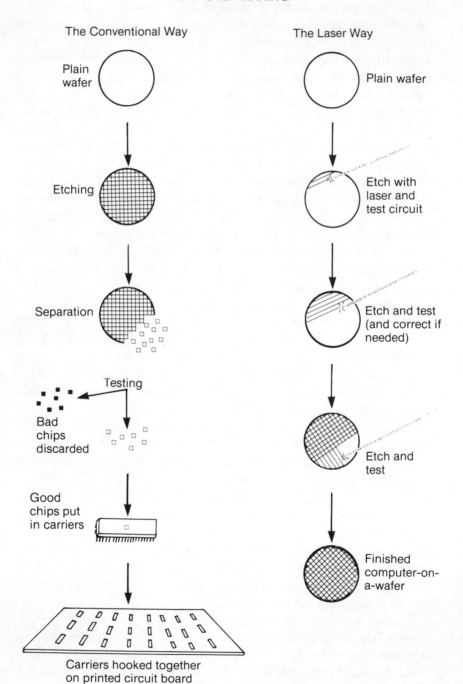

The Conventional Way

Plain wafer

Etching

Separation

Testing

Bad chips discarded

Good chips put in carriers

Carriers hooked together on printed circuit board

The Laser Way

Plain wafer

Etch with laser and test circuit

Etch and test (and correct if needed)

Etch and test

Finished computer-on-a-wafer

The beauty of the process, Bruce said, became clear only when it was compared with the way silicon chips were normally made. Traditionally, plain wafers of silicon were dipped in light-sensitive chemicals and then covered with a mask, not unlike a photographic negative, that had a picture of the desired circuitry. Light, more chemicals, and the repetition of the process built up layer after layer of circuitry over the face of the wafer. After this etching, the wafer was broken into several hundred separate chips meant to be encased in carriers, hooked into printed circuit boards, and wired into the complex assemblages known as computers. But before that, they were tested for defects.

Defects were the big hurdle, Bruce said. Even in the space-age haunts of Silicon Valley, where impurities such as dust were controlled with all the expertise money could buy, as many as half the chips from a single wafer had to be discarded because of defects. The problem was often illustrated by analogy. If Manhattan were a microchip, for instance, one pothole would stop all traffic. And there was no way to repair the pothole. Defects thus determined the overall size of chips, Bruce explained. If they were made much bigger than the size of an aspirin tablet, tiny errors in the circuitry caused by dust specks and other impurities were sure to make them all rejects. The result was that chips had to be small.

"The probability of random defects increases as the area of the chip gets bigger," Bruce said as he jotted a few equations on the room's blackboard. "The likelihood of a chip being good decreases as its size goes up. But size is what we want—monster chips. So our process has to be sequential. Rather than building layer after layer over the whole surface of the wafer, we start in one corner and work our way across, etching and testing as we go. If we find defects every so often, we can take care of them."

If the manufacturing process could be perfected, Bruce said, it would be possible to make the wafers almost any size. However, four or five inches in diameter would be the practical limit because of another consideration. "One small wafer is going to put out the heat of about ten electric irons," he said.

The solution to this problem had been worked out by Dave Tuckerman, the physicist who went to Lowell with the idea for a gamma-ray laser. By etching thousands of tiny grooves on the back of the wafer and pumping water through them at high speeds, Dave had discovered a way to remove dozens of times more heat than had previously been thought possible. The wafer would not melt. Instead, it would glow with the awesome power of logic gates opening and closing at rates that were billions of times faster than neurons in the human brain.

The group was slightly ahead of its time in its push for wafers, as suggested by the number of researchers around the world who had failed at similar projects. Bruce and his colleagues were quite aware of this dark history, and knew that without good luck and hard work their project too would end up on the scrap heap.

The potential benefits of big chips had beckoned to experimenters for decades. In the 1960s and 1970s scientists at Texas Instruments, International Business Machines, and Toshiba had all given it their best—to no avail. In the 1980s a second wave of wafer fascination swept through the semiconductor industry, affecting virtually all the major manufacturers and many fledgling companies as well.

An example was Trilogy, a pioneer of wafer technology founded by Silicon Valley veteran Gene M. Amdahl and based in Cupertino, California. The company had attracted $250 million in initial financial backing, including $80 million from such giants as Digital, Sperry, and CII-Honeywell Bull of France. Trilogy's plan was quite conservative by the standards of the S-1 Project. Rather than using a laser to etch the complete surface of a wafer, it focused on creating wafers by normal methods—except that each critical circuit was repeated three times. If one circuit contained a flaw or failed, then a backup would automatically take over. Although the redundancy of the circuits reduced the overall circuit density, the method did allow the use of a whole wafer and the conservative layer-by-layer manufacturing process that had long been the industry standard.

Nonetheless, the goal was too ambitious. Trilogy at first gave up plans to make supercomputers out of its wafers, deciding to leave the problems of packaging and the addition of other hardware to its customers and clients. Then, in 1984, it gave up the goal of monster chips altogether. It had proved too difficult.

At Livermore, a small group of graduate students and young scientists had set their sights on something more ambitious—to etch, step by step, a whole wafer into a supercomputer. "Some people think we can't pull it off," Bruce said as we left the conference room and headed for his wafer-making facility. "Clearly our approach is one of the boldest."

We walked out the back door of 1877 and headed for a smallish building. This was 182. It was a real building—not a trailer—with metal siding and a concrete foundation. All trailers at the lab were numbered in the 1000s, all buildings in the 100s. Next to 182 were truck-sized, whirling fans and air conditioners that were connected to the building through three-foot-wide flexible tubes. Inside the building was a vast array of benches covered with monitors, lasers, computers, metal pipes, and large bundles of wires. There were tanks of compressed gas. There were metal racks the size of telephone booths covered with neat rows of dials, meters, and knobs. Scattered about the rest of the room were many smaller objects—hammers, screwdrivers, nuts, bolts, goggles, tape measures, small bits of hardware, aerosol cans, hex wrenches, and soldering irons. Across one bench stretched a large, blue laser, six or seven feet long. Hanging from the ceiling were two large, black-cased Sony TV monitors. In general it was the kind of high-tech mess that made perfect sense to somebody who helped create it but utterly stupefied an outsider.

Bruce explained that one particular pile of objects on a bench—prisms, lenses, mirrors, television cameras, metal carriers, and a host of other hardware—was in fact a prototype for a wafer-making machine.

As Bruce talked, some of the chaos came into focus. Light from the big, blue laser on the bench was refined by the optical system to create a mini-blowtorch. At the center was a chamber where the wafer was processed. Instead of moving the light source, whose optics were extremely delicate, the system worked by shifting the wafer back and forth. Its platform moved by means of tiny motors and gears. Pipes carried gases in and out of the reaction chamber. Mirrors and prisms focused not only the laser but also an arc lamp that lighted the overall process so a TV camera could monitor the operation. Under the bench was a powerful, compact computer that orchestrated the whole process. It released different gases into the reaction chamber and adjusted the output of the laser and the movements of the wafer in order to create the tiny circuits. The whole thing was automated. TV monitors hanging from the ceiling allowed humans to observe the process.

The prototype apparatus was in the midst of disassembly, said Bruce, while a larger, more sophisticated version was being built on a nearby bench. He also noted that some of the construction chaos in the room was due to the installation of a laminar air-flow device meant to remove tiny specks of dust that might disrupt the wafer-making operation.

Getting the process to work at all was the first big hurdle. The next was writing the software instructions for the computers so the operation was automatic. It was one thing to make individual transistors, and another to knock them out at the rate of a thousand per second. Hon Wah, Bruce said, was writing the software for the apparatus—a "silicon compiler."

We walked outside the building and Bruce showed me an attached shed filled with dozens of metal cylinders and pressure gauges— different types of gases for the reaction chamber. "Danger," warned a sign in red letters. "Toxic Flammable Chemical Storage and Work Area. Authorized Personnel Only." He pointed with pride to a big blue cabinet and said it controlled the flow of gases into the reaction chamber. Its face was covered with a hundred tiny lights in neat rows that indicated the status of different gas bottles, whether they were full or empty, open or closed.

Back in Building 1877 he left me with Hon Wah, who was designing circuits in an office across from the small conference room. As Hon Wah gave me a demonstration, the display of his computer came alive with symbols for logic gates, wires, transistors, and other bits of hardware that make up the heart of a computer. Holding a tiny control in his hand, his eyes glued to the screen, Hon Wah rearranged the wiring diagram with a few deft motions.

Only a few years ago people performed such tasks with pencils, blueprints, and months of patient work. Hon Wah was doing it with electrons and light. I looked down and realized his machine was a Valid Logic terminal. "Valid SCALD System," read its label. An idea born at the lab had come back to aid the group's quest for bigger and better achievements.

The young scientists would need all the help they could get. Lowell had set them a task whose scope was many times greater than almost anything attempted by industry. The overall budget of the S-1 Project was about $30 million. By contrast, Trilogy had started with resources of $250 million and still failed to meet its goal. At Livermore, there was no way to predict the chances of technical success. The whole thing was a gamble. So far the young scientists had created a few circuits. They still had a long way to go. Market forces provided the discipline at Trilogy. The young scientists had Lowell. Would their final machine be a one-of-a-kind creation? Or would it be one of a family of computers that had been tested over the years to get out the bugs? It was a critical question. The ultimate challenge for a machine that was helping to coordinate a strategic defense might come only once, with no exact warmup, no exact preparation. After all, a shield would be attacked by objects whose characteristics and behavior would always be a matter of speculation.

As I mused about the challenge, Larry came along with Andy Weisberg, computer whiz, rocket enthusiast, and player of nuclear war games.

Tall and gangly, with long black hair and a big toothy grin, Andy, 29, was born in New York City and graduated near the top of his class from Stuyvesant, a prestigious science high school in the city. His schoolmate there was Hon Wah. They and some hundred of their classmates went on to college at MIT, where Andy took three degrees—mechanical engineering, electrical engineering, and aeronautics and astronautics. In 1975, at the age of 20, Andy became a Hertz fellow and started studying at Stanford while working at the weapons lab. He almost single-handedly got the wafer project off the ground. He had left O Group in the late 1970s, but had recently returned, specifically asking to work on issues related to creating a defensive shield for the nation.

"Lowell continues to supply these pushy goals for S-1," he said as we headed for the conference room. "They are very pushy, I must admit. It means that sometimes great things happen. But the other side, which I do admire Lowell for and which I don't quite have myself, is that he can forgive himself and anyone else when it doesn't happen. He'll just push the deadline back a few weeks."

What Andy was currently working on was of key importance to whether pop up would work and whether the group's computers would have enough time to perform their complex calculations. He was "red-teaming it," meaning he was simulating moves the Soviets might make to try to outwit a defense. In American military circles the red team was always the bad guy and the good guy was blue. In Andy's case, he wrote computer simulations of Soviet rockets, trying to foresee what the Soviets could do to make them less vulnerable to X-ray lasers and other elements of a shield. Andy's work was top secret and quite sophisticated. But it nonetheless bore some resemblance to the "Missile Command" battles fought by kids in video arcades across the country.

As we talked a loudspeaker in the hall came alive. "Attention all laboratory personnel," it warned. "The security department will be holding exercises in a limited area using blank ammunition. These exercises will last until approximately midnight." The men in battle fatigues from the cafeteria were obviously getting ready to conduct mock raids. Andy said that sometimes when he arrived in the morning he would find empty cartridges scattered on the ground.

Andy shied away from discussing his current work, which he said was "sensitive." But generalities about defense and pop up were fine. "It's a whole new ball game," he said, "one that's very much to America's advantage. I disagree that you want things that are to the advantage of both powers. We're only playing one side of this game. My feelings about nuclear freeze are that we tried it inadvertently during the Nixon era and the Soviets kept on building.

"There're so many weapons in place now," he continued. "And there're an awful lot more on the way. If instead of building new weapons we built new defensive ones for the same cost—and if for every defender we put in place we could deny the Soviets one and a half or two offensive missiles—then I would argue that there's no argument for putting in more offensive capability. These things are a very good exchange for offensive weapons."

Although he strongly supported the development of advanced weaponry for the defense of the nation, Andy, like some of his colleagues, had strong reservations about doing the work himself. "I have tried over the years to keep my hands clean," he said. "I have not entirely succeeded." He emphasized that his dabblings in weaponry never had anything to do with nuclear bombs. He had managed to avoid that line of work entirely.

In general, Andy said, pop up was feasible, but he was concerned about the inevitable gap between the ideal and the real—between bright ideas in the lab and hardware in the field. "The military has always had manpower problems, and I get a little worried about the complexity of the defensive systems we are talking about, which have to function autonomously. This isn't too difficult a technology for technocrats like us. But with the maintenance staff you get in the volunteer Navy, I worry about a system that smart. Our smartest satellites are not very smart."

Still, Andy said, occasional failures did not matter in the overall scheme of things. Even if some X-ray lasers malfunctioned or some Soviet missiles slipped through a shield, a defensive system could still perform a valuable function. "Even if it's only 20 percent effective, it's considerably more than 20 percent effective at deterring the Soviets, because the 20 percent that gets protected is an enormous retaliatory capability."

Of course Andy's view was very different from the one expressed by President Reagan in his "Star Wars" speech. The President held out the hope of an era in which offensive weapons would vanish from the face of the earth. What Andy was talking about was protecting some fraction of the nation's thousand or so land-based missiles from enemy attacks. Larry too had mentioned the retention of missiles, saying a shield would increase an enemy's uncertainty over being "slaughtered." There was some irony in all this, since what made the President's speech noteworthy was its dismissal of the nuclear status quo, including the nation's arsenal of land-based missiles.

"In some sense it makes MAD possible with a hell of a lot fewer weapons," Andy remarked. This might be so. One reason there were so many missiles was to ensure that some survived for purposes of retaliation after a Soviet first strike, and an American shield might help protect a reduced number of missiles. But shields also introduced a complicating factor when both sides had them, a Soviet one perhaps being able to defeat a small force of American missiles. Andy's "fewer weapons" implied that only America had a good shield.

"I think it creates a certain uncertainty in the minds of people pushing red buttons," Andy continued. "They can't be certain of winning. They could lose very big. And we're increasing the range of losing very big because God only knows how effective the defensive system would be. It can never be tested—certainly not in the kind of rate saturation we're talking about. The pop-up system in particular, which you don't see in orbit, has the ability to create uncertainty in the minds of the offense as to whether the defense will do some good."

Uncertainty in itself was not always a good thing, according to some critics. An American shield might raise doubts in the Soviet military not only over the wisdom of aggression but also over the ability to retaliate after an American first strike. During an international crisis, the Soviets might decide it was better to quickly launch their full arsenal against an American shield, despite the unknowns, rather than wait to try to penetrate it with the few missiles that might survive an attack on their silos. In this scenario, a shield would lessen an enemy's chance of aggressive success but also would paradoxically encourage such aggression. This was one reason critics said strategic defense was dangerous. It could raise the risk of war.

I asked Andy if defensive weapons couldn't be viewed as enhancing the utility of an offensive arsenal. Wouldn't they allow an aggressor to brush aside a feeble retaliation? Unlike Larry, who emphasized the benign aspect of the weapons, Andy clearly saw the other side of the coin.

"Sure," he said, "they'd make your existing capability far more deadly. That's why the idea is not to increase that existing capability, but to instead increase your defensive capability—to trade those strategic dollars into defense."

We switched from talk of weapons to reflections about the group of young scientists. Andy described how many of its members had been recruited and his feelings about those methods.

"Of course you know about the Hertz connection. That's the way most of the manpower has been drafted. The Hertz Foundation concentrated all the applicants. The interviewers combed them even further. And those who were willing to hire on here were already self-selected for this kind of interest." Hertz fellows were indeed an elite group. Only one out of fifteen Hertz applicants was accepted, and those fifteen already had at least A-minus averages.

"I've toyed with the notion that Hertz operates on the model of *The Child Buyer*," he continued, referring to a novel by John Hersey in which a shadowy company in the Southwestern part of the United States buys young geniuses to work on highly classified defense projects. "Here are all these people, after all, with these nice resources, picking out the best and the brightest. Let's face it, no one in industry is giving away these kinds of scholarships. But I really had no qualms once they explained the national defense clause. The Hertz Foundation was a very enlightened way to go through graduate school. They said it was a matter of personal conscience. But I think they did want to find out if defending the country was part of my values. I certainly didn't want to swear that I'd let the government define what constituted a national emergency, because they could have defined it as Vietnam. I missed the draft by a year and was profoundly glad about that. Nobody at the time seemed to mind that the prime of American manhood was getting turned into gunship fodder or drug experiments in Southeast Asia."

Andy went on to describe what life was like at the weapons lab. The picture he painted was one of remarkable tension between the isolation of the Livermore area and the offbeat attractions of Lowell and the group. Andy viewed the situation from a slight remove. He lived in San Francisco and came to the lab only a few days a week.

"There is a real aspect of debate here. Many of the interactions are thinly veiled aggressive displays. It's not just male society, it's a particularly self-selected variant of it. I used to call it 'ego war.' I remember certain evenings sitting around eating popcorn with Rod and Lowell. Their basic notion of amusement was to set problems for one another that could potentially damage each other's ego, testing the pecking order of who knew most about what. That didn't appeal to me at all. I found I've always done better in life by politely losing arguments and letting others talk—which takes some doing, because I tend to talk a lot.

"At any rate, there's not much entertainment at Livermore. It might not be bad if you're a jock. You see them jogging in vast numbers. With the males around here you can talk technolese over hamburgers till the cows come home. That's no substitute for a love life. It's not the same thing as an intellectual life. There are subsocieties here in the group, like the people who go to the symphony and the ones who go to rock concerts. There are large dinner groups and movie groups that go into Berkeley. But basically Livermore is no place for a single male to live."

I sped down Interstate 580 in my Hertz rental car, moving across the valley toward San Francisco. The sun, sinking behind the Bay Hills, touched the ranches and the grasses with gold. I was late for a dinner date with George Chapline, a Livermore physicist in his early 40s who had helped Peter Hagelstein get the nuclear X-ray laser off the ground. George had suggested that we meet at a restaurant about twenty-five miles from the lab.

Skirting the edge of the Bay Hills, I got off the interstate at Diablo Road. Behind me was Mount Diablo itself, a benign giant covered with trees and the rays of the setting sun. Somewhere ahead of me was the Danville Hotel, where George had suggested we meet. Also ahead of me were whizzing compact cars and hundreds of little shops. It was strange to suddenly find myself surrounded by the culture of suburban California.

The "Danville Hotel Restaurant and Saloon" was one of those fancy re-creations of the old West, its courtyard filled with flowers, wagon wheels, and little curio shops. Inside, it was thick with polished wood, rich carpets, ornate turn-of-the-century lamps, cut glass, immaculate tables, fancy crystal, and young waitresses in long gingham skirts.

George was a large man with an open collar, a kindly face, and thick eyebrows that came together every so often in an expression of puzzlement. He looked a lot like the college professor he used to be. He worked not only on nuclear weapons but on such questions as whether the universe had ten dimensions.

Over dinner he explained some of the early history of the nuclear X-ray laser. Long before pop up and the President's speech, the device had been avidly sought by physicists—mainly out of curiosity, he said.

"It was partly that nuclear device technology had been pretty well developed for applications such as ballistic missile warheads and even enhanced radiation devices. These had reached a certain point of maturity. It was natural to start thinking about what other sorts of things you could do with nuclear devices. I would say that this is one of the main forces behind the development of third-generation ideas—intellectual curiosity.

"Of course, philosophically speaking, there are those people who believe that nuclear devices are intrinsically bad and that you should get rid of them, period. But there are other kinds of people who are just curious—apart from politics or morality. Given the existence of these things, what are their potential uses and applications? For good or bad, I fall into the latter category. I evolved into it. Before coming to the lab I had no interest in nuclear weapons. I didn't come from a military family and my father didn't work for the military. My real interest has been in pure science. After coming to Livermore, applied physics became my main occupation and pure science became sort of a hobby."

Born out of curiosity, the weapons had acquired one of the most pivotal and challenging missions in the history of Western civiliza-

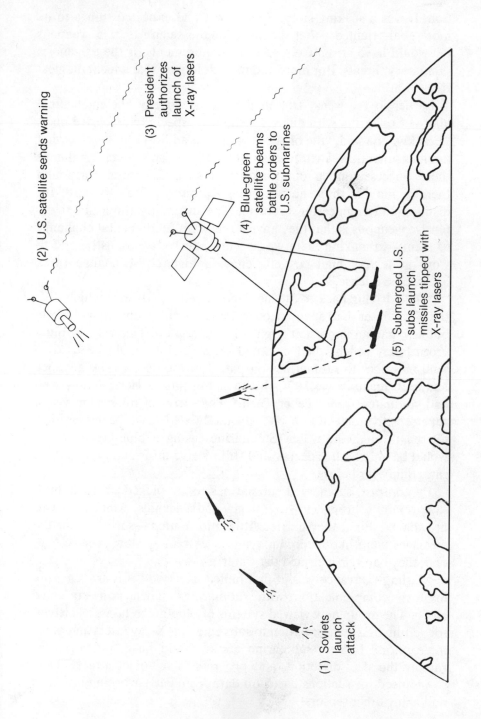

(1) Soviets launch attack

(2) U.S. satellite sends warning

(3) President authorizes launch of X-ray lasers

(4) Blue-green satellite beams battle orders to U.S. submarines

(5) Submerged U.S. subs launch missiles tipped with X-ray lasers

tion. It was a striking story. Somehow I had expected things to be more goal-oriented—that the work of the scientists at a weapons lab would have arisen from security requirements or the exigencies of military threats. But more and more it looked like a technological free-for-all.

Earlier in the week, Lowell too had spoken of the intellectual allure of tinkering with nuclear weapons, especially defensive ones. "Frankly," he said, "the offensive game, in addition to its somewhat dubious intent, is awfully easy. There just isn't much challenge there. Success consists of shrinking off an inch here and a pound there or moving the center of gravity a half an inch forward. It's distinctly an engineering problem. The intriguing thing about defensive weapons is that they have a real, semifundamental challenge to them—to making them work, work effectively, robustly, and to work at a very high cost-efficiency, a high cost-exchange ratio, against the offense."

While driving back to the lab, I pondered an advance which, like the X-ray laser, had spontaneously arisen in the group years before, but now had an important application to pop up. This was the blue-green laser, which when mounted on a satellite could be used to send messages to submarines on patrol in the ocean. The advance had been made in the 1970s by Jack Marling, a Hertz fellow who had graduated from "Teller Tech." The secret of his system was a supersensitive detector to pick up modulated laser beams as they filtered through the water. Submarines using a blue-green system would be able to dive deeper and still receive information at greater rates than ever before.

By contrast, submerged submarines today picked up their messages mainly through low-frequency radio signals, which had two drawbacks. First, they carried little information—so little that the messages were like records playing at extremely slow speeds. Second, they barely penetrated the water.

Marling's advance was at first hailed as a good way to generally improve communication with submarines. Then pop up came along. The group now viewed systems of blue-green lasers as critical for getting timely information to subs carrying X-ray lasers and other interceptors. Indeed, submarine crews would have to learn very rapidly the size, direction, and progress of a Soviet attack. They would need instructions based on data from early-warning satellites and many other sensors.

Submarines were crucial for pop up because of the curvature of the earth. An X-ray laser fired into space from the United States would have to travel thousands of miles before it could "see" missiles rising over Asia. There was no time for that luxury. X-ray lasers therefore had to be based much closer to the Soviet Union, preferably in submarines.

Like George's reflections on the birth of the X-ray laser, the blue-green saga showed how the work of Lowell's group was not always driven by defense ideology. In many ways O Group was charged with making a broad assault on as many frontiers of military science as possible. Then insights could be clustered to bear on particular problems.

The process by which the group's high-tech advances were applied to important defense missions was usually a point of pride at Livermore. But on at least one occasion the phenomenon had come to irk Teller, who had been accused of unfairly trying to profit from the blue-green idea. In 1980 Teller had purchased 40,000 shares of stock in a company known as Helionetics, based in Irvine, California, when he became one of its directors. Soon after President Reagan's "Star Wars" speech of March 23, 1983, Jeff Gerth in *The New York Times* wrote that Teller had an apparent conflict of interest in advising the President about the feasibility of strategic defense because of his Helionetics stock. Gerth wrote that the company's laser technology included "a high-powered ultraviolet laser that can be used in space-based weapons and communications."

In a letter of rebuttal to the *Times,* Teller denied any impropriety. "Contrary to Mr. Gerth's report, Helionetics does not have a weapons laser. The Helionetics laser is useful in manufacturing solar cells and may be useful in communications, but it is totally different from a laser which could be used in antimissile defense. There is no conflict of interest between my advice to the White House on antimissile defense and my ownership of Helionetics stock since there is no relationship between the company's products and antimissile defense."

Narrowly defined, Teller's assertions may have had merit, although the secret nature of research at Helionetics left the weapons question open to doubt. But one laser being developed openly at Helionetics was a blue-green one for communication with submarines—an item of obvious importance to pop up. The company had contracts with the Navy for its development.

Other controversies had swirled around pop up, especially those touched off by the rapidity with which it had to be deployed. One fear was that the President would not have time to authorize the use of its nuclear weapons. And the alternative, authorization by computer, was seen by critics as dangerous because of glitches, false alerts, and the possibility of an accidental Armageddon.

A month before my visit to the lab, President Reagan's top scientific advisers had testified on these issues before the Senate Foreign Relations Committee. According to Lee Byrd of the Associated Press, they said a system to attack Soviet missiles in their boost phase would have to be triggered on extraordinarily short notice by computers—so fast that it might preclude a decision's being made in the White House.

"Has anyone told the President that he's out of the decision-making process?" demanded an irate Senator Paul E. Tsongas of Massachusetts.

"I certainly haven't," said George A. Keyworth, II, the President's science adviser.

Robert S. Cooper, director of the Pentagon's Defense Advanced Research Projects Agency, volunteered that the President could be guaranteed to be in the decision loop by carrying a strategic defense trigger "even into the bathroom."

Senator Joseph R. Biden, Jr., of Delaware pressed the issue of whether an error might provoke the Soviets to launch a real attack. "Let's assume the President himself were to make a mistake . . . ," he said.

"Why?" interrupted Cooper. "We might have the technology so he couldn't make a mistake."

"Okay," said Biden. "You've convinced me. You've convinced me that I don't want you running this program."

War by computer was feared because of the long history of false alerts—the 46-cent computer chip, for instance, that failed in 1980, setting off alarms and sending B-52 pilots racing for their bombers. After such dramas, the military always explained that humans were in the decision loop, evaluating the information from various sensors and computers. False alerts would always be found out before it was too late, the military insisted. And so far they always had been. The position of the generals implied a healthy distrust of early-warning technology. Even the ultimate computer, they seemed to be saying, might break down or generate bogus data.

One of the young scientists had told me that a computer error and false alert wouldn't matter. "So what if you deployed defensive armor?" he said. "Unlike the consequences of unleashing an offensive arsenal, people would not be killed, cities would not be destroyed." What he said had an element of truth. Yet how would the Soviets respond when they saw American submarines launching pop-up interceptors, which might be difficult to distinguish from offensive missiles? Would they wait to see if these were X-ray interceptors mistakenly sent aloft? Or would they quickly unleash their own arsenal, fearful they had better use it or lose it?

Complex hardware and its frailties made up only half of the computer controversy. The other half was programs—which in their most advanced form started to endow a computer with artificial intelligence. Circuits that operated billions of times faster than the synapses in the human brain were of little use unless the computer had a good program that orchestrated them. It was the difference between a baby's brain and that of an adult—one had circuits while the other had circuits and some very good "programs" that produced such things as skill, compassion, cunning, and kindness.

The problem with programs might not be mistakes but getting things to work at all. AI, as the field of artificial intelligence is known, had been pursued for more than two decades with little to show for the effort. Headway was being made, but the extent of the challenge was illustrated by the state of research in artificial vision—an aspect of AI that researchers thought would be easy to master. After two decades of effort they had yet to teach machines the seemingly simple act of recognizing everyday objects and distinguishing them one from another.

This discouraging history had implications for pop up. In outer space, a smart battle station might have to locate missiles, plot trajectories, tell decoys from real missiles, and compensate for ambient light conditions. Would a Soviet nuclear explosion in space throw off the program? Would a meteor shower? Would a satellite spewing thousands of tiny flares? These were the kind of problems that a smart battle station would have to handle very quickly and accurately. A solution might be possible, but it was light-years ahead of the state of the art.

A final complicating factor in the whole vision of strategic defense was what happened to Soviet warheads hit by pop-up interceptors. This was seldom discussed by the young scientists. At best, warheads might blow up or fall back intact onto enemy territory. At worst, their payloads of plutonium—one of the most toxic substances known to man—would be scattered through the atmosphere to eventually rain down on the earth as radioactive fallout. Amadeo F. D'Adamo, a biologist at York College, wrote *The New York Times* to call this possibility a "fatal flaw" in Star Wars, adding that in the worst case "atmospheric winds (and the force of gravity) would deposit the plutonium in so wide a layer that it is difficult to see how life could be sustained."

It was close to 10:00 P.M. by the time I got back to the lab. At the gate a guard volunteered to escort me to the O Group buildings. The streets of the weapons lab were deserted. Most lab employees had headed for home and their families long ago. But the young scientists were just beginning to cook.

Suddenly, two men in battle fatigues dashed across the road—guns drawn, knives strapped to their sides. They raced toward the heart of the weapons lab. The incident was over before I knew it, although the knot in my stomach lingered.

Back in Building 1877, things were hopping. People were roaming the halls, and someone's stereo was pounding out a Rolling Stones song. It seemed to be "Sympathy for the Devil."

I tracked down Fred Mitlitsky and we headed for his work area, which was in a room of Building 182, near the wafer-making apparatus. Fred was a graduate student from Columbia University whom I had met at the Dyson lecture. In contrast to some of the veterans of the group, Fred was in his early 20s and enthusiastically in pursuit of his Ph.D. His raw energy helped power the wafer project. His task that night was to use a scanning electron microscope to inspect some silicon wafers he and his colleagues had recently etched.

Compared with the mess of the wafer-making area, his room was immaculate. Its centerpiece was the microscope, a towering assemblage of knobs and stainless-steel tubes that could magnify objects a hundred thousand times.

Fred flipped some switches and began to warm the device up. It had two distinct parts: the microscope and the control console. The microscope itself was a chrome tube about two feet long. At its bottom, Fred inserted a wafer. Beams of electrons would systematically crisscross the wafer's surface, knocking out secondary electrons whose intensity would be measured by a sensitive detector similar to a TV camera. The impulse from this detector would be carried to the console before which Fred sat. There were a TV screen and a panel covered with knobs that controlled the electron beam and the movement of the wafer. The whole setup was fantastically rich for a graduate student, compared with the usual university lab.

"I guess this is a typical night," said Fred as he fiddled with the knobs. "It's 11:30 P.M. and I expect to be doing analysis for about the next five hours. Today I came in about 2 P.M. because I'd been here early the previous morning. There're some people that do a regular 9 to 5. This is just a phase I slipped into a few days ago. It's typical. A lot of the O Groupers tend to be people who keep working when they're on a roll."

He twisted the knobs and the TV screen zoomed in on a series of fine horizontal ridges and valleys that were crossed by a single, bold, vertical line. It was the surface of a wafer, the bold line having been created by the laser. Though large on the screen, the line, a simple conductor of electricity, was a hundred times smaller than a human hair.

"This is a magnification of 1600 power," he said as he looked at the screen. "Hey, that's a damn nice line."

He zoomed closer. "These patterns," he said, indicating ripples on the surface of the line, "are typical of material which has been molten and then solidified."

Fred tweaked the knobs and searched the moving TV image for other structures. "Some of these things are going to look like volcanoes," he noted. "If you point the laser at the surface and keep cranking up the power, eventually you get a little death and destruction."

Lowell walked in suddenly, and Fred called out, "Hey, we have beauty again, sheer beauty."

Lowell leaned down behind us and began to explain what the TV picture was all about. "We're basically learning how to draw conducting lines over insulators," he said. "The line we're drawing here goes over hills and valleys. As it plunges into a valley, it's important that it be not only continuous but the same thickness. Otherwise, where it tends to neck down, it will prematurely pinch off during its lifetime."

Fred and Lowell discussed the line for a moment, and Lowell quickly began to ask for more.

"You're authorized to flip to another section of the wafer," he snapped. "Did you pre-fill the holes, like you promised last week?"

Fred explained that this experiment had been performed a few weeks earlier and was only now being analyzed.

I noted a bizarre structure on the screen. "Yes," said Lowell, "let's zero in on that protuberance. Fred is famous for his truly exotic anomalies—the Mitlitsky Towers."

"We've actually got one on this wafer," said Fred. "I believe we didn't close the shutter in time and got five orders of magnitude more exposure than we requested."

Lowell was not satisfied with the answer and proceeded to interrogate Fred for ways the structure could have been formed, such as the gas being accidentally let out of the reaction chamber while the laser was running.

"The lines on the amorphous silicon were a lot nicer," said Fred, clearly discouraged with the tone of the examination.

"None of these are on amorphous silicon?" Lowell asked, his eyebrows rising.

The tone of the exchange suddenly altered, Lowell realizing that he had misunderstood the nature of the experiment. Fred explained that the screen showed a repeat of an earlier test, except that it had been performed on a more challenging substrate.

"Really?" Lowell asked, moving closer to the TV screen. "Well, that's very nice. Fine, fine. That's very impressive then."

Etching lines on pure silicon was much more difficult than doing the same on amorphous silicon, which had a rough, noncrystalline structure that was better for bonding and adhesion.

During the exchange, Fred had kept his hands on the controls and his eyes fixed on the screen as Lowell switched from tough inquisitor to impressed superior.

Turning to me, Lowell mentioned that earlier in the evening he had seen Peter Hagelstein and asked if he had a minute to come talk. "He claimed he was on a 4 A.M. to 6 P.M. schedule," said Lowell. "I caught him right at six. He said he was about to drop and had to go home and get some sleep. He said he couldn't possibly come down but promised if I just let him go he'd call you tomorrow."

The mysterious Hagelstein had again eluded my grasp. It was getting late and the day had been long. I tried to suppress a yawn.

Fred picked up the beat and said he had better go home to get some sleep.

"No," said Lowell, "you should not be getting to sleep. You should be getting to work."

Lowell and I left Fred to his wafer adventures and headed for Windy Ridge, driving through the deserted streets of the lab. Simulated terrorists were nowhere to be found.

It had been an interesting day. Pop up was predicated on all kinds of hardware, some of it in early stages of development. The blue-green laser system and the computer hardware meant to orchestrate a defense were clearly meant to be breakthroughs, although their rudimentary designs were a long way from finished systems that could be used in a defensive shield. Reaching that point would be a challenge. Some experts disparaged the large S-1 mainframes as falling short of their goals. Yet these machines were the least ambitious part of the whole supercomputer quest. The real challenge would be wafers. Here giant industrial firms had failed to achieve even modest goals. Yet the young scientists of O Group and the S-1 Project were struggling with wafer aims even more ambitious. Another challenge would be artificial intelligence, a field that had frustrated scientists for decades. And even if the various hurdles could all be overcome, there still would be intrinsic issues raised by pop up and its need for extremely quick responses. Would there be enough time for humans to evaluate warnings? Would the President be in charge? Or would nuclear weapons be deployed at the beck of computers? And, most difficult of all, would computer errors touch off accidental war? Such issues were certainly discussed at the lab. But the vast majority of its energies went elsewhere. Bruce was doing his best to master a demanding technology. Andy was fighting war games. Fred was struggling to get a Ph.D. The diversity of their technical interests was unusual in that they all worked for a laboratory whose primary responsibility was the design of nuclear weapons.

The view from the top of the ridge was again breathtaking, stars strewn across the sky. Then the abstractions of the day started to hit home. This was where, during a war, man's creations would outshine the stars.

WARRIOR BLUE

Peter Hagelstein never wanted to work on weapons—not in the beginning, at least. He wanted to win the Nobel Prize by creating the world's first laboratory X-ray laser, a device that would have no use in war but wide application in biology and medicine. Its radiation of extremely short wavelength would allow the holographic imaging of tiny molecules from the human body, providing clues to the riddle of cancer. This humane and ambitious project was perfect for Peter, a talented generalist who plays violin and piano. Indeed, Peter labored day and night on his laser of peace.

Along the way, however, he got caught in a very different quest, one he had long avoided—the design of nuclear weapons. He did so even though his girl friend objected and threatened to leave him. She was emphatic, at one point marching with protesters outside the laboratory's fences. But Peter stuck to his guns, as she did to hers. Amid a bitter breakup and ensuing depression, Peter invented an altogether different kind of X-ray laser, one of enormous power that could be efficiently pumped by a nuclear bomb.

This tale had been outlined for me repeatedly by different people at the lab—unfortunately, never by Peter. All the versions were in agreement up to the point where they speculated on why he designed the weapon; then there was discord. One reason was said to be his intellectual curiosity. Another was the allure of access to millions of dollars worth of equipment, Peter getting the lab's full backing for his peaceful laser experiments only after inventing the nuclear weapon. Another was that he acted out of fear, his paranoia being carefully whetted by lab authorities who encouraged him to read Alexander Solzhenitsyn's tales of Soviet horror. Another was that Peter wanted to outshine senior scientists such as George Chapline, who was also working on the X-ray challenge. Curiously, no one suggested that Peter did it because he wanted the nation to have a defensive shield.

The rumors were interesting but less revealing than Peter himself would be. So far, however, I had been unable to meet him and had the sinking feeling I never would, despite his having said he would call or stop by the small conference room.

It was the fourth day. I decided to gather as much information as I could about Peter and his scientific quest. My plan was to visit the site of his peaceful laser work, where he was still trying to create a laboratory X-ray laser that might yet win him a Nobel Prize.

I drove with an escort from the group's squat buildings to a modern brick structure that rose to five stories in some places. Peter's experiments were performed here, a laser facility known as Novette, or, when completed, Nova. Everything about the building and its surroundings suggested permanence and solid financing— fine bricks, artful landscaping, tasteful displays in the foyer. It was an interesting contrast to the ragtag trailers of O Group and the S-1 Project, which looked as if they could be removed in a day without a trace left behind.

I joined a few visiting scientists on a standard tour. All visitors donned special coats and booties to minimize the chance of contaminating the laser's optics with dust and dirt. We were then ushered into a cavernous room filled with a massive, white steel frame that held individual lasers. These blue tubes, a foot or two in diameter, crisscrossed the room, getting larger and larger as they neared the target area. This whole assemblage was known as Novette. It was almost the length of a football field, the ceiling above it soaring three stories. Novette had two beam lines, each 500 feet long if straightened out. When all ten laser lines of the project were operating, the $176 million facility would be known as Nova. The main target area for Nova was still under construction in a large, adjacent building.

The goal of both was controlled fusion—using lasers instead of A-bombs to ignite hydrogen isotopes. It was called "controlled" because the fuel pellets were very small, in effect, miniature H-bombs. According to Livermore scientists, such fusion might be used to turn generators and make electricity for the nation. In order to start the thermonuclear reaction, a burst of laser light was directed at a target barely visible to the human eye, a fuel pellet a few tenths of a millimeter in diameter. This was compressed and heated by the laser light to temperatures and densities similar to those in the sun, at which point it was meant to ignite.

The project was a good example of how Livermore's mandate had broadened over the decades to include work on projects other than nuclear weapons. It also illustrated the enormous challenge of some of those projects. Despite more than a decade of effort, laser fusion had yet to achieve "break even," the point where the energy released by the fuel pellet exceeded the amount pumped in.

Although the primary goal of Novette was controlled fusion for energy production, the big laser was also used for other kinds of experiments, including Peter's search for an X-ray laser, as well as classified research related to weapons design.

At one end of the room, about a story above the blue lasers, was the target chamber where Peter and the other scientists carried out their experiments. It was surrounded by catwalks for the technicians. The spherical target chamber was about six feet across, while the point inside where all the beams merged was the size of a pinhead. The chamber looked even larger because it bristled with long rod-like devices meant to detect what happened during an experiment.

We left the laser room itself and entered a high-tech control area cluttered with color TV monitors and panels and buttons and scientists busy preparing for the next shot. A technician cleared all personnel out of the laser room and the countdown began. A key was inserted into a panel that started the electrical buildup in the laser's capacitors—large devices that slowly soaked up electricity from the commercial grid and stored it for quick discharge into the laser.

What was about to happen was the creation of an intense pulse of visible light—but one that was very special. Regular light is made up of electromagnetic waves of many different frequencies and phases that often interfere with one another, just as waves on the ocean surface often cancel each other out. In contrast, waves of laser light have exactly the same frequency and direction of motion and are perfectly in step with one another. They are a pounding rhythm of light.

Although sometimes very powerful, laboratory lasers were seldom used as weapons because of their size. They were giant beasts meant for displays of delicacy and precision, as was the case with Novette. By contrast, laser weapons were often meant to be small, portable, and fit for displays of brute force.

A buzzer sounded. "Attention in the laser bay," boomed a technician over a public-address system. "In two minutes power conditioning will begin an automatic charging sequence. At this time, all personnel clear the laser bay." A scientist explained that the high voltages stored by the capacitors might accidentally kill a bystander.

A short time later the buzzer sounded again. "Attention in the laser bay. On my mark, power conditioning will initiate an automatic charging sequence. Three . . . two . . . one . . . mark. At this time, all personnel clear the laser bay."

The computer was now in control. It would charge the capacitors and fire the laser. "Sequence started," said a synthesized voice from the control panel. Arms folded, the scientists and technicians gazed silently at a color TV monitor as a yellow arrow slowly moved down a long list of steps being completed by the computer. "The laser will fire in 120 seconds," said the synthesized voice.

Near the end of the countdown, a technician held his hand over a red abort button so he could stop the whole process at the last second if need be. Here humans were, ultimately, still in control. The computer voice began the final count: "Five . . . four . . . three . . . two . . . one."

There was a barely audible, distant snap. In the laser room itself, however, there had been a vast transformation of energy, vaporizing the target. When the laser was fired, the Novette capacitor banks sent ten billion watts of power into flashlamps and laser amplifiers.

The key to transforming this raw energy into a powerful beam of coherent radiation lies in the electrons of the lasing material. Any electron, if properly jostled, will emit a photon of light. In a laser, billions of electrons are jostled all at once. With Novette, the electricity from the capacitors is turned into a burst of regular light that hits the lasing material, causing a significant number of its electrons to rise from their ordinary configuration into higher-energy states. This is called "pumping" the electrons. (Novette is pumped by light. A nuclear X-ray laser is pumped by a bomb.)

The nature of the lasing material is such that its electrons are briefly held in a state known as a "population inversion." When one of these electrons spontaneously decays back to a lower-energy state, it releases a photon of light. What makes a laser a laser is that such spontaneous photons start to trigger stimulated emissions as well. They trick excited electrons into emitting other photons that have exactly the same frequency and phase and are headed in the same direction. It is the beginning of a cascade. What emerges from the end of Novette is a powerful beam made up of coherent photons. This is what constitutes a laser, originally an acronym for Light Amplification by Stimulated Emission of Radiation.

Novette's beam was of fairly long wavelength, being in the near-infrared portion of the electromagnetic spectrum. As the beam emerged, however, its wavelength was cut in half as it passed through special crystals that forced it into the green portion of the spectrum. This light had a wavelength of 5320 Angstroms. (An Angstrom is one ten-billionth of a meter, or about four billionths of an inch.)

For decades, the quest in laser making has been to construct devices of ever shorter wavelength. First came lasers in the microwave region of the electromagnetic spectrum, then the ruby-red laser, then the ultraviolet, and so forth, the wavelengths getting shorter and shorter. This was also Peter's goal—to create the shortest waves ever. Whereas wavelengths of visible light range from 7000 to 4000 Angstroms, X-rays are considered to be less than 100 Angstroms. A brilliant success in the X-ray region would be the achievement of a laser with a wavelength of 1 Angstrom. One reason for the allure of this goal is that shorter wavelengths pack more punch. X-rays have 100 to 10,000 times more energy than visible light and react with matter in a very different manner. Light, for instance, does not penetrate human flesh, whereas X-rays do, a fact that doctors have long exploited to "see" bones inside the body.

Peter's challenge was to take Novette's light of 5320 Angstroms and somehow use it to produce a laser in the neighborhood of

1 Angstrom. To lase at these tiny wavelengths, target materials were selected that had electrons very tightly bound to their atomic nuclei. It took a powerful punch to knock these electrons into highly excited states, to create a population inversion. A universal rule of laser making is that the power required to attain lasing goes up as the inverse cube of the desired wavelength—an enormous rate of growth. This challenge is one reason why the quest for X-ray lasers has attracted and frustrated so many scientists over the decades. It was a huge mountain to climb. It's also why the pumping source for an X-ray laser has to be something powerful, like Novette or an H-bomb.

For years Peter had struggled to find the best way to achieve this lasing action—and not by mere trial and error but by understanding the fundamentals of electron transitions, by learning how, when, and why electrons move from one atomic state to another. Since X-rays are different from waves of visible light, purists such as Peter said they were searching not for X-ray lasers—where the "l" stands for light—but for X-rasers, standing for X-Ray Amplification by Stimulated Emission of Radiation. Peter's masterwork was XRASER, a computer program meant to simulate and predict such electron movements and thus aid in the selection of materials and designs for the creation of an X-ray laser. XRASER was huge, containing more than 40,000 lines of code. (In the computer world, a programmer is considered quite good if he can write a few hundred error-free lines of code a month.)

Peter's experiments, which were not operating during my tour of Novette, took the powerful, visible light of the large laser and focused it on tiny targets of metal film, whose tightly bound electrons became quite excited. After nearly a year of work, however, there had been no signs of success.

I had heard much about the X-ray laser saga from Peter's peers and from Lowell. But now, seeing Novette, the scope of the drama had become clearer. Both the challenge and the tools were very large. And the end of the quest was nowhere in sight. The world's most powerful laboratory laser and one of the world's brightest laser scientists had so far failed to create a coherent beam of X-rays. Peter's quest with Novette was all the more frustrating because he had already made a breakthrough in a very different realm—creating an X-ray laser pumped by a nuclear bomb.

* * *

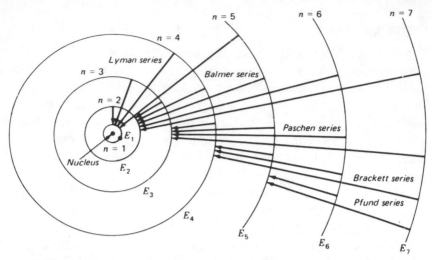

Quantum transitions of single electron in hydrogen atom. Electron transitions are the basis of laser light. The complex atoms of metals have dozens of electrons, complicating the task of mapping transitions.

My escort took me back to 1877 where I awaited the arrival of the mysterious Hagelstein. Early in the week Lowell had gone on at length about how Peter stood out among his peers. "He has the enormous advantage of being not only exceedingly competent in a technical sense, but quite creative," he said. "Most capable technical people are as dry as chips when it comes to innovation."

References to Peter's breadth and creativity had come up often in conversations at the lab. Peter was said to have run marathons in college and to have been on the swim team. He studied piano. He played violin in a string quartet during his freshman year at MIT, also joining its symphony orchestra and touring with it nationally. He read French literature—in French.

Lowell had interviewed Peter for a Hertz Fellowship, and after getting a feel for his diverse interests asked why he pursued them. "His answer," Lowell recalled, "was that they made life worth living."

Many people had commented on Peter's eccentricity. Andy Weisberg, a close friend, had gone on about how Peter was intellectually driven and full of rigor but left himself open for all sorts of mundane problems. "He's an insomniac in general but especially before important meetings," Andy said. "He works incredible hours the day before and then can't sleep, and shows up looking like a dead fish."

Larry West had been impressed with Peter's ability to concentrate all his energies on a single goal. He recounted how Peter had worked around the clock on computer codes to predict the electron transitions of laboratory X-ray lasers in the 1970s. "He was working fourteen or fifteen hours a day, night and day, seven days a week." Larry added that Peter's meals often consisted of peanut butter sandwiches and a Coke. "He'd run to the refrigerator, open the bread, slap down some peanut butter, and go right back to the computer terminal. In O Group you have to be smart enough to do the job or crazy enough to do it. Peter was both. He worked night and day calculating atomic energy levels. There were millions of things he had to do, all of which were very exotic and relied on the most advanced physical theory. He didn't even have a physics background. He learned the most advanced quantum physics by simply reading the technical literature, which was amazing. He worked that way for about seven or eight years."

Larry also said he thought Peter felt some ambivalence about his role as a creator of third-generation weapons. "He still doesn't want to be known for weapons," Larry said. "He feels that the perception of the general scientific community is that it's evil. So he's very cautious about ever having his name attached to anything having to do with weapons, even if he believes they may help the world."

Finally, after weeks and months of rumors and stories, after failing to track him down in his many haunts, Peter appeared at the door. He was 29 years old and had a round, unlined face, pale complexion, and silky blond hair. He was taller and heavier than I expected, looking a bit like an overgrown choirboy. His manner was withdrawn, his gaze cast downward. He apologized for not having stopped by sooner. I asked him to start at the beginning and tell me something about himself. Little by little, hesitantly at first, Peter told his story.

Peter had grown up in Los Angeles. He had shown an early talent for mathematics, which his father, a mechanical engineer, encouraged. His parents broke up when he was about ten, and Peter, like Larry, lived with his mother. Throughout this turbulent period his love for the perfect world of mathematics continued to grow. In the sixth grade Peter entered a mathematics competition in Los Angeles County and placed thirteenth out of some 50,000 applicants. He would have done better but, as Peter had recalled, "during the final round the pressure freaked me out and I didn't handle it well."

Peter went on to excel in math and history at Canoga Park High School, which Peter said was strong in the humanities and fairly weak in the sciences. He started to write music. "I came to the conclusion that the interesting compositions were too hard to play and the ones I could play were too dull," Peter recalled. "So I started writing my own. That started in 1971 and continues to this day. Recently a copyist went over some of my work and I hope to get it published. It's a joy to compose music. My techniques are not professional but some of the work is sort of interesting."

Though he loved the humanities, Peter got his highest marks in math. In his senior year he took a correspondence course in linear algebra from the University of Washington, where his mother had gone to school. He also started to feel a strong attraction for the physical sciences, even though they were not emphasized at his school. He became a tutor for an advanced-placement physics course at a nearby high school, teaching and learning much of the material at the same time. He took the final and got a perfect score. "I had a gift," Peter recalled. "And it was something I enjoyed."

Most of his friends planned to go to Stanford or the University of California at Santa Barbara. Peter, graduating in 1972 with a National Merit Scholarship, had applied to many colleges. He was quickly accepted by MIT, which offered him a hefty package of financial aid. Peter and his mother were far from wealthy, so he set off for Cambridge.

Set in an old Boston suburb, MIT is an elite educational mecca for computer jocks, math prodigies, and whiz kids of all sorts. While Caltech excels in pure science, MIT has few peers in computer science or electrical, mechanical, and chemical engineering.

Peter found it intimidating at first. He said Asian students always seemed to sit in the front rows and have all the answers. "I knew I wasn't the smartest," Peter recalled. "But the material was compelling."

Peter took a double load, as well as courses during the summer. After his second year at MIT, he was ready to graduate with an undergraduate degree from the Department of Electrical Engineering and Computer Science. In the spring of 1974, he was admitted into MIT's graduate school. Financial aid had paved his way as an undergraduate, but now he worked, first as a research assistant and then as a teaching assistant. Belatedly, Peter began to look through MIT's fellowship file. Hertz stood out as having one of the highest stipends of all.

Peter had his interview with Lowell, and in addition to clinching a fellowship was offered a job at the weapons lab for the summer of 1975. Never having heard of the lab, Peter hesitated at first, but eventually accepted.

Did Lowell explain the nature of the laboratory? "He said that in some ways it was like anyplace else," Peter answered. "He said they were working on lasers and laser fusion, which I had never heard of before, and he said there were computer codes out there that were like playing a Wurlitzer organ. It all sounded kind of dreamy."

At the age of 20, Peter drove down Interstate 580 through the Livermore valley toward the weapons lab. What he saw was sharply at odds with the green trees and ponds that had been depicted in a laboratory brochure. "I got out here at the end of May," Peter recalled. "It was close to 100 degrees and the hills were burnt brown. The place looked disgusting. I was driving down the free-way and the sign said the population of Livermore was 35,000. It seemed there were more cows than people.

"The lab itself made quite an impression," he continued, "espe-cially the guards and barbed wire. When I got to the personnel department it dawned on me that they worked on weapons here, and that's about the first I knew about it. I came pretty close to leaving. I didn't want to have anything to do with it. Anyway, I met nice people, so I stayed. The people were extremely interesting. And I really didn't have anywhere else to go."

For the next year or so Peter flew back and forth between Massa-chusetts and the weapons lab. In 1976, after four years of study, he graduated from MIT with B.S. and M.S. degrees in electrical engineering and computer science. He proceeded to take up full-time work at the lab. As was often the case in O Group, he main-tained his academic status, working toward a Ph.D. at MIT and receiving a yearly stipend from the Hertz Foundation in addition to his lab salary. As Peter saw it, he was an MIT student working at Livermore temporarily. It, after all, had the right tools.

In 1976, Peter was interested only in trying to create a labora-tory X-ray laser, an advance that he felt would bring a host of biomedical discoveries. He read widely in organic chemistry and neurophysiology, imagining the secrets his revolutionary tool would reveal. The laser's very short wavelength would allow it to "see" all sorts of biological processes, cell structures, and molecules that previously had been hidden. Moreover, the images would be three-dimensional. Just as lasers at visible wavelengths could take 3-D holographic "pictures" of large objects, such as Coke bottles, X-ray lasers would be able to do the same in the microscopic world of atoms and molecules, revealing the fabric of life.

Scientists at the frontiers of biology longed for such pictures. They had already discovered the chemical composition of many biological molecules, and desperately wanted a way to understand how these complex structures fit together in three dimensions, forming biological membranes and other structures. The pictures would shed light on all sorts of biological processes, including why cellular machinery went awry in the phenomenon of cancer.

Another attraction for Peter was that so many scientists had tried and failed to create an X-ray laser over so many decades that its final achievement would spark a worldwide sensation and possibly lead to the Nobel Prize. Indeed, Peter's excitement grew rapidly as he began to understand the scope of the challenge. But the bureaucratic machinery of the weapons lab and the federal government remained cool to the notion of funding any work on a laboratory X-ray laser.

The principal American patron of the X-ray effort in the early 1970s had been the Pentagon's Defense Advanced Research Projects Agency, which contributed about $1 million a year to the nationwide quest, some of it going to Livermore. But having paid all the bills for years and gotten no experimental success for its trouble, the agency in 1976 decided to abandon the effort. Unfortunately for Peter, the decision came almost simultaneously with his arrival at the lab.

All was not lost. In order to pursue his X-ray experiments, Peter hoped to rely on the internal financial resources of Livermore and, more importantly, on access to its huge lasers, which were the biggest and most powerful in the world. But such support failed to materialize. The lab's laser group, known as Y Division and headed by John L. Emmett, was busy doing weapons studies and chasing the holy grail of laser fusion and had little time for the shy graduate student from Lowell's group. Such neglect was all the more frustrating to Peter after Y Division in 1977 switched on its beautiful, new $25 million laser, known as Shiva, after the Hindu god of destruction and reproduction.

So Peter kept himself busy by mastering physics, learning quantum theory, studying the literature, developing ideas, and writing computer codes late into the night. In the perfect world of higher mathematics, with the help of his trusty computer terminal and the huge stable of supercomputers harnessed to it, Peter simulated the experiments he had been denied in real life. Andy, in describing this period, had called Peter "a lone voice crying in the wilderness." The description was apt. Peter's devotion to the problem, his discipline, his sacrifice, his asceticism, were prophetic in their intensity.

But Peter was not the only person at Livermore to dream the dream of X-ray lasers. Others had too, and they eventually succeeded in persuading Peter to join their distinctive efforts.

The search for the X-ray laser at Livermore had actually gotten underway in the late 1960s, the pace picking up considerably when Lowell and George Chapline teamed up to pursue it. George, in particular, never stopped pondering the elusive goal. During the mid-1970s he occasionally worked on the problem—but from a different angle than Peter. George wanted to pump an X-ray laser with a power source many billions of times more powerful than the biggest laboratory laser on earth. He wanted to use a nuclear bomb.

Such thoughts had occurred to others before. Indeed, for decades the weapons enthusiasts at Livermore had envisioned using nuclear bombs to dig ditches, blast asteroids, create black holes, and pump all kinds of exotic beam weapons. But Chapline in 1977 came up with a novel idea for how to go about building a nuclear-pumped X-ray laser. In one of those odd coincidences, that year also marked the appearance of the movie that would eventually become the rallying cry for the work—*Star Wars*.

Chapline's idea was compelling enough to call for a nuclear test. His experiment was to be piggybacked onto a detonation that had already been scheduled for the Nevada site. There was no prospect for the much more expensive alternative—a dedicated test. After all, Chapline's idea at this point was risky. Skeptics at the lab kept pointing to the long, unsuccessful pursuit of the X-ray laser.

Chapline's test occurred fairly quickly, but in general the creation of nuclear detonations in the Nevada desert often takes years of planning. Hundreds of scientists, engineers, machinists, guards,

and laborers have to be mobilized to draw blueprints, to build the bombs, to make special detectors, to check safety and security, to get clearances, and to deliver the prototype nuclear device to the test site. Such efforts have often been made and have often been rewarded. Since the atomic age began in 1945, the United States has detonated more than 700 nuclear bombs at test sites in New Mexico, the Pacific, Alaska, Colorado, Mississippi, and Nevada. The Soviets have conducted more than 500 tests.

The 1,350-square-mile Nevada Test Site is located about seventy miles northwest of Las Vegas. Its arid landscape is dotted with mesquite, yucca, and Joshua trees, and with craters formed by the collapse of underground caverns that had been carved by nuclear explosions. During a large detonation, an observer detects a distant rumble, followed by a gentle, wavelike rocking of the earth.

For Lowell, Peter, Bruce, Larry, and the rest of the young weapon designers, this gentle rocking motion is the closest they can ever come in peacetime to personally experiencing the effects of a nuclear explosion. Since the advent of the Limited Test Ban Treaty in 1963, all American and Russian tests have been confined to beneath the earth. The new generation of weapon makers at Livermore are all too young to have participated in a detonation in the earth's atmosphere.

In Nevada, most of the twenty or so nuclear tests conducted every year are Department of Energy (DOE) shots that try out new bomb designs or make sure weapons already in the stockpile are still fresh. But the one that Chapline tagged onto was different. This was a Pentagon test conducted by the Defense Nuclear Agency (DNA). There are only one or two of these explosions a year. Rather than testing and monitoring the bomb itself, their aim, as is the case with all DNA nuclear tests, is to take a bomb whose reliability and features are already known and use it to study the effects of its radiations on different kinds of military equipment. The DNA shots are much more elaborate and expensive than those conducted by DOE, many costing more than $40 million each.

In preparation for a DNA test, engineers dig a long horizontal tunnel beneath the Nevada desert and erect a large metal pipe inside it. At one end of the pipe they build a big metal box for the bomb and at the other end a test chamber. Before the test, all the air is pumped from the pipe in order to mimic the void of outer space. When the bomb is detonated, radiation races down the pipe at the speed of light, bathing the test chamber with neutrons, X-rays, and gamma rays. A fraction of a second later, trap doors in the pipe slam shut to keep the bomb's debris from smashing into the test chamber.

In the DNA test that Chapline tagged onto, the main focus was to study the effects of nuclear radiation on the MX warhead, making sure it could survive a nuclear attack in space as it sped toward the Soviet Union. The warheads were clustered on bulkheads in the chamber, about a thousand feet from the bomb. In all, four hundred separate points of data from various experiments were meant to be taken by scientists during the expansion of that nuclear fireball deep beneath the Nevada desert.

One of those experiments was Chapline's. Pounded by intense radiation from a bomb rather than from a large laboratory laser like Novette, the target material in Chapline's experiment would,

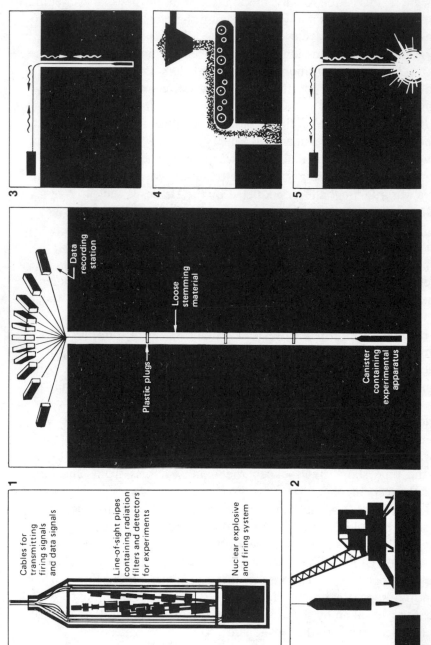

(1) Nuclear weapon and detectors for vertical test in Nevada. (2) Assembly lowered into hole. (3) Cables checked electrically. (4) Hole filled. (5) Weapon exploded and data recorded.

Cables for transmitting firing signals and data signals

Line-of-sight pipes containing radiation filters and detectors for experiments

Nuclear explosive and firing system

Data recording station

Loose stemming material

Plastic plugs

Canister containing experimental apparatus

with luck, undergo a population inversion and lase at X-ray wavelengths. It would be a "nuclear" X-ray laser only in the sense that it was pumped by a nuclear bomb. Its atomic nuclei would in no way contribute to the lasing. As always, the lasing itself would be the product of the coordinated movement of billions of electrons.

Code-named Diablo Hawk, the explosion took place on September 13, 1978. The bomb went off, but the elaborate apparatus of detectors and sensors for measuring the output of the X-ray experiment broke down. No one knew whether Chapline's innovative idea was a success or a failure.

George was disappointed but not about to give up. He talked to everybody he knew in positions of power about the idea and its merits. Then a bureaucratic miracle occurred. Congress directed that $20 million be split between the nation's two weapons labs to try a dedicated nuclear test of something new, risky, and different. If ever there was anything that matched that description, it was Chapline's idea for the nuclear-pumped X-ray laser. George at last had the money to finance a dedicated experiment. Rather than piggybacking onto somebody else's test, his idea could become the focus of its own multimillion-dollar effort. Scheduling was such that the soonest possible date for the detonation would be in late 1980. Instead of a horizontal DNA test, it would be a standard DOE shot in which a nuclear bomb and detectors were placed at the bottom of a deep vertical shaft dug in the desert floor.

Curiously, this period of bold new vistas in the manipulation of nuclear fire coincided with an effort by the Carter administration to end nuclear testing altogether. In May 1978, President Carter instructed his negotiators to seek a complete, worldwide ban on nuclear tests as a way of applying a brake to the arms race. The move, however, brought a groundswell of opposition from the weapons labs and the weapons bureaucracy in Washington. By 1980, the proposed ban was a dead letter.

As months rolled by and plans moved forward for Chapline's dedicated test, engineers and technicians prepared new hardware and new detectors. But their careful work was about to be upset by the appearance of a rival idea for a nuclear X-ray laser—a design put forward by Peter.

Throughout 1979, Chapline and the laboratory's main bomb builders who were interested in the nuclear X-ray laser had been holding regular meetings to discuss it and the impending test. Had they overlooked anything? What was the physics? Was there a better way to try to go about it?

Lowell and Peter were present at some of those discussions. Peter's input was especially welcome, for he had been working all those years on laboratory X-ray lasers and knew the general X-ray laser theoretics better than anybody else at the lab. But Peter's impulse was to resist. He hated bombs. He didn't want to be associated with anything nuclear. This feeling, moreover, was strongly reinforced by a woman he dated at the time, Josephine Stein.

Peter and Josie had met at MIT in the early 1970s and had gotten to know one another while playing together in the symphony. She was a mechanical engineer who could talk about stress values or Schubert. Peter was a high achiever who excelled in sports, school, and music. Their attraction was natural—but it was only an attraction and not yet a romance. Throughout their years at MIT they remained friends.

Josie had graduated two years after Peter, in 1978, and stood out in the senior yearbook. Other members of her class listed such extracurricular activities as Math Club, Varsity Pistol Team, Rugby, Amateur Radio Club, Astronomical Society, Chess Team, Electronics Research Society, and Science Fiction Society. Josie's listings were unusual in that they were devoted exclusively to music— Symphony Orchestra, Choral Society, Chamber Music Society, Bach Society Orchestra.

During the summer of 1978, Josie moved from Cambridge to Berkeley to begin work on a master's degree at the University of California. She looked up Peter in nearby Livermore and the two were soon seeing much of each other. They played music together and went to movies, concerts, and parties thrown by members of O Group.

As Josie learned more about the lab and what it did, she became vocal in her opposition. She said bombs were bombs, and would always be agents of death and destruction. She accused Peter and his friends at the lab of ignoring the reality of their work. She told Peter that Lowell and Teller were using him for their own ends. She encouraged Peter to quit, and to interview at other laboratories for a job.

Peter was sympathetic. He had never liked the notion of working on weapons, and had usually managed to do things at the lab that in his own mind had no relation to bombs whatsoever. Now he felt pressure to make some kind of nuclear contribution. He fought it, going out to Bell Labs in New Jersey at one point to interview for a job.

Throughout 1979, moreover, Josie became more and more militant in her criticism of the weapons lab, at one point joining protestors outside its gates. She argued her points not only with Peter but with his friends, especially Jerry Epstein, whom she and Peter had originally met at MIT. Jerry, a Hertz fellow at Berkeley who worked part-time with O Group, even joined with Josie on one occasion to march in a protest.

"What Jerry did at the lab was totally unclassified," Larry had recalled. "But Josie felt it was too much. Doing anything within three hundred miles of the lab was too much for her."

Despite Peter's aversion to nuclear labors and Josie's support of this sentiment, one day he accidentally started down a fateful path. It was during the summer of 1979, at one of George's meetings. There Peter let slip a suggestion that changed forever the focus of the nation's nuclear X-ray laser program—and may yet change the strategic postures of the superpowers as well.

The day before the meeting, in typical fashion, Peter had been on a binge, working day and night. He arrived at the meeting in his "dead fish" mode, slightly disoriented and dazed.

For years Peter had pondered how to make X-ray lasers, his mind turning the problem over and over. Now, zonked from too much work and not enough sleep, his subconscious seemed to take over. He viewed himself from a distance, as if through the wrong end of a telescope. It was the kind of psychological state that comes after an accident or great stress. There was Peter. There was Peter at the meeting with George and Lowell and the others. There was Peter saying something that had not been said before, something new in the arcane world of nuclear X-ray lasers.

"I had been up twenty hours," Peter recalled. "It had something to do with being stretched out. The mouth just said it."

In the days after the meeting, Lowell lobbied hard for a test of the approach that Peter had broached. Chapline resisted. In the end, lab officials decided that the impending test of Chapline's nuclear X-ray laser should be modified to include Peter's idea as well, even though making the changes would entail some expense.

One bomb would pump two sets of hardware, each meant to produce an X-ray laser. It was to be a competition—senior physicist versus graduate student.

"Flash of insight" was the way Lowell described Peter's idea. Peter was more circumspect. "It takes five minutes to make a suggestion, and it just happened to be one that hadn't been made before. Then I got my arm twisted to do a detailed calculation. I resisted doing it. There were political pressures like you wouldn't believe."

Peter was asked to do much more than scribble for a few minutes on a yellow pad of paper. He was being asked to sit at his computer terminal day after day, pouring his special expertise into the calculation of what might happen when a certain lasing setup was pumped by a nuclear explosion. The raw material was to be his mammoth computer code, XRASER, which he had written to understand the electron transitions that power all X-ray lasers. His creation was quite personal. XRASER had a subroutine named after Josie. The complexity and depth of the code meant that only Peter could bring it to bear on the nuclear question. XRASER was a tool meant for his hands alone.

But Peter felt he had better things to do. His work on laboratory X-ray lasers, although still derided by Y Division, was nonetheless picking up speed. Two of Peter's friends from MIT, Jerry Epstein and Jordin Kare, had come to the lab and were helping on various aspects of his Nobel project. He was struggling to finish his Ph.D. Couldn't the mad bombers see he was busy? Couldn't they leave him alone?

Despite the protestations of Josie and his own apprehensions, Peter went ahead and worked on the calculations for the nuclear-pumped X-ray laser. Why? Certainly there were the "political pressures" Peter had mentioned. Both Teller and Lowell were eager for him to work on what was perhaps the most innovative (and still highly classified) idea in nuclear weaponry since the H-bomb. Long afterward, Peter liked to joke about Teller's general influence on people, citing a line out of *Star Wars:* "The Force has a powerful effect on the weak mind."

Moreover, during this period Peter read *The Gulag Archipelago,* Solzhenitsyn's three-volume portrait of the nightmares of Soviet concentration camps. During our conversation, Peter said he had indeed read the *Gulag* volumes during this period, but insisted that years earlier he had started and dropped them, and was in no way naive about the Soviets, having read much Russian literature and history in high school and college. "I've got a fairly moody and depressive personality," he said. "I read the *Gulag*. I'm afraid I like reading that kind of thing. I don't think the *Gulag* was pivotal. I was depressed and it lifted my spirits." In contrast to Peter, other members of the group said his reading of the book made a discernible difference in his attitude toward work on nuclear weaponry.

During our conversation, the factors Peter emphasized were his rivalry with Chapline and his hopes of advancing the understanding of the physics of the X-ray laser, whether pumped by a laboratory laser or a nuclear bomb. "Chapline and I never got along. I was a graduate student and he was a senior person. He made life very hard." There might indeed have been a temptation to try to beat the elder physicist at his nuclear game. After all, George was threatening to win the race for the X-ray laser with what Peter considered a cheap shortcut.

There was also the technical allure. By 1979, despite long years of pleading, Peter still lacked the big tools he needed to try to achieve his laboratory X-ray laser dream. But if things worked out with the nuclear variety, he might be allowed to step up work on those that were more benign. After all, people would at last be convinced that the X-ray quest was more than a personal obsession. At last Peter might get the kind of access he wanted to the expensive hardware of Shiva and Novette.

In addition to factors mentioned by people at the lab, two other forces seem likely to have played a role. One was Peter's desire for Lowell's approbation. Fred's late-night work on supercomputer wafers showed that Lowell could be a stern master, dispensing a bevy of barbs and snide remarks. That episode also showed that Lowell could be sincere in his praise. It was a powerful combination—disparagement alternating with a pat on the back. With shy Peter, the smile of approval must have been sweet indeed.

The other factor was friendship. Peter was being asked to participate in what was, after all, an important part of the laboratory's agenda—work on nuclear weapons. Surely he could refuse, but his relationship with the place might never be the same. There probably would be no overt display of displeasure on the part of Lowell or lab officials. But subtle changes might make him feel uncomfortable and compel him to leave. This would mean giving up his friends, his home, and one of the few places in the world where his special talents had really been appreciated. On that first day at the lab, Peter had almost turned back when he saw the barbed wire, guards, and guns. But, as he put it, "I met nice people, so I stayed."

The young scientists of the group were close friends. They were smart and sassy and could play pranks like nobody else. Being with them was fun. O Group once took up a collection to buy Lowell a costume of Darth Vader, the character in *Star Wars* who epitomized the dark side of The Force. But they scrapped the idea, afraid Lowell would actually wear it as he wandered the halls urging them to work harder.

The fabric of friendship extended even to the language they spoke. Classified projects led to classified jokes. After a while, the young scientists began to be cut off from the spontaneity of the outside world. A visitor could engage them in polite conversation, but so much of their world revolved around secret research that free-ranging discussions could occur only with other "Q-cleared" people. It was like the Gulag. Stalin's concentration camps were the only place in Russia where people could really criticize the state. Freedom came only in captivity.

Whatever the reasons in the murky world of motivation, Peter sat at his terminal and worked on the calculations for the design of the weapon. Moreover, they seemed to show promise. It looked as if Peter's off-the-cuff suggestion had considerable merit.

During this period, his relationship with Josie started to fall apart. "At first I tended to agree with her," Peter had recalled. "But she was terribly adamant. The more she talked the less sense she made."

Though a parting of the ways was almost predictable, Peter eventually became very depressed. Of the two, he had been more passionately involved in the relationship. At his lowest moments, after the breakup, the stereo in his office played nothing but Requiems. Lowell said it sounded like a funeral parlor.

The underground test itself, code-named "Dauphin," occurred at the Nevada test site on November 14, 1980. Lowell and George were there, worrying and fussing and sweating over the details. Peter was not, having stayed behind in Livermore.

The test was a success for both devices, although Peter's results were vastly superior. (The dual success was perhaps why Lowell

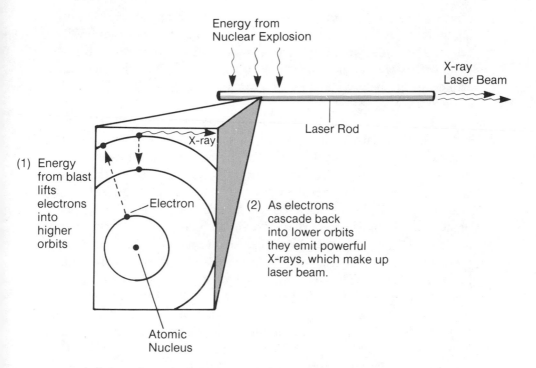

Energy from
Nuclear Explosion

X-ray
Laser Beam

Laser Rod

X-ray

(1) Energy
from blast
lifts
electrons
into
higher
orbits

Electron

(2) As electrons
cascade back
into lower orbits
they emit powerful
X-rays, which make up
laser beam.

Atomic
Nucleus

kept two sections of electrical cable in his office.) Lowell flew back from the Nevada test site. To celebrate, he and Peter and several other members of O Group drove into the heart of downtown Livermore and had ice cream at the Baskin-Robbins 31 Flavors.

"My view of weapons has changed," Peter recalled. "Until 1980 or so I didn't want to have anything to do with nuclear anything. Back in those days I thought there was something fundamentally evil about weapons. Now I see it as an interesting physics problem."

Josie went far in the opposite direction. In 1980 she received a master's degree in mechanical engineering from Berkeley and then, after her breakup with Peter, returned to MIT to work on her Ph.D. In Cambridge she played with a group known as "The No Nukes Trio." In the months after the breakup, her views of nuclear weaponry and the people who ran the lab deepened and became more pronounced. By a remarkable coincidence, her opinions were first set before the public in a biweekly MIT student newspaper called *Link* that was dated November 3 to 16, 1980, corresponding with the date of Peter's successful nuclear test.

"Fellowship for Work on 'Human Problems' Linked to Livermore," read the headline. It was a detailed account of the recruiting practices of the Hertz Foundation, a picture of Teller in its center. The understated charge was deception—that the foundation, ostensibly set up to fund graduate education, in truth recruited unsuspecting students to work on bombs. The by-line was Josie Stein.

In the article Josie did not mention Peter by name. But the fact of the article's existence suggested that she had strong feelings about why he had ended up at Livermore. The article started off by noting that another MIT newspaper, *Tech Talk,* had carried ads from the Hertz Foundation meant to bring its fellowship program to the attention of MIT students. One of the ads was reproduced. "The proposed field of graduate study," it read, "must be concerned with applications of the physical sciences to human problems, broadly construed." In the article Josie commented: "From the information in the announcements, one would never guess that the administration of the fellowship has close ties with the Lawrence Livermore National Laboratory, one of the two national laboratories dedicated to the research and development of nuclear weapons."

She then drove the point home, noting Teller's place on the Hertz board, the foundation's address, and the fact that Lowell was both the foundation's chief recruiter and the head of O Group, which "is largely composed of Hertz fellows and Hertz alumni."

At the end of the article she asked whether the competition for Hertz Fellowships was "in reality a deceptive campaign to recruit the most capable young technologists to work on nuclear weapons–related projects at Lawrence Livermore Lab? Such a premise would be very difficult to substantiate. However, prospective applicants for the Hertz Fellowship would be well advised to carefully consider the implications of involvement with the Foundation and Livermore."

For Peter, the implications of his work on nuclear weapons multiplied in the wake of the successful test, his device rapidly becoming the basis for the nation's nuclear X-ray laser program and playing a direct role in the genesis of the "Star Wars" speech.

The name bestowed upon Peter's creation was "Excalibur," after the Arthurian legend in which the young king-to-be pulled a magic sword from a stone. At Livermore a separate bureaucracy was set up around it, R Program, with an O Group member, Tom Weaver, at its head. Depending on whether or not R Program was about to conduct a nuclear test, the size of its staff could swell into the hundreds. R Program also became the primary sponsor of Peter's work on laboratory X-ray lasers. Peter now had the access he wanted to the laboratory's big laser.

In the wake of his bittersweet nuclear triumph, however, Peter began to feel that the original reason for pursuing research on peaceful X-ray lasers had vanished. Techniques with electron microscopes and regular X-rays had improved to the point that they were better suited to achieving the long-sought biomedical goals. Even if a laboratory X-ray laser was successfully created, Peter felt there would be nothing useful for it to do.

Hints of this turnaround were contained in Peter's doctoral dissertation, which he submitted to MIT in January 1981 under the title "Physics of Short Wavelength Laser Design." In essence it was a primer on the theoretics of building a laboratory X-ray laser. Its 451 pages were thick with equations and scholarly references, but the document broke from its esoteric pace at one point to suggest "future applications." There was no mention of biological imaging or molecular insights or solving the riddle of cancer. Instead it pointed to three works of science fiction—*Ringworld* by Larry Niven, *Mote in God's Eye* by Niven and Jerry Pournelle, and *Tom Swift and His Cosmotron Express* by V. Appleton.

In one of them, *Ringworld,* a spaceship was hit by beam weapons as it approached a foreign world. "We have been fired upon," cried a character in the book. "We are still being fired upon, probably by X-ray lasers. This ship is now in a state of war. Were it not for our invulnerable hull, we would be dead."

For Peter, the reference to death rays bespoke a deep change of attitude. "Originally I had gotten into this business thinking X-ray lasers would be used for the holography of biological molecules," Peter said. "That was my original incentive for working as hard as I did. But by the time my thesis got written, it was fairly clear to me that X-ray lasers wouldn't be able to make much of a dent in terms of biological problems. They would be interesting, but if I were a biologist and needed an answer, I could think of lots of places I'd go before turning to the X-ray laser.

"Writers of science fiction are supposed to look into the future. So I started looking to see what they had in mind for X-ray lasers.

It turns out all the science fiction references are to blowing things up."

When I first saw Peter's dissertation, before coming to the lab, I thought the references to science fiction bespoke not defeat but militancy—that he had been inspired by death rays. But when we talked he said the references were descriptive, not prescriptive. "Livermore is now putting in more than five million dollars for these experiments at Novette. But suppose we were to make one work fabulously—beyond our wildest dreams. What in the world could we do with it? We don't know yet. It gives you a certain feeling of frustration. Here's this neat effect and apparently the only use of consequence for it is to blow things up. It's fairly discouraging."

In contrast to Peter's analysis, others in the group said various types of laboratory X-ray lasers would eventually have application not only to biological holography but such processes as etching compact circuits on silicon chips. They added that Peter's moodiness often made him needlessly pessimistic.

No matter what the potential uses of a laboratory X-ray laser, Peter was forced, in writing his doctoral dissertation, to document the disconcerting fact that it did not exist. His pursuit of it over many years had been a failure. Unstated in the document was the fact that the only working X-ray laser in the world was nuclear. Out of frustration, his thesis was laced not only with references to death rays but with a certain bitterness. In its foreword, Peter thanked many individuals at the weapons lab for their assistance in his work, citing many members of O Group and the S-1 Project. Then Peter spoke of Lowell, a man who "first suggested the approach to me and led me into this folly when I was too naive to know better. He has been a constant source of encouragement and ideas of all sorts (including the notion that the X-ray laser design is a summer project for a graduate student, and that Y program would carry out the X-ray laser experiment in their spare time out of sheer good will). The man has been called a dreamer by some and is clearly a technologist, many of whose ideas are ahead not only of his own time but ahead of probably several generations of descendants' times as well."

In short, over the years Peter had become a designer of third-generation weapons by default, although few of his friends back at

MIT knew of the transformation. After all, the nuclear X-ray success and the rapid bureaucratic response of the weapons lab had been accomplished amid complete secrecy. The government demanded it. The mere existence of the nuclear X-ray laser was a top national secret.

The silence was unofficially broken by an article in the February 23, 1981 issue of *Aviation Week and Space Technology,* a weekly trade publication known in the Pentagon as "Aviation Leak." Its author, Clarence A. Robinson, Jr., detailed what he reported to be all the basics of the secret Nevada test, calling it a "breakthrough" for Livermore that "has the potential to blunt a Soviet nuclear weapons attack." The nuclear X-ray laser beam was said to have a wavelength of 14 Angstroms—very close to the 1 Angstrom criterion for a brilliant success.

Robinson said the test cost about $10 million. A projected application, he continued, would be to surround a nuclear warhead with a ring of about fifty laser rods and have them fire at missiles. Each rod would be pointed at a target, then the bomb would be detonated. "The X-ray lasers based on the successful Dauphin test, when mounted in a laser battle station, are so small that a single payload bay on the space shuttle could carry to orbit a number sufficient to stop a Soviet nuclear weapons attack." Critics have repeatedly disparaged this assertion and others like it, which they characterize as the worst kind of high-tech fantasy.

A slick drawing accompanied the article. It showed a battle station in space that bristled with long laser rods. Subsequently, this picture was widely copied throughout the media as stories proliferated about the new type of nuclear weapon.

The *Aviation Week* article did not cite Peter or anyone else at Livermore by name. His work was still shrouded in anonymity. But it did give some clues as to the novel feature of Peter's idea. It said that "the lasing material in a series of lasing rods is an atomically dense substance in solid form"—in other words a metal or a number of different metals drawn into a long rod. Conventional lasers, in order to amplify their output, often have a resonant chamber in which photons of light bounce back and forth. But the X-ray laser rods conjured up another vision: the length of the rod would help determine the amplification. The more atoms that could be lined up in the form of a long rod, the greater the overall laser output. A practical limitation for an X-ray battle station in space would be the ability to quickly move a long, thin rod and have it point accurately at a distant target.

The article also said an earlier test of a nuclear X-ray laser at the Nevada site had failed because of problems with instrumentation—in other words, Chapline's 1978 test. It said the earlier experiment had been based on the use of krypton fluoride, a gas.

A few months after the appearance of the *Aviation Week* article, a series of events took place that ultimately culminated in President Reagan's "Star Wars" speech. In May 1981 George A. Keyworth, II, was named the President's science advisor. A nuclear physicist from Los Alamos, he was intimately familiar with the X-ray secrets and had been strongly recommended for the job by Teller.

Also in 1981, a small and very select group of scientists, industrialists, and military men began to meet in Washington, D.C., at the Heritage Foundation, a conservative "think tank." Their goal was to formulate a plan for creating a national system of defense and to convey that plan to the newly elected President. Among the group's members were Teller and such members of the President's "kitchen cabinet" as Joseph Coors, a beer executive. The group's top officer was Karl R. Bendetsen, once Under-Secretary of the Army, later Chairman of the Board of the Champion International Corporation, and a long-time overseer of the Hoover Institution on War, Revolution, and Peace. Since the 1940s he had known Teller, who in addition to his position at the weapons lab also held a post at Hoover. All group members received security clearances so they could learn about and discuss secret details of new weapons, including Peter's nuclear X-ray laser.

The group's first meeting with the President took place in January 1982, followed by two other White House visits prior to the "Star Wars" speech of March 1983. In addition, Teller had a private meeting with the President in September 1982 during which he stressed the importance of the technologies being developed at Livermore. In all, Teller met with the President four times over the course of little more than a year.

Throughout this period the government maintained a news blackout on the subject of the X-ray laser. No official was to acknowledge that it even existed, despite the detailed leak that had appeared in *Aviation Week*. That silence was officially broken by Keyworth, the President's science advisor, in a talk at Livermore on January

14, 1983. According to reporter Keith Rogers, he hailed the "bomb-pumped X-ray laser" as being "one of the most important programs that may seriously influence the nation's defense posture in the next decades."

But there were skeptics. Long before the President's speech, rumors of the X-ray breakthrough had reached Bethe, Teller's erstwhile friend. In February 1983 curiosity brought him to Livermore for a two-day visit. Bethe was briefed on all the secret details of the X-ray laser, his security clearance having been maintained over the years. At the end of the first day he was still skeptical. He had strong doubts that the device worked as claimed. Numbers from the nuclear test site were not enough. He wanted to know in a fundamental way why the X-ray laser was said to work.

During the second day of Bethe's visit, Peter was recuperating from one of his all-night bouts of work. He was home sleeping when the phone rang. It was Lowell. He complained that Peter was twenty minutes late and everybody was waiting for him. Hadn't he received notice about the meeting with Bethe? "I threw on some clothes and came scrambling in, trying to wake up," Peter recalled. "I'd had something like three hours of sleep." Out of breath, Peter paused to compose himself and then walked into Teller's office, high atop Building 111.

"Bethe had hassled a lot of people in the program and wasn't getting any satisfaction," Peter recalled. "Teller was there initially that day and then went out because he had work to do. Lowell was there to witness what went on. Bethe was certainly asking the question that was the basis of everything. In fact, it was kind of surprising that nobody had given him a fair answer before. It took me a little while to figure out what in the world he was asking. Then it was obvious. I hadn't gone through the arguments recently. But I thought, well, I know the numbers will work out. So I turned to the blackboard and said, here's the answer and let's try to work out everything that leads up to it."

Forty minutes later, Peter had finished. "By the time I was done, the equations had come out right. Hans Bethe was very pleased and impressed, and his criticisms had fallen apart."

Bethe's curiosity had been satisfied in relation to the physics of the X-ray laser, but he still had strong doubts that it or its brethren could ever stop an armada of Soviet missiles, especially ones that had been specifically designed to foil such a weapon. After his visit, he told *Time* magazine: "I don't think it can be done. What is worse, it will produce a Star War if successful."

Teller in his Congressional testimony painted a picture of the Bethe visit and described its significance for him. "He listened for a day carefully," Teller recalled. "The morning of the second day he came back with a considerable number of intelligent objections. In the course of the second day, all his objections were answered to his satisfaction. He said in front of me, 'You have a splendid idea.' But did he change his public position? No. Instead of objecting on scientific and technical grounds, which he thoroughly understands, he now objects on the grounds of politics, on grounds of feasibility of military deployment, on other grounds of difficult issues which are quite outside the range of his professional cognizance or mine."

During this same day of testimony, Teller outlined for the congressmen all the essentials of pop up, an idea for the deployment of nuclear X-ray lasers of which he was the author. Teller was clearly giving himself, and perhaps Bethe, insufficient credit.

I asked Peter why nobody else at the lab had been able to answer Bethe's question. "It was probably a combination of things," he answered. "Tom Weaver would have been able to answer it fairly easily but he wasn't around. And so they kept serving him up seconds. And when all is said and done, it is hard to get hold of information in the program.

"Bethe's question was the first and foremost of the basic questions you'd ask. Different people had asked it. The kind of thing that Hans Bethe wanted was something fundamental that he could write down and remember. The program had thrown up a fair amount of smoke on these issues because there were so many different ways you could define the answer. Hans Bethe had been shown reams of calculations and output and all kinds of stuff. But that just didn't answer his question. He wanted something simple and fundamental. He asked it in a way that I thought everyone should have been looking at it. I could write down the energy levels and so forth and he knew exactly what was going on. He knew what processes were important and why. What do you expect from a man who more or less founded the field of atomic physics?"

Peter, the creator of the nuclear X-ray laser, and Bethe, the skeptic, had come to a shared understanding in a way unique to physicists. It was a meeting in which Lowell, often aggressive and domineering, had sat on the sidelines. It was a drama that Teller had missed. Bethe at the time was 76 years old. Peter was 28. Bethe was a Nobel laureate. Peter was an electrical engineer who had taught himself physics.

Before my visit to Livermore, Bethe had told me that the X-ray laser "as far as the physics goes is a very ingenious job. It is likely to go. Now, of course, the engineering and the actual deployment is another matter. Such a device is a long way from actually working, even in a test circumstance, and to translate this into an operational device is a fantastic business."

Bethe also said he had been shown all the other proposals for third-generation weapons at Livermore. "None of them impressed me," he said. "These are mostly half-baked or quarter-baked ideas. That does not apply to the X-ray laser, which has been quite carefully thought out."

Bethe said he thought there was some cynicism among officials at the laboratory about the third-generation weapons, whereas the young scientists were probably sincere. "Enthusiasm is very good," Bethe said. "And this is certainly a very important component in this business. The young people want to show something for themselves. Yet many, many people in the nuclear weapons enterprise have stated that there isn't much more to be done about offensive weapons. So, they say, 'If we want to continue in this field, let's try defensive weapons.' That's a little bit harsh, but I'm afraid this is a big component of it all."

Rather than trying to build a defensive shield and new kinds of nuclear weapons, Bethe said the nation should try to stabilize the arms race with treaties and by working on nonnuclear technologies, such as smart munitions, that would raise the nuclear threshold in Europe. "We need to try to understand the other fellow and negotiate and try to come to some agreement about the common danger," Bethe said. "That is what's been forgotten. The solution can only be political. It would be terribly comfortable for the President and the Secretary of Defense if there was a technical solution. But there isn't any."

In the months following his visit to Livermore, Bethe used his influence to help launch studies and critiques of the X-ray laser and to argue against its use in a defensive system. The war over Star Wars had begun in earnest. Most of the studies focused on what the Soviets could do to outwit the system, the easiest approach being simply to overwhelm it. One of the first of these reports was published by the Cambridge-based Union of Concerned Scientists. It was coauthored by Bethe.

Before meeting Peter, I had expected him to be a gung-ho enthusiast like Larry, ready to offer a series of quick comebacks to the critics. The science fiction in his Ph.D. thesis reinforced my expectation. His invention, moreover, had helped pave the way for the "Star Wars" speech and its promise of a new strategic era. Here, I thought, would be a key spokesman for the "technical solution" to the threat of nuclear war.

But Peter had no quick comebacks. The science fiction references had been part satire and part ironic comment on the seeming futility of his higher ambitions for the laboratory X-ray laser. It was not militancy, not death rays. Peter had indeed done the calculations for the bomb-pumped X-ray laser, for whatever complex of reasons. But his work clearly had little to do with wanting to create an impenetrable defense for the nation. Perhaps the implication of Josie's article was correct—that the Hertz money had been used to trick Peter and his peers into working at the weapons lab. But even if subtle coercion played a role, Peter nonetheless took credit for his creation by defending it in his meeting with Bethe. It was clearly the source of a certain amount of pride. Yet Peter also seemed to feel a deep ambivalence about his brainchild. After the events of 1980, he began to find weapons an "interesting physics problem." It was not exactly the way a king-to-be should talk about his magic sword.

During our conversation, Peter shifted back and forth on the issue of whether a shield was feasible. His manner did not evoke visions of a high-tech warrior who believed that all problems could be solved with hardware. It suggested a troubled young man who preferred to ignore the military uses of his creation and, when asked to contemplate them, tended to see limitations. As we talked, he stressed not technical solutions to the arms race but political ones, such as cultural exchanges between the superpowers. At times he sounded like Bethe.

"Defense is clearly interesting and feasible," he said. "I suppose if I say something like that they'll want to classify it. With respect to whether it will make war less likely, I doubt that, I mean in terms of man's drives. You're not going to stop war. It would be very nice if we could develop a defensive network that would blow away all Soviet ICBMs. But I don't think we can do that. We could take out some. But I don't think we could take out all of them. Even if we could, that would not stop war or get rid of the nuclear threat, people being what they are. I'm more or less convinced that one of these days we'll have World War Three or whatever. It'll be pretty ugly. A lot of cities will get busted up. I don't really understand how in the world to defuse the situation or get rid of it. I tend to blame the Soviet government for a lot of it. But as these things go, our own government is sometimes more earthy than its voters realize or would like to know. When all is said and done, the Russians are not as flaky as we are in a lot of respects. I bear no grudges, at least with respect to the Soviet people. In terms of making the situation better, I think something that would make a big difference is if there were large-scale cultural exchanges between the Soviets and us—so we could at least get to know one another. Maybe that would help. We're in a bad situation, though. And getting up a defensive system might help things somewhat. But it wouldn't keep cities from being obliterated."

KNOW THINE ENEMY

★

There would be no debate over the feasibility of pop up and other defensive systems if their success depended solely on a thorough understanding of the laws of physics. But unlike the moon landing, a feat of pure technology that centered on a struggle with the force of gravity, defensive systems would have to deal with an unpredictable and intelligent enemy. Both defenders and detractors of Star Wars agree on the likelihood of a strong Soviet response. The question is how strong, and whether it would doom the quest for defense. The Russians could attack the system itself, protect their offensive missiles, deploy a variety of decoys, or simply pommel a shield with increased numbers of missiles and warheads. In short, they could employ countermeasures.

Advocates of strategic defense often say the Soviet Union is technologically backward and could never defeat American expertise. Critics say the Soviets, though sometimes behind, will always be advanced enough to outwit any high-tech shield.

With pop up, the debate centers on whether the Soviets could build very fast missiles whose period of bright flames and rapid acceleration would be completed not in space but much closer to the ground, while still surrounded by the protective blanket of the earth's atmosphere, where X-rays could not penetrate. If so, the hope of boost-phase interception would suddenly disappear. Nuclear X-ray lasers popped up from American submarines would find themselves unable to hit Soviet rockets, and instead would face thousands of hard-to-detect cool warheads zooming toward the United States through the void of space. They would be hard to distinguish from decoys, and difficult to destroy. The beam of an X-ray laser might crumple a fragile booster but only scrape the paint off a hardened warhead.

The debate over the strength of Soviet technology is mirrored by a long-running dispute over its people. One view is that Russian society is inherently backward and that East-West conflict is rooted in this fundamental difference. The other is that no real differences of values or interests divide the peoples of the superpowers, and that conflicts often arise because of misunderstandings and the lack of a conciliatory spirit. The first view calls for keeping the Soviets behind bars, the second for cultural exchanges.

It was the fifth day. Yesterday I had learned something of Peter's views about the Soviets. Now I was scheduled to meet Rod Hyde, 31, a math prodigy, weapon designer, and enthusiastic foe of the Soviets, one who saw both their technology and people as flawed.

Rod's first love was space. During the past decade at the lab he had designed a number of sophisticated spaceships, his dream being to visit the stars. But he feared that the Soviets might thwart his ambitions. As Lowell's second in command, he was now in a position to do something about it. He passed judgment on the feasibility of advanced ideas in nuclear weaponry and other areas explored by O Group. Not just a technologist, he studied Soviet history and politics. Nobody followed the workings of the Politburo like Rod, said his young peers. And nobody joked so earnestly about rearranging Soviet society with a few well-placed H-bombs.

"Working here is fine by me because I don't trust the Soviets worth beans," said Rod as we settled down in the small conference room of 1877. "My idea of the future is to get off into space—not just one or two people, but in a big way. There'll be technical challenges. You also have the problem that the Soviets can drag wild cards into the game. I guess my biggest worry is that the Soviet leaders want only power. If they owned the planet I don't think they'd allow the evolution of technology to continue. There'd be a radical change. They would essentially shut down any advance. That's clearly the safest way to stay in power. The only reason they are going with technology is that they can't afford not to."

Rod didn't look or act like a whiz kid. He obviously was bright but spoke in a slow drawl. He had longish hair, a full, scraggly beard, and glasses with thick horned rims. He was scruffy. Every so often a wry smile broke through his beard.

"To me," Rod continued, "working for the future has two parts. One, coming up with spaceship designs to actually realize the vision. Two, making sure the ground rules stay the same—that the Soviets don't stop us before we're able to get into space in a big way. After that, I don't worry about the Soviets anymore.

"They're very cautious, so the ground rules might hold. They've been in power a long time and don't want to take risks or do anything to upset it. They also have this stupid belief that Communism is going to win, that it's historically inevitable. I don't know to what extent they believe this, but obviously they have to pay lip service to it. I think it's crazy. But it's fine if it prevents them from attacking us or taking risks. So they're very conservative. Basically that's the reason defense is so attractive. If you increase the uncertainty of success in war, that's good, because if war is sufficiently uncertain, I don't think they're going to risk it. And in the long run I think we win because in technology and space we're always going to beat them. Their economy just doesn't work.

"What I want more than anything is essentially to get the human race into space. It's the future. If you stay down here some disaster is going to strike and you're going to be wiped. If you get into space and spread out there's just no chance of the human race disappearing."

Rod grew up in Corvallis, Oregon, with one sister and two brothers. He read science fiction, played chess, and took college courses in science and math while still in high school. Rod was one of the members of O Group whose formal education had been light in the humanities. After college, however, Rod developed an interest in Soviet history and the classics, especially Thucydides and the Peloponnesian wars. A hero was Alexander the Great. "He had class," said Rod. "He was so damn talented to do what he did at his age. He was 32 when he died, and he had conquered the known world at the age of 26."

While still in high school, Rod proved himself extraordinarily adept at the complexities of math and science. "I guess what started it all was that my father accidentally introduced me to calculus while he was taking a course at the university. One day he left this calculus book lying around, and I immediately went through the first ten chapters. It was a revelation. This was ninth grade or so." Calculus is the perfect mathematical tool for the analysis of change—the motion of missiles, projectiles, planets, pendulums, and anything else that moves.

For Rod, the vision of its power suddenly and irrevocably opened a chasm between him and his peers. Frustrated by high school classes in mathematics, he took courses at the local university. Soon Rod was torn over where to go to college full time. Caltech had a better overall reputation and was more exclusive from Rod's point of view. Throughout high school he planned on going there. But in his senior year two factors tipped the balance in favor of MIT. One was that his interest had swung from pure to applied science—from chemistry and calculus to space travel and the design of engines for starships. Throughout adolescence his love of space had been nurtured by a stream of science fiction, most especially by authors Gordon Dickson, Keith Laumer, and Robert Heinlein. Now Rod decided to pursue the academic study of space flight. And in such areas as aerospace engineering, MIT had a better overall program than Caltech. The decisive factor in his switch, however, was that MIT would accept the college credits he had accumulated in high school.

"I chose MIT basically because it looked like they'd let you get away with more," said Rod. "I had two courses, differential equations and second-year physics. The advantage at MIT was that I was able to advance place not only those courses but everything beneath them. I had about a third of the units I needed to graduate. It became clear that Caltech wouldn't accept that sort of junk. They're very paternalistic, or at least they were in those days.

"When I entered MIT the idea was to get two degrees, space engineering and physics, and to combine them to work on space propulsion. When I got there I took it easy the first half-year. Then I decided I was getting bored and that I could probably get out faster if I stuck to one degree. I had to work hard, but in two years I had my degree in astronautical engineering."

In the process he got straight A's, except for one B in an economics course (which he had to take in order to fulfill the school's minimum requirements in the arts, humanities, and social sciences). Rod's schedule allowed little time for extracurricular activities—except for chess, which he played recreationally and in tournaments. Upon nearing graduation, Rod set his sights on a quick Ph.D. He started to search for graduate fellowships, the standout being the one from the Hertz Foundation.

"I met Lowell during a Hertz interview," Rod recalled. "He offered me a job at the lab that summer working on laser fusion rockets. I knew nothing about laser fusion at that time. The attraction was that it was my first technical job. Before that I had been working in canning plants in Oregon."

A college graduate at the age of 19, Rod joined Lowell at the weapons lab. He came as a summer intern in 1972 to design the engine of a starship. The idea was to drive it with small fusion explosions produced by a battery of lasers. A magnetic nozzle would protect the rear of the ship and direct the force of the blast. Indeed, Rod soon came up with the outline of a novel design that allowed the starship to travel thousands of times faster than before—on paper at least.

But a distraction arose. Late that summer there was to be a world championship chess match between the reigning Russian master, Boris Spassky, and the challenger, an upstart American, Bobby Fischer. The fact that competition was to take place in Reykjavik, Iceland, in no way dampened Rod's enthusiasm. Fischer was one of Rod's heroes. Rod would be there, even though it meant stepping up the pace of his summer study.

The match was to be a minor superpower confrontation. Fischer was a chess genius, recluse, and iconoclast who had dropped out of high school to pursue the game. He always carried a transistor radio so he could listen to rock music. Before the match, Fischer announced that he had been called upon to do battle with the evil Soviet empire. "They cheat in other sports, not just chess," he told authors Larry Evans and Ken Smith. "The Russians have been committing international crimes for so long—spreading lies and political propaganda all over the world, cheating at sports—someone has to stop them. I've been chosen. I intend to teach them a little humility."

This was a battle Rod was not about to miss. Toward the end of the summer, he worked day and night on his starship. A solid design started to emerge. The ship had huge wings, not for flying through planetary atmospheres but for radiating excess heat generated by the fusion explosions. Its winged radiators would glow red.

As the match approached, Rod locked himself in his office and worked around the clock for four days, just as he had done occasionally at MIT. His final paper describing the ship went on for dozens of pages, had more than a hundred equations, and contained two dozen tables and diagrams. Lowell then drove the dazed graduate student to the airport, where Rod boarded a plane for Reykjavik to watch the Russians lose their world chess title.

Not just a personal triumph, the design Rod produced that summer soon caused a national sensation. In late 1972 he and Lowell flew to New Orleans so Rod could present a declassified version of his starship paper at a scientific conference. Its details were secret because the design of fusion pellets revealed much about the construction of H-bombs, something the government kept closely guarded. The graduate student was a hit. Most of the scientists at the session on "Advanced Propulsion Concepts" had previously considered the subject in terms of the Space Shuttle, which didn't come close to what Rod had in mind.

Rocket performance is usually measured by the length of time it takes one pound of fuel to burn while producing one continual pound of thrust. This is known as the "specific impulse." The higher the number, the hotter the engine. For the main engines of the Space Shuttle the specific impulse is 455 seconds. For the rocket Rod had in mind it was at least 300,000 seconds, and perhaps closer to a million.

The audience was struck not only by the raw numbers but also by the aura of secrecy that surrounded Rod's work. At the time, laser fusion was new and highly classified. Rumors spread at the conference that Lowell had gotten Rod's paper past government security censors only after something of a struggle. The incident was so noteworthy to scientists that it was eventually written up in *The Man-Made Sun,* a book on laser fusion by T. A. Heppenheimer. The science fiction fan from Corvallis was starting to make waves in the world of real science.

Rod virtually never left the lab after the frenzied initial contact, at first working part time and jetting back and forth from MIT as he finished his education. He received his M.S. degree in 1973 and started working full time at the weapons lab in 1975, finally receiving his doctorate in 1976. Hertz paid the way.

At Lowell's house there was a painting of one of Rod's starships, a long, thin object shooting past the rings of Saturn. It was a shiny cylinder with portholes and "USA" stenciled prominently on its side. Stretching out behind it was a long series of pipes and radiators that ended in the fusion area. The engine was surrounded by a gentle glow.

In light of Rod's devotion to futuristic rocketry, his contempt for Soviet technology was somewhat understandable. The Soviets had never distinguished themselves in rocket design. Their poor record, moreover, was not always evident from reading the news. After all, the Soviets launched huge numbers of large boosters every year and held all the endurance records for manned space flight.

But closer inspection showed that they indeed lagged in certain aspects of rocket technology. This was most clearly illustrated by the history of the moon race. During the 1960s, as America perfected the Saturn 5 moon rocket, the Soviets tried to build their own moonship, which in American aerospace circles was known as the Type G booster. It failed miserably. It never successfully got into space, and blew up on more than one occasion. Not only that, but the Type G booster utilized an antiquated fuel technology that America soared beyond in the 1960s.

All rockets need oxygen in order to burn their fuels. For both Soviet and American rocket programs, the oxidizer is usually liquid oxygen, which must be kept at 298 degrees below zero. (A jet engine needs no oxidizer because it gets its oxygen from the air.) The liquid fuel and oxidizer are pumped into a combustion chamber where they mix, burn, and explode out the end of the rocket, producing an equal and opposite reaction that moves the rocket forward.

The fuel used by the Soviets for their moon rocket seems to have been kerosene, which has a specific impulse somewhere in the 200s. An advantage of kerosene is that it is liquid at room temperature. The disadvantage is that it packs little punch. A much better fuel is liquid hydrogen, which is more difficult to master, partly because it has to be kept at 423 degrees below zero. But hydrogen has great rewards. It can generate a specific impulse in the 400s. Rockets with high specific impulse are more efficient and can carry heavier pay-

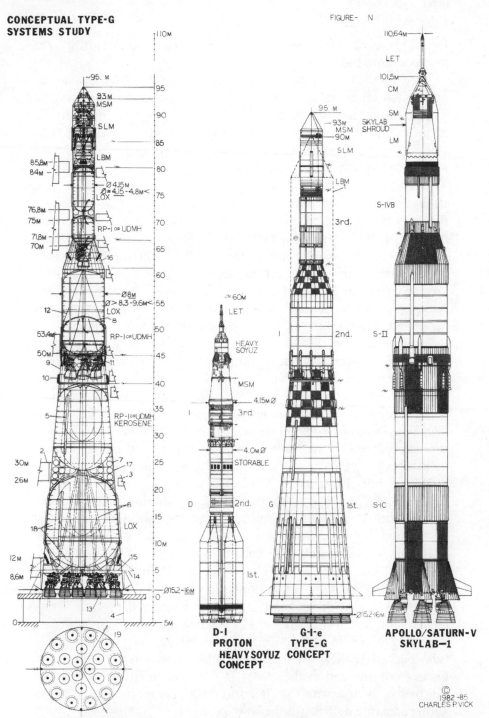

**D-I
PROTON
HEAVY SOYUZ
CONCEPT**

**G-l-e
TYPE-G
CONCEPT**

**APOLLO/SATURN-V
SKYLAB—1**

American and Soviet moon rockets. Soviet engines were so weak that the crew and moon lander had to be lifted into earth orbit on separate rockets. Despite less demanding technology, the Soviet Type G rocket failed to get off the ground.

loads. Those with low specific impulse must be extraordinarily large to carry more fuel.

Even today, more than two decades later, the Soviet space program often relies on boosters that burn kerosene and liquid oxygen. These rockets are big because they have to be, but that may be about to change. According to aerospace magazines such as *Aviation Week,* spy satellites have recently shown that the Soviets have a new family of rockets under development on launch pads at Tyuratam in central Asia. All about the site is equipment for the storage of liquid hydrogen. Moreover, one of these boosters dwarfs the Saturn 5, the most powerful rocket America ever built. According to the Department of Defense publication *Soviet Military Power 1984,* this giant booster may be able to lift up to 150 tons into low orbits around the earth—about seven times more than the largest operational Soviet booster, and five times more than America's biggest booster of the moment, the Space Shuttle. It's taken two decades, but the Soviets seem on the verge of catching up.

In a similar way, Soviet rocket technology seems to have lagged in the design of missiles meant to loft warheads between continents, which are sometimes known as ICBMs or Inter-Continental Ballistic Missiles. In both East and West such rockets follow the same general rules. Their engines ignite, burn, shut off, and fall away. Their payloads—up to a dozen or so individual warheads—coast through space until they reenter the atmosphere and plunge toward their targets. For most of their flight, the warheads fly through the void of space. Each side's missiles can also dispense a bevy of decoys, metallic balloons, chaff, and other materials and electronic devices meant to confuse radars and complicate any attempt at destruction of the real warheads.

But there the resemblance ends. The Soviets tend to use liquid fuels, the Americans solid. The American military started using solid-fuel engines back in the 1960s. In principle these have a great advantage in that they can be stored for years and fired at a moment's notice with the turn of a key. They are like Fourth of July firecrackers. There are no delicate pumps and pipes—just a big tube packed with a sophisticated, rubbery material that quickly burns from one end to the other. The challenge is to manufacture the fuel in such a way that it burns at a very even rate, thus insuring accurate delivery of the warheads.

By contrast, liquid fuels are corrosive and hard to handle. In their most primitive form they must be kept in holding tanks pumped into a rocket only when needed. More advanced liquid fuels can be stored on board a missile, but there are still dangers of corrosion over time. According to Robert P. Berman and John C. Baker in *Soviet Strategic Forces,* the Russians have nonetheless for the most part stuck with storable liquid fuels on their military missiles, only recently testing a new generation of solid-fueled rockets.

This tidy picture of American excellence and Soviet retardation is blurred by one fact. Liquids tend to work. The Soviets fire their intercontinental missiles out of operational silos all the time, sometimes in coordinated exercises with other types of missiles and weapons. By contrast, the U.S. Air Force has never successfully launched a solid-fuel rocket out of an operational silo. During the 1960s, four attempts took place. Three missiles failed to ignite, while the fourth blew up a few seconds after liftoff. From that point on rocket tests were conducted much more carefully. Engineers would take the designated missile out of its operational silo, ship it to a special facility at the Vandenberg Air Force Base in California, give it a careful going over, and then fire it toward a test range in the South Pacific.

In short, each superpower has chosen a rocket technology with certain strengths and weaknesses. The Soviets have aimed for reliability and low cost, the Americans for power and high technology.

Rod was a theoretician who could work wonders not just years ahead of his peers in the world of military technology, but decades. He knew all about the history of military missiles, both Soviet and American. To him, the pattern of the past pointed to nothing but victory for us and defeat for them. The Soviets, he said, had little chance of outwitting pop up with fast rockets because they would be unable to build them. He pointed to their current generation of big, slow boosters. "In the long run I think we win because in technology and space we're always going to beat them."

In sharp disagreement with Rod are the critics who have disparaged pop up. For instance, the 106-page report by the Union of Concerned Scientists, written by Bethe and his coauthors and published in March 1984, said an X-ray laser in space would be able to penetrate the earth's atmosphere only to a depth of about seventy miles. It also said fast-burning Soviet boosters would be

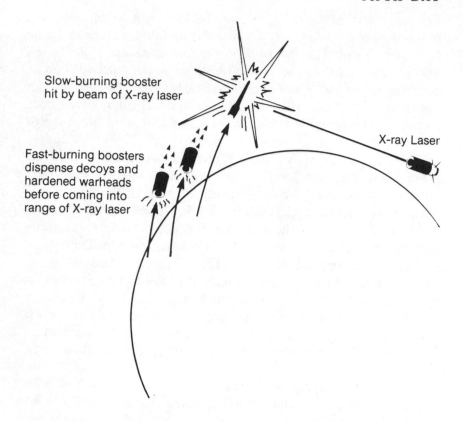

Slow-burning booster
hit by beam of X-ray laser

X-ray Laser

Fast-burning boosters
dispense decoys and
hardened warheads
before coming into
range of X-ray laser

able to finish firing their engines before crossing that threshold. "In conclusion," it asserted, "the X-ray laser offers no prospect of being a useful component in a system for ballistic missile defense."

A second report taking issue with Rod's view was written for the Congressional Office of Technology Assessment (OTA) by Ashton B. Carter, a fellow at MIT. It was published in April 1984. "Fast-burn boosters," it said, "would be a potent, even decisive, counter-measure against almost all concepts for boost-phase intercept."

Perhaps the critics were correct. But Rod too had a point. Today the most threatening part of the Soviet missile fleet is made up of SS-18s, lumbering, liquid-fueled giants with ten nuclear warheads that turn off their engines high above the atmosphere after firing them for about 300 seconds. They would be sitting ducks for a nu-clear X-ray laser. Evading pop up would require the development of Soviet boosters that burned out after about 60 seconds. The gap between 300 seconds and 60 seconds—between current technical reality and the misty future—was what the critics said could easily be closed. It was an assertion Rod ridiculed.

"I don't think pop up is dead," he said. "The OTA stance is that when the Soviets come up with a fast-burning ICBM, then pop up becomes essentially impossible. And I agree with that. But the fact is that the Soviets are behind us in the technology of solid-fuel boosters. We've had two generations of solid-fuel boosters already, and our next one, the MX, is only marginally fast-burn, something on the order of 170 seconds. It's going to take them a while to come up with a fast-burn thing, even with their stealing things or knowing that it can be done. If fifteen years from now their boosters are fast-burn, by that time sensor and decoy detection will have improved to the point that I think we can start picking out decoys in mid-course. Booster kill is made much harder by fast burn, but there are other options to play. Anyway, that whole issue comes up in fifteen years. And so I'm not going to let it influence what I do now."

In response to this kind of argument, critics make two points. First, they say X-ray lasers might not be deployable for years—perhaps as many as ten or more. So the Soviets would have some time to learn to build fast-burn boosters. It is not as if their missile force would be instantly vulnerable for the next fifteen years. Second, even though the Soviets have historically relied on slow-burning liquid fuels, it is within their capability to switch to very fast-burning fuels. Before, there was no urgent need. But the Soviets could do it if pop up loomed as a threat. In general, the Soviets do not have to excel at technology to outwit a defensive shield, the critics say. They just have to be competent. Defeating a defense is always much easier than trying to build it.

The brunt of their argument is borne by history. The critics point to the past and say that the Soviets, though backward in some areas of technology, have always caught up when they tried. They point to the history of the A-bomb. America had one in 1945 and the Soviets had theirs four years later. So too, America had the H-bomb in 1952 and the Soviets had theirs three years later. They point especially to the history of MIRVs, or Multiple Independently-targetable Reentry Vehicles. These are the separate warheads on a missile, each one aimed at sites that may be a hundred miles apart. MIRVed missiles were introduced by the United States in 1970 as the ultimate technological edge over the Soviet Union. Military planners confidently predicted that it would be decades before the Soviets mastered this high-tech art. Much to their chagrin, the Soviets had them about five years later. In fact, the repeated failure of the technical edge is one reason the critics argue against defensive shields in general. It is pure folly, they say, to think that the United States can gain a permanent advantage that will allow it to stay ahead in a critical area of technology. All it will do is provoke another spiral of an already expensive arms race.

The critics also have noted that American debates about Soviet capabilities can be quite influential, in the past persuading the military to take dramatic action. During the 1950s and 1960s, anticipated (not demonstrated) advances in Soviet technology led to the abandonment of plans to deploy the Nike-Zeus and Nike-X defensive systems as protection against Soviet warheads. The Pentagon found so many ways to outwit the systems that military planners decided that the Soviets could easily do the same.

Despite the polarized views of Rod and the critics, they do have something in common—technological optimism or, more bluntly, faith. In a very American way, Rod and his friends at Livermore see the future as a broad sweep of unlimited technical opportunity to be shaped solely by their individual talents and hard work. The curious thing about the critics is that they too have faith, but it is faith in the prowess of Soviet scientists and engineers. The critics say history is on their side; Rod and his peers at the weapons lab say the future is on theirs.

Rod's contempt for Soviet science is deepened by what he sees as a Soviet distrust of technology in general. They hate what he loves. "To me there is a rational reason for being anti-Soviet now," he said. "We are trying to do something which I consider fundamental—getting into space. The only thing that can stop that is a Soviet takeover. I don't think the Soviet leaders believe in communism or any shit like that. I think they believe in power. If they owned the entire world, I don't think they would persist in any way with technology. It can only be a threat to them.

"I want the future to be up in space because there is just so much more out there," Rod continued. "Here you can't play games with new political systems because every piece of land is already owned by someone. It's a zero sum game. Out there, it's absolutely limitless. There're no more frontiers here. Space is one big frontier."

Rod put his convictions about space to work. He was a member of the Citizens Advisory Council on National Space Policy, a group founded by science-fiction author Jerry Pournelle and sponsored jointly by the American Astronautical Society and the L-5 Society. The *L* is for Lagrange, the French mathematician who identified the set of five points at which the gravitational pulls of earth, moon, and sun are equalized. L-5 is the fifth Lagrange point, where the society would park a space platform.

The Soviets, too, had devoted energy to the development of space stations—in fact, far more than the United States. Over the years their Salyut manned laboratories had set many of the records in orbit. And the Russians, of course, put the first man into space.

Rod did not cite these facts. When he disparaged Soviet technology he honed in on their rocket engines or on a truly curious area of apparent backwardness—their work in the field of computers. Here the Soviets have struggled to catch up with the West and at the same time have worried about the potential for political decentralization that lies in the proliferation of personal computers. "The basic stance of [Yevgeny] Velikhov, the Vice-President of the Soviet Academy of Sciences, is that there aren't any personal computers in the Soviet Union and he doesn't intend to let them be introduced," Rod said. "They're not considered socially proper. The state's job is to tell you what computer power individuals should have. In general they've decided individuals do not need it at all, the state institutes do."

Lowell came into the conference room at that point, listened for a minute, left, and returned with a computer print-out of a newspaper story. "Here is an article on how the Soviet Union is coping with the communications and information revolution," he said. "They say explicitly that they are not going to allow personal computers." The dateline was Moscow and the story had been published in the *London Telegraph*. It was an interview with Velikhov, who the paper said was responsible for the Academy's newly formed Department of Information Science, Computer Technology, and Automation. "Soviet officials," it read, "talk about domestic computers as a hypothetical possibility, to be carefully planned and prepared for. A top scientist responsible for 'guiding the new trend' has stressed that home computers should be available only to people who 'need' them, under a 'state system' ensuring 'the development of this technology in the required directions.' "

Lowell expanded on the theme, saying that not only personal

computers but all information technology was under tight control. "A few computer buffs will probably make their own computers," he said, "but the party does not allow people to exchange software. The party does not permit nationwide computer maintenance organizations. They've suppressed that very vigorously even though the costs have been very high. You'll never have computer networks of either the government or private-sector type that you have in this country. You won't have nationwide software distribution. The party reserves to itself nationwideness. You have to have a monopoly on something rather fundamental in order to maintain control, in order to stay in power. The party decided that one of the things was communications. It's pretty effective. Look what the Polish government did when it imposed martial law. It essentially knocked the nation back on its back by merely suppressing intercity telephone calls, radio broadcasts, and transport. It just cut off cities from each other and broke the back of Solidarity. The Soviet Union will never have to do that because it never allowed it to happen in the first place.

"The Soviets spend $1 to $3 billion a year just to suppress the reception of foreign broadcasts," Lowell continued. "They can't jam the whole country but they jam around the cities. They have several times as many transmitters for jamming as they do for broadcasting. They're extremely concerned that the population remain uncontaminated by foreign communications."

Rod took Lowell's point a step further, saying the Soviets not only controlled their own news and information but tried to control ours as well. The Soviets have agents, he said, throughout the Western press.

Lowell added that Soviet dissident and former weapon designer Andrei Sakharov had made that charge in a letter. "He pointed out that the Western press in particular has been heavily penetrated by KGB, and that even Western press reports are no longer very reliable when they are on politically sensitive topics," said Lowell. "It was one of the most remarkable statements in a remarkable letter."*

---

* Months later, Lowell sent me a copy of Sakharov's letter as it appeared in the Summer 1983 issue of *Foreign Affairs* magazine. Although we had subsequently discussed many points of Sakharov's letter, only one was highlighted—in bold yellow magic marker. The paragraph made no mention of the KGB or Soviet agents, but it did warn of "pro-Soviet elements." Wrote Sakharov: "One must take into account that, in the countries of the West,

Not everyone was as pessimistic as Lowell about the Soviet leadership's ability to keep a lid on the information revolution. In his book *Behind the Lines,* Donald R. Shanor of Columbia University described how Soviet citizens were increasingly using new, compact shortwave radios, television sets, and video and audio tape recorders to capture Western broadcasts and to form underground networks for distributing such material. "Satellites launched to improve Western Europe's television transmission and to bring in American programming are beaming down signal 'footprints' that can be picked up across the Soviet border," he wrote. The book's message was decidedly at odds with Lowell's—that the evolution of technology was starting to erode the power of Soviet censors.

Lowell left the room and Rod started to explain that his own Soviet views predated his arrival at the lab. As he spoke it became clear that his feelings were indeed based on more than disdain for Soviet technology.

"During high school in the late 1960s the Vietnam war was still going strong and you were still subject to the draft. There was a huge peace feeling and antiwar feeling. Certainly all the intellectual types at our high school were very much into that. I always disagreed and I could always hold my own in arguments. I think the Soviets are the only reason there's any threat of nuclear war. If we were the only guys who had nuclear weapons, I don't think there'd be any problem. Witness the fact that when we were the only guys who had them, there was no trouble."

I mentioned that we exploded two atomic bombs over Japanese cities.

"Sure, we dropped a couple—but that was during a war that the other guys started. When we had a monopoly for those four years after the war we could have really changed the way the world organized itself. But we didn't. On the other hand, everyplace the Red army goes, it stays. I guess Turkey and Iran have been exceptions."

I noted that the Soviets also pulled out of Austria after the war.

"That's right, they pulled out of Austria and Greece but they were never formally in Greece. It was just a resistance movement—guerrilla-type games.

---

pro-Soviet propaganda has been conducted for quite a long time and is very goal-oriented and clever, and that pro-Soviet elements have penetrated many key positions, particularly in the mass media."

"Look at what they have done to their own people. Stalin was no nice guy. He probably killed 30 million. I think the peak rate was in the transition between Lenin and Stalin. Lenin was no prize either. He started the gunning down of the kulaks." (These were the private farmers in the Soviet Union who resisted collectivization of the land.)

Rod said his feelings about the Soviets were one of the main reasons he worked on bombs. "I can't see how you could work on nuclear weapons if you didn't care about the Soviets taking over. At least for me, I have to be anti-Soviet first. I don't give a shit what they do to their own people. As far as I'm concerned the Russian people have had dictators for a thousand years now. I think it's something in their culture. They just need a strong authority figure. They also have a much higher tolerance for suffering than I consider rational or sane. To me that labels them as a people who can take adversity very well but who are never going to produce anything. Because to produce something you need intolerance to suffering in the world. You need to be impatient and want to change things."

In part, Rod's views on the Soviets were updated and given detail by his daily ritual of scanning the news on the group's computer network. The use of keywords, he said, allowed him to electronically search a large number of newspapers and wire services for stories of particular interest. Rod shared the fruits of his news watch with the rest of S-1 and O Group, as indicated by the computer printouts of newspaper articles on the walls of 1877. The computer network also was the source of the article on the purported fate of personal computers in the Soviet Union.

We left the conference room and walked down the hall to an empty office so Rod could demonstrate his technique. He saddled up to a terminal and started to punch in commands that would connect him to a distant computer. He was on the Arpanet, the military's computer network. Rod was sending electronic impulses through the group's computerized gateway and entering a global network—a highway of electrons that stretched from sunup to sundown, from Britain to Korea.

The screen of Rod's terminal flashed "password" and he tapped in a reply. It then flashed "account number" and he again responded. We were deep inside a distant computer. Rod said he was going to search for stories related to Israel. He typed the word

"ISRAEL" on the screen and told the computer to restrict its search to stories since yesterday. "Let's see," he said, "nine stories. I usually hit the most recent one and work my way backwards."

We scrolled through one story after another. After a few minutes, Rod sent a command that told the computer he wanted to sign off, at which point it flashed a parting bit of wisdom: "The wise shepherd never trusts his flock to a smiling wolf." Rod groaned and said the sign-off messages were sometimes worse than that.

As we walked back to the conference room I asked whether the Soviets lagged far behind in the development of nuclear X-ray lasers.

"I don't know," he said. "Peter's view has been that if you look at the early literature on laboratory X-ray lasers, more of it was written by the Soviets than us. Then, all of a sudden, Peter says, the Soviets just stopped writing on this subject. He finds that suspicious. The trouble with their weapons community is that there's just no way of knowing. They have closed labs. But their literature on the subject dried up around 1977."

It was a curious contrast. As opposed to Rod's disparagement over fast-burn boosters, the allusion here was to possible Soviet technological advances, perhaps even ahead of the United States.

Rod talked of yet another type of advanced Soviet technology, one threatening to turn America into a radioactive ruin. He said one of the best reasons to deploy American X-ray lasers was that they would increase the "uncertainty" over whether new, super-accurate Soviet missiles could destroy our land-based arsenal in a preemptive strike. Echoing many of his peers, Rod said the expansion and evolution of the Soviet missile armada was so great that it could now knock out 90 percent of our Minuteman missiles, a thousand of which were scattered across the American heartlands. "That is new," he said. "That wasn't the case in the 1960s or even the early 1970s."

What Rod was referring to was the "window of vulnerability" that got so much attention in the early days of the Reagan administration. But in 1983 while investigating the alleged vulnerability, the President's Commission on Strategic Forces, headed by Lieut.-Gen. Brent Scowcroft of the Air Force, retired, had found that the window was a myth. So great was the commission's faith in the security of America's land-based arsenal that it said the MX missile should be placed in the very Minuteman silos that had previously been declared so vulnerable. The commission also said that anticipated increases in the accuracy of Soviet missiles were a real issue—though not cause for alarm. For the future, it recommended several possible modifications of the U.S. arsenal to keep it safe from a debilitating first strike. One was that America should develop a fleet of small, mobile land-based missiles.

In contrast to finding conventional ways to stabilize the arms race, Rod said the United States should adopt a defensive shield to protect its big land-based missiles. This might be expensive, he said. But the price was worth paying.

"The worst that can happen with defense is that you increase the arms race," he said. "I think Sakharov hit it right on the head in his *Foreign Affairs* paper when he said there are worse things than the arms race—nuclear war, for instance. If you look at the money we spend on strategic arms, it's not very much. It's like $30 billion a year for us. Of our total budget that's nothing. It's zip. So what if defense ultimately caused an increase in spending on strategic weapons, which would not clearly be the case? If defense systems get very good, you can cut offense spending. If they get moderately good, you may well need more spending on both. If that extends the uncertainty and prevents war, who cares? The expense is just nothing when compared to the gain of preventing war. Too much of what the liberal press seems to concentrate on is that this will spur another increase in the arms race, in contrast to this will continue to prevent war. That's what dominates the discussion for me."

Rod did not mention that Sakharov in his letter had gone beyond costs to question the feasibility of defense. "Much is written about the possibility of developing ABM systems using superpowerful lasers, accelerated particle beams, and so forth," he had written. "But the creation of an effective defense against missiles along these lines seems highly doubtful to me."

Also, the "uncertainty" Rod spoke of cut in many directions, such as the one in which critics said an American shield might paradoxically encourage an enemy to take the risk of starting a nuclear war. There was another kind of uncertainty as well, one that went to the heart of the debate over Soviet technical prowess. Our missiles were allegedly threatened because of big, new, accurate Soviet missiles. This was new, Rod said. Somehow the backward Soviet engineers had been able to come up with good missiles. The other uncertainty lay in the critics' charge that the Soviets could keep forging ahead technically and develop fast-burn boosters that would outwit a defense. Would such boosters allow the Soviets to strike with impunity? That too was an uncertainty, one that threatened us rather than them.

Finally, the critics said that discussions such as Rod's were too narrow, focusing only on visions of land-based missiles. In fact, these held less than one-fourth of America's arsenal of warheads. The nation also had bomb-laden aircraft and submarines, both of which were said to be nearly impossible to destroy in a premeditated attack. Because of this balance of forces (known as the strategic triad), critics argued that the United States was far less vulnerable to a "counterforce" strike (an attack on enemy weapon systems) than the Soviet Union.

After Rod left the conference room, I tried to call Livermore's spies, a group of low-profile experts who were said to know the truth about the state of Soviet technology. Cryptically, with the lab's usual penchant for single-letter designations, it was known as Z Division. Its staff of more than 60 radiochemists, engineers, economists, and political scientists worked with some of the highest intelligence agents in the federal government. The shadowy group was said to have performed an unclassified analysis of Soviet literature on laboratory X-ray lasers. I called Z Division, identifying myself as a reporter and asking about the analysis. The secretary said someone would call right back. I waited. Nothing. I called again and got the same response. Nothing. Privy to some of the top secrets in the land, the members of Z Division apparently enjoyed their anonymity.

Lowell appeared at the door and suggested we go to dinner. We set off in his Volkswagen through the traffic of downtown Livermore to El Lorito.

Over an order of nachos, Lowell told a long story that threw my nighttime confrontation with the nuclear raiders into a different light. Livermore and all the government's nuclear weapons labs and factories and reactors had been undergoing a series of security tests and upgrades, he said. There were drills, raids, and nighttime helicopter landings by Department of Energy auditors who posed as terrorists and Soviet spies. It all started, he said, in the early 1980s, when a team of Congressional investigators from the General Accounting Office found lax security conditions at a site where the Department of Energy makes plutonium and tritium for bombs. Moreover, a similar incident occurred at the Los Alamos National Laboratory, convincing auditors that a terrorist group would be able to actually steal a bomb. The episodes touched off widespread attempts at reform which were sweeping the laboratories.

We drove back from dinner, passing the lab's fences, barbed wire, and other paraphernalia of security and secrecy. It was there not just to stop terrorists but also to frustrate the flow of information to the Soviets—for two very distinct reasons, each illuminating a different side of the debate over the strength of Russian technology. One view, pointedly expressed by weapon makers and the federal government, was that secrecy was needed to keep American high technology out of the hands of enemies. The Soviets were behind and we intended to keep them that way, went the argument. A very different argument was less forcefully expressed. It held that the Soviets were very clever and could be quite sophisticated in their development and application of technology. American weapons might be easily countered if the Soviets knew all the details. For example, if they learned about the workings of a blue-green laser satellite, they might be able to jam it, cutting off this link to American submarines.

It was after midnight when Lowell and I drove back to Windy Ridge. We sat down in the kitchen and started talking about secrecy and security. In the United States penalties were relatively mild and attitudes quite humane—but not in the Soviet Union, Lowell said.

He told the story of an American spy who was under diplomatic cover at the U.S. embassy in Moscow. One day the agent went to look at a Soviet military base. He had no camera and took no notes. He had no miniature transmitter. He merely wanted to look at the base, burn its details into his memory, and later write a memo for his superiors. As the agent observed the base a Soviet police vehicle pulled up and opened fire. The agent dived under his car amid a hail of bullets. This lasted for several minutes, all the while the agent screaming at the top of his lungs that he was an American citizen with diplomatic immunity. Finally the police lowered their weapons. "The Soviets fire first and ask questions later," said Lowell with a satisfied grin.

Not mentioned in Lowell's comparison of superpower secrecy

was America's own dark history during the McCarthy era. It was
the alleged theft of American atomic secrets that led to the sentenc-
ing of Julius and Ethel Rosenberg, who were executed as spies.

As the night wore on, Lowell's voice became increasingly doom-
laden. Not only were the Soviets dangerous, he said, but they posed
a threat to the continuation of life on earth. They were dabbling
with the creation of deadly new organisms. He said his worst sus-
picions had recently been driven home by an article in *The Wall
Street Journal* by William Kucewicz. The Soviets were trying to
hook the gene for making cobra venom onto the virus that causes
flu. It could, said Lowell, create a nearly unstoppable plague that
would take its victims one by one. "The germs would drift through
the air and land at will for their nasty work," he said.*

Soon it was past 3:00 A.M. I wondered how many young scientists Lowell had entertained with his late-night tales of Soviet
horror. He seemed to have a world view that said the Soviets were
bad. Period. It was an attitude that drew on facts that were un-
deniably ugly. The Soviet Union was a closed, militarized society
that flouted its own laws, tyrannized and took over its neighbors,
and drove its best citizens into exile. It was a police state that had
imprisoned and murdered millions of its own people. And Lowell
was right in saying that they could shoot first and ask questions later,
a lesson driven home by the death of 269 people on Korean Airlines
Flight 007.

But there was another side to the Soviet Union, one conspicu-
ously absent in Lowell's harangue. Russia had produced musicians,
poets, chess masters, and Nobel laureates. Peter said getting to
know her people was important for mankind's survival, and suggested that the superpowers should engage in cultural exchanges—

---

* I later examined the article, a copy of which Lowell had given me. It did
go into detail about alleged Soviet developments in germ warfare. To its
credit, it also carried something of a disclaimer: "U.S. intelligence analysts,
military scientists, and independent researchers stressed the difficulty of
creating a recombined germ-warfare agent that could survive outside a petri
dish in the laboratory. . . . Soviet scientists, they said, would require a
level of biotechnological knowledge and honed technique that would put
them at the very edge of the frontier in Western recombinant DNA research. However, U.S. scientists and intelligence experts could not rule out
that possibility. The Soviets, they said, are working hard enough on genetic
research that a new weapon, if not already developed, could become a
reality in the future."

implying, perhaps, that reform of the Soviet system might come from within. Lowell was smart and surely knew the other side of the Russian story. But he ignored it. He found it more satisfying to keep the Soviets behind bars, as did Rod.

In contrast to their unwavering hard line on Soviet society, Rod and Lowell exhibited a curious flexibility in their portrayals of Soviet scientists, engineers, and industry. These were so backward, Rod insisted, that the Soviets would be hard-pressed to build rockets fast enough to foil pop up. But then he went on to say the Russians had built missiles so big, accurate, and threatening that America needed X-ray lasers to defend itself. Lowell in his gloom over Soviet biotechnology took the whole paradox one step further, putting the Russians at the cutting edge of modern science. Lowell said Soviet biologists were brilliant and ready to infect the world with a suicidal plague. Maybe he was right. Maybe Rod was too. Rocket engines, inertial guidance, and biotechnology were all different types of technology, based on different types of expertise. But their views seemed extreme just on the basis of internal evidence. Soviet society could not be as bad as Rod and Lowell made out. And Soviet science could not be conducted only by idiots and mad geniuses. There had to be a middle ground.

BATTLE PLANS
★

The holy of holies at the weapons lab was Building 111, a seven-story edifice of reinforced concrete able to withstand the tremors that occasionally shook the area. It was home to the lab's director, to Teller, and to the divisions that turned promising ideas into powerful weapons. Of the hundreds of trailers and buildings at Livermore, it was the tallest. Moreover, Building "111" was actually number one. All the other structures at the lab had numbers that were larger.

It housed the top bureaucrats of the lab's two main groups for nuclear design, A and B Divisions, which traced their history to the founding of the lab. In addition, it had recently gained a third tier of weapon designers who had gone far beyond the fusion and fission bombs of the past. This was R Program. If O Group was the spark-plug behind many of the third-generation ideas, R Program was the engine. It was the place where ranks of scientists, engineers, and machinists turned ideas into action. They built bombs, measured their output, designed systems for tracking targets and pointing laser rods, and developed overall strategies for their application.

The core of O Group had a dozen scientists and graduate students, mostly in their 20s. By contrast, the average employee of R Program was in his 40s. From their offices in Building 111, the head of R Program and his lieutenants had the authority to call on the talents of many of the lab's 8,000 employees, the ranks of R Program swelling into the hundreds when nuclear tests were scheduled for the Nevada desert. Members of O Group might offer ideas about how to build or use third-generation weapons, but R Program was the place where ideas were tempered by pragmatism and experience.

It was late in the afternoon of the sixth day. As arranged earlier in the week, I was scheduled to have dinner with Tom Weaver, head of R Program. In the informality of his home, I hoped to find out how far third-generation weapons had been developed and what the current strategies were for their use.

Tom, 34, was a tall redhead with a bushy beard. A high bureaucrat, he nonetheless dressed informally—open collar, casual slacks.

We headed toward his house in our separate cars, planning to pick up his son, Mark, on the way. Tom was a single parent, divorced about five years. He lived in Walnut Creek, a little more than half an hour from the weapons lab, in the shadow of Mount Diablo. He was an astrophysicist who had worked for many years in O Group. After the success of the X-ray laser, which Tom had helped design and build, he talked with Teller and in 1981 was appointed the first head of R Program. He had testified on Capitol Hill in this capacity, appearing in April 1983 with Teller and Lowell at a hearing on "Third-Generation Systems" before the House Armed Services Committee. Not just a scientist and administrator, he was also a recruiter. He was on the Hertz Foundation board and was the assistant coordinator of its Fellowship Project, a position directly under Lowell. According to a recent tax return of the foundation, Tom received $4,350 for this work. In short, Tom was a rising star at the weapons lab, with good political connections that derived from his relationship with Teller.

We drove off the interstate into the thicket of suburban California and pulled up to a school. Tom got out and came back with Mark, about seven years old.

At Tom's house we were greeted by Plato, a friendly mutt who desperately wanted to be petted. Mark obliged. In the dining room was an old, beat-up piano and several posters of wispy nebulae.

Many of these were remnants of supernovae, stars that had exploded long ago with the brilliance of entire galaxies. Tom was an expert on supernovae. He and his colleagues tended to look on the night sky as a laboratory of interesting nuclear processes as well as a thing of stark beauty.

During dinner Tom talked at length about Bethe. They were both astrophysicists and had shared data on several occasions. "Tom Weaver is a very solid and competent physicist," Bethe had told me. "He has done very good work on supernova explosions. He is a very solid citizen."

Mark was calm throughout dinner, talking about school and his day. Then the phone rang. It was Lowell. A transformation came over Mark as he chatted on the phone. He started to quiver and shake with anticipated pleasure, much as Plato had done when we arrived at the door.

Mark hung up and said Lowell was going to stop by later. This prospect clearly excited him, Mark recalling other occasions when he and Lowell had played together. Once, Mark said, Lowell told him how important it was to learn how to "hassle people" and to lie with a straight face.

Mark demonstrated. "No, madam, I did not do it," he said, his head thrown back in mock indignation. Tom dryly observed that this performance was not very convincing. Mark laughed and happily finished his dinner.

"I guess when I was Mark's age I got into reading a lot of books on science, and decided that I was going to be either an astronomer or a carpenter," Tom said in the living room. During his senior year of high school in Winter Park, Florida, Tom was one of 40 national winners in the Westinghouse Science Talent Search. From there he went straight to Caltech on a National Merit Scholarship. By the time he graduated in 1971, with honors in physics, Tom had already been interviewed by Lowell for a Hertz fellowship. He was 21 years old. That fall he started graduate work at the University of California at Berkeley, financing his graduate education with a Hertz fellowship and commuting back and forth to the weapons lab.

"After I started my thesis research I was out at the lab a lot, particularly because I was using the lab's computers and was collaborating with some of the people there. The last couple of years I was more or less an absentee graduate student as far as Berkeley was concerned." Tom graduated in 1975, his thesis entitled: "The

Structure of Strong Shock Waves, with Implications for Deuterium Synthesis in Supernovae."

That year Tom began full-time work at the weapons lab, studying why stars go through various stages of birth, evolution, and explosive death. He also labored on more down-to-earth projects, such as developing fuels for the mini H-bombs of laser fusion. From the start, Tom worked with Lowell and his young colleagues. "To some extent O Group and extended O Group consists of people Lowell by hook or crook has managed to convince to come to the lab," said Tom. "At some point there is a critical mass of bright people. O Group began around 1975. Before that there was what you'd call a proto O Group right up next to Teller's office. It sort of scandalized the director's office because all these scrungy graduate students were hanging around up there. One guy in particular always came in barefoot, and he would come in past the director's receptionist. Once a barefoot guy in a beach shirt walked into the director's conference room to ask Lowell a question right in the middle of one of these director's meetings. We heard about that for a long time.

"The laser fusion stuff I did was mainly with Lowell, and the astrophysics mainly with George Chapline. George was 29 when I showed up at the lab. Lowell was 30. They were the Young Turks, bright and aggressive and stirring up trouble all over the place."

Suddenly Lowell arrived, a whirlwind of action and commands. He carried a six-pack of 16-ounce bottles of Coke, a popcorn popper, and a brown envelope. It was going to be a party, O Group style. There was commotion in the kitchen as Lowell and Mark joked and made popcorn.

As Lowell entered the living room, I mentioned Mark's performance at dinner and asked about lying with a straight face.

"Oh, it was Rod who taught him that," he said, digging into the popcorn.

I asked Tom what I considered a relevant but harmless question—whether people in R Program actually worked with plutonium to fashion bombs for third-generation weapons.

Tom hesitated. "Well, there's a project group that's actually not part of R Program per se, although it's . . ."

"Stop beating around the bush," snapped Lowell. "Yes, indeed, his people do it."

I suggested to Tom that he needed to learn how to lie with a straight face.

"That's the thing," said Lowell. "He stammers so much that everybody knows when he's blowing smoke. What Tom is trying to say is that one of his project group-leaders does design nuclear explosives for the purpose of pumping X-ray lasers."

"Clearly," Tom continued, "we have to model in great detail the physics of the laser, and that generally involves large numerical models that run on the big computers. We have to try to understand what the optimal pumping conditions are, what sort of radiations the bomb should put out to optimally pump the laser. We need to understand what sort of laser geometry, one, works at all and, two, gives the best laser output."

He paused. "If I hesitate, it's because I'm trying to understand what I can and can't say."

"Don't worry, Thomas, I'll interrupt when you step over the line."

I asked whether the major effort in R Program went into computer codes and simulations, or actually exploding bombs and analyzing data from tests in the desert.

"There's a big overhead to doing tests at all," said Tom. "If you take the effort as a whole, there's a lot of people who'd say they weren't formally associated with R Program at all, but in fact dig the holes and rig the recording gear and so forth."

It was not clear to me just how far work had actually progressed on third-generation weapons other than the X-ray laser. Every so often I heard rumors that R Program had conducted another test in Nevada, such as event "Romano" in December 1983. Was this an X-ray laser or something more exotic? Bethe had suggested that the other ideas were preliminary at best. I suspected that the other weapon ideas were "paper designs" at this point. But I had no way of knowing. Moreover, the public's limited knowledge of what went on at the Nevada test site was getting even more limited under the Reagan administration. In 1983 it reversed a long-standing government policy of announcing all nuclear tests and started keeping the existence of small ones secret.

"R Program per se is focused on X-ray lasers," Tom said in answer to a question. "My feeling has been that if you're going to have a different third-generation concept, it's better to have that be independent in a lean way. We're busy enough trying to do as much as we possibly can with inadequate resources. We're not terribly conservative, and so we're always biting off more than we can chew. It then takes a heroic effort by a lot of people to pull it off."

So you're not testing or working on the fabrication of other third-generation weapons? I asked.

"That's right. There are people in R Program who propose other third-generation concepts, and we are liberal in allowing them to do so. We're just not willing to pay for the experiments."

I was curious about the calibration of equipment for the detection of X-rays produced in the nuclear tests. At Stanford University in 1983, protests had erupted when researchers from Livermore petitioned the school for access to government-funded particle accelerators at the Stanford Linear Accelerator Center that could be used to generate powerful X-rays. Fifteen faculty, 180 staff members, and 2,000 students signed petitions objecting to the secret-weapons-related research.

I asked Tom whether the press reports were correct—that some of that research was meant to aid development of the nuclear X-ray laser.

"It's fairly peripheral to our program," he said. "We're interested in diagnostic development, and they have some capability to do that over there. But that's more long-range research. It's not closely tied in. Most of that is long-term diagnostic development for the normal test program. Occasionally, we'll ask some of those people to help us on a shot. It's interesting and has some relevance, but it sure isn't going to make or break our efforts."

Lowell came into the room with a fresh bowl of popcorn. "Did Tom manage to obscure the Stanford situation while I was out?" he asked. "There's massive figleafing on both sides. You have to watch closely to see the courtship. The lab agreed it wouldn't drop bombs on the Stanford faculty, and Stanford agreed it wouldn't inquire very closely about what happened to those detectors once they were calibrated."

I wondered if Lowell's remarkable mix of irony, sarcasm, and candor would help with questions of strategy—the battle plans outlining how well X-ray lasers might operate in space. Lowell, seeming to read my mind, pulled a thick manuscript out of a brown envelope. He said it was a rebuttal to the most definitive criticism

of the X-ray laser to date—the paper written by Ashton B. Carter
for the Congressional Office of Technology Assessment.

"Let's get down to cases," Lowell said with relish. He wanted to
read through his rebuttal point by point, excerpting and explaining
it for me. Lowell said the rebuttal was based on a secret document
and had blanks where classified material had been deleted.

"I don't think this is terribly appropriate," said Tom, who clearly
seemed more comfortable speaking in generalities.

Lowell was firm. "People have criticized your program in the
open literature. Do you have any responses you can make on an
unclassified basis? If you don't, I will."

"Well, why don't you comment and I'll comment on your comments."

Tom, as head of R Program, had risen to a bureaucratic position
that was superior to Lowell's in terms of determining what was
secret and what was not. By the letter of the Department of Energy's
classification laws, it was Tom, not Lowell, who decided what could
be said about the X-ray laser. The situation was somewhat awkward
since Lowell had originally been Tom's superior.

"OK," said Lowell, turning to me. "I'm going to summarize in an
unclassified fashion and Tom can agree or disagree."

He handed me a xerox copy of the Carter study. Certain sections
had been carefully numbered and underlined. Lowell had ignored
the bulk of the 98-page document, highlighting only those points
that raised his ire.

The Carter study, published a month before my visit to the
weapons lab, had already aroused much debate in Washington.
"Perfect or near-perfect defense," it said, "is so remote that it should
not serve as the basis of public expectation or national policy."

Carter had gone to Yale and graduated with degrees in physics
and medieval history. As a Rhodes scholar he had attended Oxford
University, graduating in 1979 with a Ph.D. in theoretical physics.
He had then worked for OTA and for the Office of the Secretary of
Defense. At the time he wrote the study he was a research fellow
at the Center for International Studies at MIT. Twenty-nine years
old when the report was published, in many respects he was a young
scientist on the "other side" of the debate over the feasibility of
strategic defense.

A main objection to Carter's report, Lowell said, was that he

had talked only about "the laser under study," and had proceeded
to say it would never damage Soviet missiles.

"Contrary to his assertions, we're studying a number of X-ray
lasers of different wavelengths," he said, reading his rebuttal.
"There's no such thing as 'the laser under study.' This is significant.
If you change the wavelength of the radiation by a factor of ten,
its penetrating capability varies by a factor of a thousand. This
variability gives you enormous flexibility in tailoring a robust attack on enemy targets.

"What you want," Lowell added, looking up, "is an impulse kill,
which is something like a hammer blow. The X-rays create a shock
wave that goes through the booster and it tears itself apart."

Lowell's voice was crisp. He was warming to the attack. He had
written the rebuttal recently and obviously enjoyed the chance to
go through it again.

Perhaps a new X-ray laser at a different wavelength had indeed
been tested since Carter did his research, as Lowell seemed to im-
ply. (Carter had received a security clearance and had access to
classified materials.) But since small decreases in wavelength called
for huge increases in pumping power, it seemed likely that a new
laser would not be startlingly different from the first. Bombs in the
Nevada desert could be only so big.

"On the next point, contrary to Carter's claim, we have yet to
determine nontrivial upper limits on how energetic, how powerful,
or, most pertinently, how bright the beam from an X-ray laser can
be. All of the limits we've encountered to date seem to be engineering ones, which have yielded to some insight."

Lowell's assertion, though impossible to evaluate, dealt with an
important point. The beam of an X-ray laser would tend to spread
slowly into a narrow cone of radiation in space, similar to the way
the beam from a flashlight disappears in the dark. A few inches
wide where it left the weapon, the X-ray beam might be hundreds
of feet in diameter by the time it reached a distant target. The only
way to get a "kill" and to compensate for this diminution was to
try to increase the concentration of radiation in the cone, to make
it brighter.

Lowell's next point took issue with a broad attack on pop up.
Carter's main objection was that the earth would often get in the
way. If based in the United States, Carter said, X-ray lasers could
never get high enough fast enough to intercept even slow-burning

Soviet boosters. The curvature of the earth meant their beams would never get close to the Soviet Union. Even if X-ray lasers were based in the United Kingdom, they still could not get high enough fast enough.

"Straw man," said Tom.

Lowell nodded his head and started to read his rebuttal. "The most attractive locations for X-ray laser platforms are probably submarines, for vulnerability reasons. These might be most advantageous if located in the Eastern Mediterranean, the North Sea, and the seas around Korea and Japan. First generation X-ray lasers with . . ."

Tom cleared his throat, cautioning Lowell.

". . . with BLANK properties will suffice to kill single ICBMs of all present and future Soviet types anticipated by the Defense Intelligence Agency. And second-generation lasers with BLANK properties will kill on the order of a dozen boosters each at maximum range from these launch sites." (Lowell said 'BLANK' to indicate where he had deleted secret material.)

Another of Carter's points was the vulnerability of subs. His tactic was to adopt an argument of conservatives who said that America's subs were more vulnerable than they appeared since their presence was announced after the firing of the first missiles, inviting counterattacks by a watchful enemy. Carter applied this argument to the launch of defensive X-ray lasers, which in order to have any chance of being effective at all would have to be stationed very close to the Soviet Union.

"Submarine patrol very near to Soviet shores suggests the possibility of attacking a submarine with shore-based nuclear missiles as soon as its position has been revealed by the first defensive launch," the Carter study said.

Lowell's rebuttal, in essence, claimed that all missiles carrying defensive lasers could be launched before a sub was located and destroyed.

"When existing American boosters such as BLANK are used in existing Polaris, Poseidon, and Trident subs by first-generation X-ray lasers, the time-line margins are such that any one of these boats should be able to usefully launch its entire complement of X-ray laser-bearing boosters, especially in consideration of the insensitivity of the mission to precisely determined submarine orientation. The X-ray laser platform mission does not require a high precision initial position or orientation of the submarine, unlike the submarine-launched ballistic missile-carrying mission."

It was an assertion that was hard to evaluate, since it seemed to rest on highly classified details of how fast missiles could be launched from a submarine.

Carter's final point had to do with fast-burn boosters. A key element in Carter's attack and Lowell's rebuttal was how far an X-ray laser could penetrate the atmosphere in an attempt to knock out fast-burn missiles. The beam would eventually be stopped at some point because of its interaction with the air.

Lowell turned to Tom and started to discuss what they might say about X-ray penetration of the atmosphere.

"What are you going to permit to be said here?" asked Lowell as he pointed to a particular paragraph of the rebuttal.

"Well, at sufficiently high brightness levels you'd have to consider bleaching," said Tom, referring to a physical effect in which X-rays would knock so many electrons out of the air that it became passable to X-rays, at least for a limited distance.

"Great," Lowell said ironically, "so how far down in the atmosphere can you attack boosters?"

"That's all I'm willing to say," Tom replied.

A powerful X-ray laser, it was rumored, might in theory be able to "bleach" its way downward through the atmosphere a dozen or more miles, reaching a point about 70 miles above the earth. In his study, Carter had criticized X-ray lasers by turning this so-called bleaching mechanism around so it transformed the X-ray laser into an offensive weapon. "A strong X-ray laser beam," he wrote, "can force its way through a column of air by bleaching the column, but a weak laser beam is completely absorbed. An X-ray laser in the atmosphere might therefore be able to attack an object in space because the beam is intense enough in the vicinity of the laser to bleach the air, whereas an X-ray laser in space *could not attack objects within the atmosphere.*" [Emphasis added.]

In short, his charge was that the Soviets, equipped with their own X-ray lasers, would be able to launch an offensive strike against earth-based targets in the United States by first attacking defensive American battle stations in space. Moreover, they could do so without having to forsake their current arsenal of land-based missiles for a new breed of faster ones.

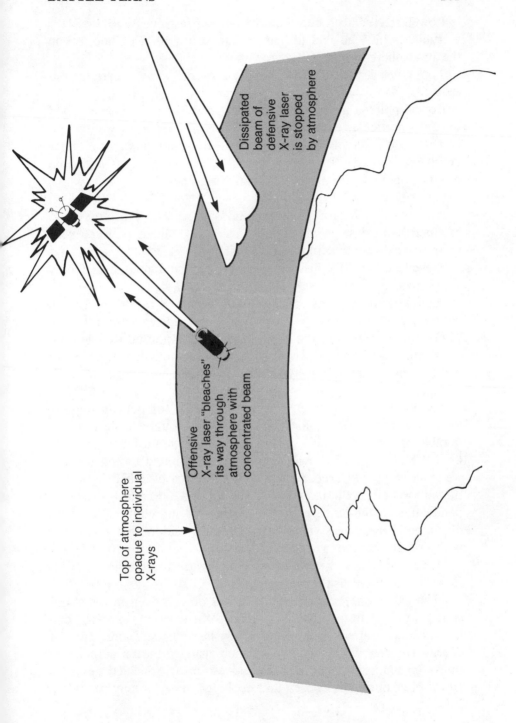

Dissipated beam of defensive X-ray laser is stopped by atmosphere

Offensive X-ray laser "bleaches" its way through atmosphere with concentrated beam

Top of atmosphere opaque to individual X-rays

Lowell started his rebuttal on the issue of fast-burn boosters. "It's a crucial point," he said to Tom. "Can you cope with boosters in the atmosphere or not? What are you going to say?"

Tom paused. "It's a quantitative question. Below a certain altitude . . ."

Lowell pointed at the rebuttal and asked Tom if it was all right to read a particular paragraph out loud.

Tom read it silently to himself. He clearly did not want the paragraph read aloud. "I would still assert," he said, "that a certain penetration goes with a laser of certain brightness."

"Or wavelength," Lowell added.

"Yes, or wavelength. Fast-burn boosters certainly force you to brighter X-ray lasers, which are harder to build and need more massive hardware to deploy, so the fast burn . . ."

Lowell cut in. "I'll just take my chances and read this on my own," he said.

"Quick burn-out boosters can't escape from X-ray laser attacks, contrary to Carter's blanket assertion," he read from the rebuttal. "They can merely force the X-ray laser off of a pop-up vehicle onto an orbital one so as to permit shooting deep into the atmosphere rather than skimming through its upper regions en route to a target in space."

My mind started to reel. The whole reason for pop up deployment was that battle stations in space were thought to be too vulnerable to enemy attack. There were also treaties between the United States and the Soviet Union that prohibited basing nuclear weapons in space. True, it would be easier to bleach deeply into the atmosphere if the laser beam was shooting straight down, perpendicular to the surface of the earth. But in rebutting Carter's objection, Lowell was taking an extreme position that conflicted with a range of earlier assertions.

"OK," said Lowell without pausing, ready to complete his attack, "the next part is the bleaching."

"That X-ray lasers in space can attack objects deep in the atmosphere has just been noted," he read. "X-ray lasers in space can always survive attack from other X-ray lasers or any other type of energy weapon with adequate—which usually means sufficiently thick—shielding. Once a threat spectrum is specified, even a BLANK of optimally chosen and deployed material may provide a quite robust multishot survivable shield for an in-space platform. In orbit X-ray lasers can thus survive and win."

"Again," said Tom, "that's a quantitative question."

"Why of course," said Lowell. "So are they all."

"I don't regard that nearly as black and white as you do."

"That's because I've worried about it more than you have," Lowell replied. "When you've studied it as much as I have and plugged as many numbers in, you'll agree with me."

There was a slight pause after this exchange between Tom and Lowell. Appeals to authority were always a problem, especially when invoked in the realm of military secrecy. In this case, moreover, there were good reasons to question Lowell's assertion. First, there were Teller's myriad statements about the vulnerability of objects in space. Second, there was the long history of questionable attempts to cope with such vulnerabilities.

Even a simple nuclear explosion in space could knock out unshielded satellites thousands of miles away, a phenomenon much less powerful than the "impulse kill" of an enemy X-ray laser. The reason was that a bomb's radiations set up extremely high electric fields in the metallic skin of a satellite—on the order of 100,000 to 1 million volts per meter, according to Samuel Glasstone and Philip J. Dolan in *The Effects of Nuclear Weapons,* the Pentagon's bible on the subject. These radiations created a type of electromagnetic pulse that knocked out delicate electric gear. For a decade the military had known about the possibility of EMP in space and had struggled to "harden" reentry vehicles, missiles, and satellites against its threat. Expert opinion was divided on the effectiveness of such shielding. Theodore B. Taylor, who directed the Pentagon's first agency to examine such effects, was quoted in an article I had written as saying that the military at first consistently tried to ignore such problems because they were nearly impossible to solve. He said there were more than fifty exotic effects from nuclear weapons that largely had been swept under the rug.

The art of protection had certainly advanced since the days of Taylor. Still, it was only Lowell's assertion that a defensive X-ray laser could be shielded from powerful attack, and that it could slice far enough into the atmosphere to knock out an offensive X-ray laser. Moreover, Lowell's new proposal abandoned the simplicity of pop up. The deeper we got into this, the fewer simple answers there seemed to be. If the Soviets could use an X-ray laser offensively, couldn't we do the same?

Undaunted, Lowell moved forward. "The Soviet attainment of fast-burnout ICBM booster technology is at least two decades away. Carter's indication of this prospect of vitiating the first generation of X-ray laser technology is quite untimely. In any event, fast-burnout booster technology will be vulnerable to orbital laser technology into the indefinite future."

Finished on one front, Lowell moved on to dealing with Carter's objections to putting laser battle stations directly in orbit—a battle plan that had suddenly taken on new importance. Carter's criticisms focused on battle stations in geosynchronous orbit, the place some 22,300 miles above the earth where satellites orbited at exactly the same rate that the earth turned, making them "stationary" in relation to the surface of the earth.

Carter's assertion was that a "perfect" X-ray laser in geosynchronous orbit would be able to intercept only a single Soviet booster. This was because all the rods of the battle station would be bound together in order to send its energies over such vast distances.

Lowell disagreed.

"A few to several dozen such advanced X-ray laser systems could potentially liquidate the entire Soviet ballistic missile order of battle, if this were salvo-launched," Lowell read, referring to the entire simultaneous firing of the Soviet arsenal. "If the Soviet ballistic missile inventory were dribble-launched in an attempt to exhaust a small orbiting constellation of American X-ray lasers, this would invite a counterforce strike on the still-loaded Soviet silos and submarines before constellation exhaustion could be attained."

In other words, the United States still might have to attack with conventional offensive missiles if the Soviets started firing missiles one by one in an attempt to outwit American X-ray lasers. The reason was that a U.S. nuclear battle station could fire only once before being consumed by its fireball. Clearly, Lowell was picturing the retention of at least part of the American arsenal of offensive missiles. It was a picture at odds with President Reagan's vision of making missiles "impotent and obsolete."

Lowell had finished with the objections to pop up and orbital deployment of nuclear X-ray lasers. From here on, Carter's study made general criticisms of space-based defense. Such a system, he said, could never be tested, yet would have to work near perfectly the first time it was used.

Lowell went into some detail in rebuttal, noting which parts of the system could be tested, with nuclear weapons being exploded underground. Then he landed his killer punch. "If it can be believed that offensive ICBMs—which have never flown over the pole, or over Soviet, U.S., or Canadian territory, or out of a real U.S. operational silo, or in any type of nuclear war environment—are going to throw warheads which have never been fired under acceleration or in the atmosphere onto Soviet targets whose details are quite unknown, then surely the same people can readily believe in the validity of defensive exercises that I've just sketched. It's simply a matter of getting used to a new idea."

It was a good point. Clearly there was no way to test completely an offensive system, so why apply a more rigorous standard to a defensive one? Yet critics maintained that a big problem remained. An offense that was ten percent effective would touch off a nuclear firestorm of unimaginable dimensions on enemy territory, whereas a defense that was only ten percent effective would transform the defender's homeland into a smoking, radioactive ruin. In short, the situations were not comparable. Defensive testing would have to be as exhaustive as possible.

Carter's second general objection to nuclear and nonnuclear defense technologies was the notion that the short response time meant the "likely need for the defense to activate itself autonomously, since there would be no more than a minute for human decision." In other words, it would be war by computer, a notion that had earlier sent the Congressmen into spasms of disbelief.

Lowell dismissed Carter's point, as well as the criticisms of the Congressmen and the answers administration witnesses gave at the hearing. "Those people are playing games or haven't listened to their intelligence briefings," he said. "They know that the President doesn't retain nuclear release authority in a lot of cases. He's already signed it off to other people. Good grief, these people are just game playing."

I would have been surprised, except that a recent book had made exactly the same point. In *The Command and Control of Nuclear Forces,* Paul Bracken, a political scientist at Yale University, argued that the button long ago had been given to military commanders in the field. One reason, he said, was that Washington, D.C., was too vulnerable to attack from Soviet submarines in the nearby Atlantic Ocean. If control had not been dispersed, he said, the Soviets might have been tempted to try a "decapitation" attack, knocking out top leadership and thus the American nuclear arsenal.

Lowell returned to his rebuttal, moving beyond the issue of the President. "The automatic and autonomous operation of the defense with less than a minute of human participation is hardly an issue, certainly, for *nonnuclear* ballistic missile defense technologies. Precisely what's the problem with shooting down a flight of Soviet ICBM boosters under any circumstances that still look threatening to a responsible American senior officer after a minute's consideration. They don't launch their civilian space flights from their missile fields, so how is a mistake at all likely?" [Emphasis added.]

Lowell developed the theme on his own. "In the absolutely worst case we receive a stiff diplomatic note and we pay $100 million worth of indemnity for accidentally stepping on the launch of their latest Venus probe. If they launch a light attack, you just knock it down with your nonnuclear stuff. If they launch 500 boosters at you, why in the world are you going to take more than ten seconds to say, 'Oops, here we go.' It's just not a credible criticism."

Lowell had a point. In some cases the mistaken firing of American defensive weapons might not be provocative. But what if American battle plans included the targeting of an enemy's early-warning and communications satellites? It was a possible scenario, given their strategic value. Would the Soviets sit idly as their electronic "eyes" and "ears" went dead? Or would they assume the worst and launch their missiles?

One of Carter's final points had to do with general ways the Soviets could foil a defense. "Booster decoys would not be nearly as expensive as true ICBMs," Carter said. "Since they carry no warheads or precision guidance system, they need not be highly reliable, and they might not need to be based in underground silos but can be deployed above ground next to the ICBM silos."

"What Carter doesn't seem to understand," said Lowell, reading the rebuttal, "is that it's the booster itself and then its silo that dominates the hardware cost of an ICBM. The warheads and the precision features of the guidance system are perturbations in the overall cost structure. Contrary to his declarations, unreliable boosters that won't fly to 80 or 90 percent of their trajectory won't be noticed, let alone shot at, by X-ray lasers, and thus are useless expenses for the offense. Booster decoys, which may cost half or conceivably as little as a third as much as a full ICBM, simply don't help the offense significantly. What Carter doesn't seem to realize is that X-ray lasers in particular, and other directed-energy technologies as well, are far less expensive and win big in the cost-exchange ratio."

Lowell paused. That seemed to be it. He had gone through all the points he wanted to rebut. Of course, as with many of his other assertions, not everyone agreed with his point on booster decoys. Some critics and other military men held they might be relatively inexpensive. Former Under-Secretary of Defense Richard D. De-Lauer had told the House Armed Services Committee in November 1983 that boost-phase decoys were a viable option. "Any defensive system," he added, "can be overcome with proliferation, decoys, decoys, decoys, decoys."

It was after midnight and I was too tired to sort through all the details of Lowell's rebuttal. But I had the general feeling that the whole evening's discussion spelled the end of pop up. There was a possibility that American submarines might launch only one X-ray laser before themselves coming under attack, and fast Soviet boosters might eventually force American planners to put X-ray lasers into orbit around the earth. That statement had caught me by surprise. The critics seemed to have succeeded in forcing an admission that the battle plan was much more complicated than it appeared at first.

Wouldn't a defensive shield create an imbalance between the superpowers? I asked. Our shield would probably be better than the one the Soviets would build at first, even if they eventually caught up. Wouldn't they fear that we might use our shield for offensive purposes to mop up the ragged retaliation after we had launched a first strike?

Tom considered this for a moment. "Hopefully it will lead them to serious arms-control negotiations," he answered. "If they think there is going to be an asymmetry which they are going to have a hard time making up, then they are going to ask what they can do to reduce the consequences to themselves. The rational thing, as they did during the first great ABM debate [in the early 1970s], is to try to get us to give it up in a treaty—to say to themselves, 'Here's an area we can't compete in. Let's give it up.' And if we're on the ball, we'll be able to extract things like across-the-board strategic arms reductions, and get them to be serious. 'Hey,' they might say, 'isn't it time to try to come to something a little less threatening all around?' I think that's a very credible scenario—as long as we don't saber-rattle and get them so paranoid that they feel the only thing they can do is launch now rather than later. I think they are not that crazy. From what I have read, the Soviet system is reasonably stable and methodical in the way it goes about decision making. I think that their perception of an impending asymmetry will make them more susceptible to negotiation."

It was an evasive but rather elegant answer. Unfortunately, it was also true that "bargaining chips" had all too often gone on to accelerate the arms race. The list went on and on—the Pershing II, cruise missiles, the MX, and so forth.

"The other issue," Tom continued, "is that if we really think we're going to force them into a corner, we could consider things like sharing technology or setting up a mutual defense system."

I asked Tom whether he thought asymmetry in X-ray laser defense was a real possibility.

"The Russians have certainly pioneered a lot of work on X-ray lasers. So as far as basic science goes, I think that we can't count on us having smarter scientists than the Soviets. Maybe we're better motivated—maybe not. It's hard to say. I like to think we're pretty well motivated. But historically the Russians have been pretty on the ball about catching up in nuclear arms."

But, I asked, what about questions of manufacturing and industrial infrastructure?

"The questions of computer manufacture are thornier," Tom said. "I think the Russians have demonstrated capability in areas where it really counts."

Such as supercomputer projects like S-1? I asked.

"Well, you can see their expertise in missile guidance. They're getting a lot better at that. They tended to lag, and I think they will lag . . ."

Lowell cut in. "The guidance system on their current generation of ICBMs is superior to the guidance system of our latest generation ICBMs. The SS-18 is quite a bit more accurate than the Minuteman III. They continued to modernize and we stopped. In about 1972 we stopped modernizing the guidance system on the Minuteman III and the SS-18 was built with gyro technology that we helped give them in 1975. It's not speculation. We've seen better accuracies on their missile tests."

According to the critics, the alleged gap in missile accuracy was one of the outstanding myths of the Reagan administration. They insisted the facts were otherwise. Some Minutemen III were built as late as 1978, with new guidance and warheads installed on 300 missiles in the late 1970s, according to Alton Frey, a former strategic analyst for the Rand Corporation. Moreover, both superpowers were struggling to deploy all sorts of new missiles with improved accuracies and guidance, the United States producing the MX, the Pershing II, and the Trident II.

Tom came back to the original point. "I think if there was a particular narrowly focused technology, they could either develop it or steal it. What they would have the most trouble with is something that required a number of integrated technologies. And to some extent, X-ray lasers in particular, and space defense do require a number of highly developed integrated technologies—integrated electronics, optics, and materials."

"What do you mean integrated electronics? Integrated circuits? What does it require beyond the megaprocessor—I mean the processor—that your people are designing or scoping or whatever?" Lowell asked.

"The Russians don't have that," said Tom, "although they probably could steal the parts for it."

"It's not a matter of stealing," said Lowell. "They can buy a wheelbarrow load of chips and that will be all they ever require."

But, I protested, the Soviets weren't even allowed to buy MacIntosh personal computers.

"These are single chips that are commercially available these days for about $10 apiece," said Lowell. "And Tom's people say you need on the order of a dozen of these things in a single X-ray laser."

"The integration thing is harder," Tom protested. "I think they . . ."

Lowell interrupted. "What integration thing, Tom? What are you integrating?"

"It's sort of like saying, 'I can buy these chips and make a computer.' It's harder than that. Some of these chips are processors in themselves. Trying to integrate those into a working system is not trivial."

"Oh, really?" asked Lowell. "How many man-centuries do you think it takes?"

I interrupted to say I was confused. I thought the issue was supercomputers, not mere chips. I mentioned that Teller in his Congressional testimony had said S-1 was extremely important to defense and to third-generation weapons. Aren't supercomputers essential for the operation of X-ray laser battle stations?

"I think when push comes to shove he's probably right," Tom said. "Our estimate for the first-order acquisition/tracking of targets is going to get mucked up by countermeasure discrimination tasks and . . ."

Lowell cut in. "The place where you need extensive computing power is in the later phases of the strategic defense battle. Nobody has made the case that you need much computing power for boost-phase intercept, because you are shooting at very few objects. They just aren't coming at you very fast. And they're coming at you a few per second. On the other hand, in the late phases of the battle, after missiles have released their warheads, objects are coming at you at rates of 1,000 per second or more."

Tom continued to take issue with Lowell on the need for powerful computers in space.

"Battle management and command and control," he said, "are very difficult. And to the extent that you need to have reasonably autonomous intelligent platforms, that might drive computer requirements higher."

"Your people," said Lowell with a huff, "have not even *begun* to make that case. Their computer requirements for doing their tasks are really quite modest for boost-phase intercept."

"I agree," said Tom. "And I think they have even overestimated it for particular tasks."

Victorious, Lowell turned to me and said: "Here's the problem. The guy has 1,500 missiles and they're burning for 150 seconds or more. That's a ten per second total that you have to handle in boost phase. If he's finally got his warheads coming down on you—and his warheads and decoys and penetration aids are several hundred thousand objects, and you only have a few hundred seconds to cope with them—then you're faced with thousands of objects per second, each one of which is of very great importance. They're much smaller. They're much harder. They're coming much faster. And they don't have a bright flame broadcasting their location like a booster does. And so your problem becomes a lot more demanding, not just because of the rate, but because of all these other nasty features. You have to get awfully close to your targets, and you have to kill them with very stringent means. And if any significant fraction of that stuff gets through, you die."

"It's not just computers," said Tom, coming back to the original point. "There're questions of high-precision manufacturing techniques, mass production techniques, that are very challenging to us and I would imagine would be even more challenging to the Russians. But if they choose to concentrate resources on that area, I would say they probably could make them. Whether they'd permanently lag several years behind is hard to say. It probably depends on their commitment. In the long run, I don't think we can count on any technological advantage."

Lowell took the argument one step further. "Not only can the Soviets do it on their own. They're awfully good at picking up stuff from us. Not just ideas, which are probably the most crucial on a pound-for-pound basis, but picking up whole technologies. I was told recently, for instance, that the Soviets have picked up an entire U.S. missile system—lock, stock, and barrel. They apparently have the shop drawings on a system which is just being deployed by the U.S. at the present time. And they're deploying it too. And as far as we can tell, it's identical—same dimensions, same performance, same everything. It looks like they literally took it to one of their production lines and said, here, produce this."

So, I asked Lowell, there's no way an asymmetry would develop between us and the Soviets?

"I think they would say, 'We obviously have to match the Americans,' and I think it would be quite easy for them to do so, completely on their own. I think that they would not, in fact, proceed on their own, since they would succeed in picking up a lot of our technology. I would be astonished if they would ever be more than

Optimum Solid-Fueled Rocket

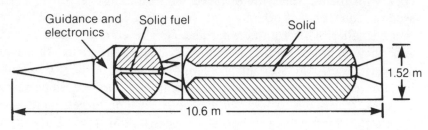

Fast-Burn Solid Rocket

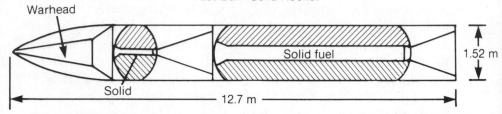

Above is Pentagon contractor's study for a future small ICBM known as Midgetman. Below is contractor's study for a fast-burn ICBM to try to outwit the Soviet system of defense. Measurements are in meters.

a couple of years behind us. If we're ahead of them, I don't believe we can get too far ahead in the strategic sense simply because we're too leaky. They don't have to be good, although they are. They don't have to be good because they can follow closely. Like a bicyclist behind a truck, they can just drift along."

This vision of Soviet expertise, of course, was very different from the picture of retardation presented just a few minutes earlier in which the Soviets were said to be so backward that it would take twenty years for them to build a fast-burn booster. It was that curious flexibility again about Soviet expertise.

I was groggy because of the late hour, and decided I'd better ask about Peter, who had been on my mind. As usual, Lowell seemed to be getting stronger as the night wore on.

Why did Peter work on the nuclear weapon? I asked Lowell.

"I strongly suspect that the single, strongest determinant in the evolution of Peter's world view was probably Solzhenitsyn. For some reason he bored through the *Gulag* during that period. It took him two or three weeks because he was working most of the time. It seemed to be a very somber period for him. He began to refer to himself as being in the Livermore Gulag, and living the life of an oppressed zek." (In Stalin's era, the zeks were prisoners who were forced to work on all sorts of projects, including top-priority ones for the development of airplanes, missiles, computers, and bombs.)

"But certainly," said Tom, "there's no doubting his commitment to making X-ray lasers work—for both the laboratory and defensive applications—although sometimes his degree of commitment is oscillatory."

I asked what was so threatening about the Soviets.

"There's one thing that keeps jumping out at you again and again," Lowell said. "The Soviets won't have to be pushed very hard to preempt." In other words, if they felt an enemy might be preparing to use nuclear arms, they would quickly be first to launch an attack.

"They're not postured to do anything else," Lowell continued. "And they don't have to be pushed very hard to do it. They are set up—and I can't go into the grubby details—but they will not preempt in a hair-trigger fashion. They will make up their minds on time scales of hours or a day and go ahead and do it. It will be done in a very methodical, cold-blooded, brutal, paranoid fashion. They'll just preempt. And they will preempt whenever they do the geopolitical calculus and decide it's better to go this way than that. They'll just go ahead and do it—kill 100 or 200 million people."

But that's not new, I said. According to such authors as Joseph D. Douglass, Jr., and Amoretta M. Hoeber, preemption had long been talked about as a Soviet military strategy.

"No," he said, "it hasn't been their strategy because they haven't had the means to implement it until about a half dozen years ago. It's only since they've developed heavy ICBMs, since they've developed a lot of missile-firing subs. These things keep jumping out at you. Someday—maybe out of the clear, blue sky, because that's the way they're postured, that's the way they're wired, BAM! It will all be over. It's chilling. It's hard to get out of your mind. This is the only way their system works for strategic command, control, and communications. You toy at it month after month, year after year. What other interpretation could you give to the fact that they have this capability and no other capability? They send out their equivalent to our Emergency Action Messages. But it isn't: 'Quick quick. Go go.' It's: 'At such and such a time on such and such a date, you'll do so and so.' It's as methodical as a guillotine blade descending.

"How far do they have to be pushed before they'll do this? It doesn't look like it's very far. They keep pointing to the guillotine blade, and keep pointing to the fact that it's held there by a hair trigger. And they say, 'Now do you really want to push us very far in this particular crisis considering the fact that you are set up to retaliate and we're set up to preempt?' So you just go back, a half a step at a time. That is the sort of thing that worries Rod. How many of those half steps are there? And how long is it going to take before we're pushed back to the point where something very desperate happens and Rod no longer has the possibility of getting the human race into space?"

Lowell was right, preemption was a terrifying possibility, but it was a threat only to America's land-based missiles. In addition, the United States had a huge mobile deterrent in the ocean. On Poseidon sea-based missiles there were more than 3,000 warheads, and on Trident missiles an additional 2,600 warheads, with more on the way. And Tomahawk sea-launched cruise missiles were being deployed on submarines, cruisers, and destroyers, their nuclear warheads planned to eventually number about 700. Only a madman would want to shoot at America's land-based arsenal and then have to tangle with its nuclear deterrent at sea.

By contrast, the Russians had most of their warheads on land-based missiles, and therefore had more reason to fear threats of preemption. And such threats had been made. General Curtis E. LeMay, once a board member of the Hertz Foundation and head of the Strategic Air Command, had written that such battle plans were standard when he presided over the nation's land-based nuclear arsenal. "We spent a great deal of our energies learning what the opposition was doing day to day," he wrote. "Believing I could foresee an attack, I was prepared to beat him to the draw and attack all of his bomber and missile bases."

In breathless detail, Lowell had described how the Soviets used their arsenal not just as the means of deterrence or preemption but as a big stick in the conduct of foreign policy. But he had failed to mention that the United States did too. The Soviets had backed down in the Berlin crisis and Cuban missile crisis partly because of the American nuclear threat. And during the Middle East crisis of 1973, the United States had used its very facile nuclear-alert system to encourage moderation on the part of the Soviets. In his memoir, *On Watch,* Admiral Elmo R. Zumwalt, Jr., recounted how the worldwide nuclear forces of the United States had been put on DefCon (Defense Condition) 3, the highest alert ever, in order to demonstrate how serious America considered the situation. Surely both superpowers excelled at the art of nuclear brinksmanship.

It was past 2:00 A.M. as Lowell and I drove down the interstate in our separate cars, Lowell going back to the lab while I headed for Windy Ridge. The evening's discussion had convinced me that the battle plans for both nuclear war and defensive shields were much more complex than I had ever imagined. With Lowell was the rebuttal, a powerful and very personal vision of how nuclear weapons might be used to bring about an era of unprecedented peace. Also with him was the popcorn popper.

AT WAR

Lowell Wood spent his youth in Simi, California, a rocky valley about forty miles northwest of Los Angeles. Back in the early 1940s it consisted of a small town and a few large ranches surrounded by the barren splendor of the Santa Susana mountains, the hills and canyons inhabited by deer, rabbits, raccoons, and coyotes. The dry, reddish hills provided Hollywood with a handy backdrop for many a Western movie. The valley itself, an oasis amid the rugged terrain, provided ranchers with a modest income from cattle, walnuts, and citrus fruit. During the 1940s and 1950s, however, the price of water and labor began to rise and the ranches started to go up for sale. Among the first to buy land during this period was Lowell's father, a real estate investor who owned residential buildings in Los Angeles. On a hill overlooking the valley he built a house for his family. There were two girls and a boy. Lowell, Jr., was the oldest.

It was the seventh day. I mused about Lowell as I wandered around Windy Ridge, which sat on a hill similar to the one that dominated his youth. Who was this man? A week of conversations had suggested some answers, especially about why Lowell was so devoted to his group of young scientists and why he advocated his ideas on defensive shields with such zeal. Lowell had a happy child-hood. He was a born leader who early in college had been sur-rounded by a powerful group of conservative mentors. He had a long history of controversial ideas and bold tactics. He had suffered setbacks. And he had always regained ground from which to wage his political and intellectual wars. More than anything else, Lowell seemed to be animated by his past. He drew emotional strength for his battles from key people and events.

But mysteries remained. Tonight I was scheduled to have dinner with several of the young scientists. Afterward I planned to talk with Lowell at length, asking him about his past and his plans for putting X-ray lasers in permanent orbit, an idea that had taken on new significance after last night's conversation.

Lowell was born on August 31, 1941, his parents at the time re-siding in West Los Angeles. A few years later the Woods moved to Simi. At first surrounded by ranches and orchards, their hill-top home was slowly encircled by tract houses over the decades. By 1984, Simi had a population of about 85,000 and was mainly a bed-room community for Los Angeles.

Back in the 1950s, however, the valley was a remote and rug-gedly ideal place for a boy to grow up. The population was about 5,000. Simi then had an elementary school, a high school, and a Protestant church, institutions which were the principal focus of the primarily Methodist community. The first bank and movie theater did not arrive until the 1960s. Lowell went to school with the ranch kids, and like them belonged to the Boy Scouts.

While growing up, Lowell every so often heard the rumble of high technology in the hills behind his house. It was a manifestation of the race for space. In 1948, North American Aviation (today the Rocketdyne Division of Rockwell International) had built a facility for testing rocket engines in the canyons of the Santa Susana mountains. There engineers would fire up engine after engine, eventually testing the ones meant to drop warheads on the Soviet Union and send men to the moon. The tests echoed throughout the valley. At night they lit up the sky.

Lowell's interest in science started to soar in the fifth grade when a neighbor, Vernon Haury, invited the youngster to visit the chemistry lab he kept at his house. "He was real bright," Haury told Karen West of the Simi *Enterprise Sun and News* after Lowell had received an award from the Department of Energy. "I tried to encourage him to keep on going and studying. I told him what I was doing and explained things to him. He picked things up real fast."

Lowell's eighth-grade teacher, Pat Havens, remembered the abilities of her star student quite well. "He was already recognized as being of genius caliber in everything, especially science," she told Bob Satterthewaite of the same newspaper.

In 1958 Lowell graduated from high school, one of 44 students in his class. He was valedictorian and the recipient of Bank of America's award for the top math and science student in Southern California.

Upon graduation Lowell entered the University of California at Los Angeles, and in his freshman chemistry class met George Chapline. They quickly became close friends. Lowell often took George out to his parents' house in Simi where they would ride horses, chase chickens, and perform some of the more dangerous science experiments Lowell dreamed up. The expansive safety of the Woods' property was the site of many an explosion.

At times, Lowell and George would climb the hills behind the house to clandestinely watch fiery tests of the huge rocket engines. "In a sense," George had told me, "Lowell has been responsible for encouraging my interest in technology. Ever since I knew him in college, he's always been very interested in applied science and in particular the far-out things. As a sophomore he had a scheme for personally doing experiments in nuclear fusion in his back yard."

During his sophomore year Lowell caught the eye of Willard F. Libby, a chemist who had just come to UCLA from a stint as one of the five Commissioners of the Atomic Energy Commission (AEC), the predecessor of the Department of Energy that controlled all nuclear projects in the United States. Libby was a Cold Warrior with impeccable scientific credentials. During the Manhattan Project he had helped create the gaseous diffusion process for the enrichment of uranium 235—a key step in the birth of the bomb. After the war he had discovered a way to measure the radioactive isotopes of carbon for the "radiocarbon dating" of ancient biological materials, an insight for which he eventually won the Nobel Prize. In 1954 he took the AEC post, replacing Henry De Wolf Smyth, a liberal commissioner who had fallen out with his colleagues after casting the lone vote to maintain the security clearance of J. Robert Oppenheimer. As AEC commissioner, Libby, in step with the Eisenhower administration and his atomic colleagues, promoted the "Atoms for Peace" program, and became involved in the fallout controversy by arguing that the risks were minimal compared with the dangers of maintaining a weak nuclear arsenal. Libby also played a role in lobbying for the creation of a nuclear-weapons lab at Livermore.

Lowell was one of the bright young undergraduates singled out by Libby to work on "199 Projects," a way for eager young chemists already doing independent research to get college credit for it. The students in the 199 club were gung-ho enthusiasts, often working late into the night, playing pranks, and enjoying each other's company. It was not unlike O Group. Lowell was quite vocal, and was considered a leader. According to Leona Libby, the chemist's second wife and a nuclear physicist herself, Lowell was something of a "bad boy" at UCLA because he refused to wear his safety glasses in the lab and instead, flaunting the rules, often donned a Mickey Mouse cap.

Libby had a good relationship with his students, having them over for dinner, lending them money, and inviting them to an annual picnic. In addition, he worked personally with Lowell on scientific projects. As a sophomore, Lowell performed research on radiocarbon dating with Libby that was eventually published as a chapter in the textbook, *Isotopic and Cosmic Chemistry.*

Moreover, during Lowell's sophomore year, Libby forever changed the course of the young scientist's career by introducing him to Teller. Libby and Teller were old friends from the days of the Manhattan Project. At the time of the introduction, Teller was a University Professor of physics for the colleges of the University of California system, having just stepped down as director of the Livermore weapons lab. The Hungarian physicist and the young chemist from Simi immediately hit it off, frequently meeting when Teller visited the UCLA campus. "He stopped by one day per month," Lowell had recalled, "and we got in the habit of talking for part of that day and usually going out to dinner together. We talked about lots and lots of things. He was a very interesting guy to talk with." One issue Teller loved to discuss in those days was the proposed ban on the testing of all nuclear weapons, which he opposed with all his might.

Still an undergraduate, Lowell had come under the influence of two of the nation's top advocates of an ever-expanding nuclear arsenal. Libby and Teller were not only at the height of their careers but were internationally known for their stance on the Soviet Union and the arms race. Teller, as soon as he was released from the restrictions imposed by his job as director of Livermore, set to work on a book to bluntly express his views, which was published in 1962 under the title *The Legacy of Hiroshima*. "In Russian Communism," he wrote, "we have met an opponent that is more powerful, more patient, and incomparably more dangerous than German Nazism."

For Lowell, the experience of gaining the confidence of two of the top conservative scientists in the nation must have been heady. He was 18 years old when he met Teller. As Lowell began his junior year, Libby won the Nobel Prize.

Like Teller, Libby was no shrinking violet, taking pains to publicly display his atomic activism while teaching at UCLA. When Lowell was a junior, Libby built a "poor man's fallout shelter" in his back yard to show that anyone could survive a nuclear war. A few months later, this collection of sand bags and railway ties was destroyed by a brush fire. According to Edward Zuckerman in *The Day After World War III*, the incident caught the eye of disarmament campaigner Leo Szilard, who quipped: "This proves not only that there is a God but that he has a sense of humor."

Lowell graduated in 1962 with Bachelor of Science degrees in chemistry and mathematics. In his senior year he had also been elected to Phi Beta Kappa, selection being based solely on grades. Lowell was in the top five percent of his class.

Fond of UCLA and the friends he had made, Lowell decided to stay on for graduate school. During his second year, however, he suffered a major motorcycle accident and nearly fatal head injuries. He was hospitalized and started a long recuperation. Throughout this trauma, Libby, now Lowell's thesis advisor, repeatedly visited his young protégé.

Throughout his years at UCLA Lowell's interests expanded greatly, not just in politics but in science as well. He became fascinated with big computers and the prospects of endowing them with artificial intelligence. He became interested in geophysics. In 1965 Lowell graduated with a Ph.D. in astrophysics, his thesis entitled "Hyperthermal Processes in the Solar Atmosphere."

Ph.D. in hand, Lowell in 1966 was invited by Teller to join the weapons lab, which he promptly did. He performed research in astrophysics and taught in the lab's Department of Applied Science, the University of California graduate school founded by Teller in 1963 and fondly referred to at the lab as "Teller Tech." One of Lowell's students was Jack Marling, the young scientist who would go on to invent the detector for the blue-green laser. Fresh out of college himself, Lowell, at Teller's request, also started interviewing candidates for Hertz fellowships.

As was usual for new employees at the weapons lab, Lowell's interests in pure science were soon crowded out by more practical concerns. He started to collaborate with John Nuckolls, the early innovator of ideas for third-generation weapons. Their main goal was to miniaturize the H-bomb. Nuckolls had already come up with designs that would shrink the device down to the size of a cocktail olive. The problem was how to ignite the fuel. One possible solution was the laser, which had first appeared in 1960. Lowell and Nuckolls in 1969 came up with a proposal to use powerful beams of laser light to compress a fuel pellet in an attempt to touch off the fusion of hydrogen isotopes into helium. The resulting explosion could be used to blow up buildings or turn electrical generators. Their idea became the basis for the nation's effort in laser fusion. So far that quest has consumed more than $2 billion in federal funds without reaching "break even," the point at which the energy released by the fuel matches that pumped in by large lasers such as Novette. Critics of the technology say that, even if successfully developed, the technique might never be economically competitive with other forms of fuel. Advocates disagree, saying the ultimate result will be a source of clean, cheap, and nearly inexhaustible electrical power. Whatever the outcome, laser fusion was Lowell's first shot at big science and technology. And it clearly turned out to be much more difficult than any of its developers ever dreamed.

Right from the start, Lowell began to recruit old friends to join him at the weapons lab. George Chapline came in 1969. Lowell's sister Paula, a biologist, came as well. John Haury, the son of next-door neighbor Vernon Haury, came to work on projects with the brother-sister team. Lowell's interest in nuclear issues also rubbed off on his other sister, Sandra, who eventually became a nuclear engineer and at times worked on problems at the government's nuclear test site in Nevada.

While Lowell and friends swung far to the political right during the decade of the 1960s, the nation, deeply divided over the war in Vietnam, moved steadily to the left. This polarization soon tore at Lowell personally. "Back in 1970 I was indicted for nuclear war crimes by a group in Berkeley known as the Red Power Family," he had said. "It was the same group that marched on Teller's house. They sentenced him to death at a war crimes tribunal, along with me and a dozen others."

The posters had appeared across the Berkeley campus in early November 1970, the message cut in bold black letters: EDWARD TELLER—WAR CRIMINAL. A poorly reproduced picture of Teller heightened his dark features and bushy eyebrows, making him look quite evil. The list of "crimes" included his work on the atom bomb, the hydrogen bomb, his role in founding the Livermore weapons lab, and his long history "as hawk advisor to Washington officials." At the bottom of the poster was Teller's address, phone number, and the suggestion that "People in the community have a responsibility to challenge Teller on his activities. You can do this by giving him a call or going by to discuss them with him. CAN YOU DIG IT?"

Toward the middle of November, the Red Power Family, a radical commune, announced its intention to hold a "War Crimes Tribunal" in a building on the Berkeley campus. On the evening of November 23, the Pauley Ballroom was packed as a long succession of speakers outlined the charges over the course of three hours. Blumberg and Owens, Teller's biographers, give a blow-by-blow account of the session, which they say was based on a tape recording. Teller was called "a leading sparkplug . . . for an even greater military nuclear arsenal" and "a paranoid anticommunist." Livermore was labeled a "scientific whorehouse." Indicted along with Teller and Lowell were Charles Hitch, President of the University of California; Glenn T. Seaborg, physicist and former chairman of the Atomic Energy Commission; John Foster, former director of Livermore; John O. Lawrence, physicist and brother of the late Ernest O. Lawrence; and Michael M. May, then the head of Livermore.

Toward the end of the evening, one of the young radicals asked the crowd: "What are you going to do when you go home tonight? You know, are you going to go home and off these labs and off these people, or are you just going to sit there and listen to this crap, huh? What are you going to do, huh? I'm gonna try and off these labs."

A general cry rose from the audience: "Let's get Teller. We want Teller."

Inconspicuously on the sidelines of the trial was Lowell, who watched the protest with growing alarm. He rushed to Teller's house in Berkeley to get the physicist and his wife Mici out and away. He also called the police, who responded in riot gear. One contingent of officers surrounded the house, while another cordoned off a road a half-block from Teller's home. Several hundred radicals from the tribunal, after burning cars and smashing store windows, arrived in Teller's neighborhood and marched on the house. The police turned them back. At a nearby intersection the mob burned Teller in effigy.

Lowell at the time was 29 years old.

The bonds between Teller and Lowell grew in many ways during the 1960s and 1970s. Under the tutelage of Teller, Lowell developed a keen eye for talent and soon succeeded in recruiting many bright young scientists to the weapons lab. Tom Weaver came in 1971. Rod Hyde arrived in 1972. To formalize the burgeoning effort and to give Lowell bureaucratic authority over the young recruits, Teller, then attached to the director's office as the lab's Associate Director for Physics, in 1973 appointed him head of a newly created "Special Studies Group" of young scientists. That same year, Teller appointed Lowell to a powerful bureaucratic position—associate head of the lab's physics department. Lowell was within reach of Teller's position, a place from which he could conceivably wage a campaign to become director of the weapons lab.

By the early 1970s Lowell was known at Livermore as a rising star who possessed not only political clout but a reputation for pushing the theoretics of nuclear design to its limits. He was fascinated with the idea of giving H-bombs a variety of exotic forms and functions. Einstein's theory of general relativity, for instance, predicted the existence of gravity waves. But none had ever been detected. Lowell came up with a scheme for creating very large ones by means of a nuclear explosion. The experiment was never attempted.

Lowell also proposed to use nuclear explosives to create black holes. In theory, ordinary black holes are collapsed stars so dense that even light cannot escape their powerful gravitational pulls. Although none have ever been detected with certainty, they are thought to widely populate the universe and individually to be many miles in diameter. Lowell wanted to create miniature ones. He developed a scheme whereby the matter for the proposed black hole would sit at the center of a special type of nuclear explosive. When detonated, the bomb would exert its force upon the matter and compress it into a tiny black hole.

In usual fashion, Lowell wanted to do something practical with his proposal—for instance, using black holes to make electrical power in space. The idea was to have a space station fire pellets of fusion fuel (deuterium and tritium) toward the mini black hole. Just before it vanished into the hole's powerful gravitational grip, the fuel would become enormously compressed, reaching the point of thermonuclear ignition. The energy radiated into space would be captured by the nearby space station and relayed back to earth. In 1974, Lowell presented this idea to a scientific meeting at the New York Academy of Sciences, where it evoked gasps and chuckles. It was, he insisted, a serious proposal.

During my meeting with Bethe, I had asked him about Lowell. "He is a very ingenious person," Bethe answered. "He is an inventor and a physicist. He has lots of interesting ideas. Many of them are quite good, and some quite bad. Once he has these ideas he gets enamored with them and wants to translate them into practice, and of course, in a big laboratory like that it's rather easy to have experiments done to test your ideas."

Bethe's remark had merit, but it also needed to be seen in perspective. In some respects, Lowell's ideas were no more farfetched than those of many researchers. Science, after all, thrives on speculation. Late in a scientific career, especially after the receipt of a Nobel Prize, many a scientist feels free to entertain his colleagues and the public with some of his wilder notions. But Lowell was unusual in that he went public with his more bizarre ideas right from the start. He did not carefully tread the career ladder, keeping his dreams to himself.

In the mid 1970s, this situation almost destroyed his career. Lowell had accidentally let some secret data slip out at an international meeting attended by Soviet scientists. By the letter of the government's classification laws, his position was quite vulnerable.

He had, as the statute put it, "knowingly transmitted Secret/ Restricted Data to a foreign national." Moreover, the full penalty was likely to be imposed because over the years Lowell's acerbic style and outspoken advocacy of extreme ideas had won him a fair number of enemies in the weapons lab and government. To his foes, Lowell was a bully and a show-off who couldn't be trusted with the conduct of pure science much less the possession of top national secrets. Now they had the security slip with which to press home their point.

A secret trial was held in 1975 to determine what should be done about Lowell's breach, the judges being members of a board of senior security reviewers from the federal government. Things went badly. It looked as if Lowell's "Q clearance" would be revoked as a first step to some kind of punishment. The end of his nuclear career was at hand. Then, at the last minute, Lowell pulled out a hidden ace—a scientific paper he had found that contained the same secret information. Among its authors was Glenn T. Seaborg, former head of the Atomic Energy Commission. The judges were in a mood to hang, but the new evidence was unequivocal: the secret data had already slipped out of the government's hands by accident several years earlier. Lowell was acquitted.

Though free on a technicality, Lowell faced repercussions from the incident. Before the trial, he had been removed as associate head of the physics department. In its wake, problems multiplied. Teller, nearly 70 years old, was then Associate Director for Physics at the lab and was to retire in 1975 from that post. Lowell had been widely seen as the inevitable successor. But now his enemies at the lab and in the government had leverage, and they pressed it to their advantage. Lowell failed to win Teller's post as Associate Director. It was a major setback.

Any ambitions Lowell had to climb the lab's career ladder now had to be abandoned. The security slip would always be there to haunt him. To make matters worse, Lowell suffered a severe emotional upset that year when his sister Paula, a pilot, died in the crash of her small plane. It was a dark period in Lowell's life. But he was not about to give up.

All that remained of his former empire at the lab was his "Special Studies Group" of young graduate students, which he formally christened "O Group" and began to expand and develop. Peter

Hagelstein, Andy Weisberg, Tom McWilliams, and Curt Widdoes all arrived in 1975; Larry West in 1977; Jerry Epstein in 1978; Jordin Kare in 1979. During this period Lowell assembled a group of trailers in a remote corner of the laboratory. It was a far cry from his former headquarters in Building 111.

Lowell's power base at the lab had vanished. His mentor had retired and remained only a figurehead, one that still had clout but was unable to aid Lowell in day-to-day battles. Nevertheless, Lowell still had considerable leverage in the form of his Hertz connection. The interest from those millions helped him hire the best and the brightest graduate students from around the country, and helped stretch their salaries at the weapons lab.

Lowell, moreover, remained a bold adventurer who was willing to take risks. Around 1977, he got involved in a battle over a technical issue that alienated some of his patrons in the Navy and resulted in a loss of research funds to his group. Lowell nonetheless vigorously defended his position, and in the process impressed some Congressmen and some of his young scientists. "He was willing to receive lightning bolts in order to defend a point that he believed was important," Larry had told me. "More than anything else, that fact won me over to him."

The issue was blue-green lasers for communication with subs. The idea had some intrinsic merit—but that was not enough for the Navy. It feared that work on blue-green lasers would erode support for the expansion of its conventional system of radio antennas and relay airplanes that were used to communicate with subs. The Navy's rejection might have been enough to kill the idea. However, Lowell found enthusiastic support for it on Capitol Hill from congressmen in Wisconsin and Michigan who had battles brewing in their states over the expansion of the Navy antennas.

Angered, the Navy in 1978 cut off most of its money to Lowell's group, killing two research efforts and almost destroying the S-1 Project, which the Navy at that time funded almost exclusively. With strong Congressional support, however, the blue-green project was funded and progress made. Lowell's group did not receive any of the development contracts—and did not want any—but the incident did serve to enhance Lowell's stature on Capitol Hill and perhaps helped him win congressional support for the S-1 computer project as well.

In short, between 1975 and 1980 Lowell had suffered two severe attacks, one from his superiors in the laboratory and one from his patrons in the Navy. Yet, remarkably, Lowell not only survived but prospered. The whiz kid from Simi, the "bad boy" prankster from UCLA, fought his way to a new kind of respectability. His group made significant breakthroughs—most notably SCALD, detectors for blue-green lasers, and the nuclear X-ray laser. The group also achieved more diverse funding, which made it less vulnerable to the whims of its patrons. Lowell's own work remained ambitious and at times controversial. But in terms of leadership, there were no doubts. He had proved himself a capable general who had been able to attract a cadre of bright and eager lieutenants. Moreover, with the birth of the nuclear X-ray laser, the election of Ronald Reagan, and the emergence of the issue of strategic defense, Lowell had an opportunity not only to carry out the conservative mandate bequeathed him by Libby and Teller but to establish himself as a leader on an issue of national importance. He had a calling and a career.

In 1982 Energy Secretary James Edwards acknowledged Lowell's work by announcing that he had won the E. O. Lawrence Award of the Department of Energy—the Nobel Prize of the weapons world. Lowell was cited for "outstanding contributions to national security in areas of directed energy, inertial confinement fusion, underwater communication, nuclear design concepts, and computer technology."

Curiously, Lowell's comeback took place amid a leadership vacuum in the lab's physics department. After Lowell failed in 1975 to win the post of Associate Director for Physics, the position went unfilled for three years. The word among employees of the physics department was that Teller was still pushing for Lowell, the lab's administration still refusing. The standoff collapsed in 1978 when pressure from within the ranks of the physics department caused a mild-mannered administrator, John Anderson, to be appointed. He quit the post in 1983 and speculation arose again that Lowell would get it. After fierce lobbying by both friends and foes of Lowell's, the lab director picked a less controversial figure. This was John Nuckolls, the early promoter of third-generation weapons and Lowell's friend.

During this period, other allies of Lowell's also began to rise, most notably those associated with the success of the nuclear X-ray laser. In 1981 Tom Weaver was named head of the newly created R Program. In 1983 George Chapline won the E. O. Lawrence Award. In 1984 Roy D. Woodruff, the lab official who had authorized the inclusion of Peter's idea in George's nuclear test, was named to the post of Associate Director for Nuclear Weapons. In a press release, the lab's director said that this appointment and other wide reorganizations were being carried out "to respond to the many new challenges for the Laboratory in nuclear weapons, including defensive technologies."

Never shy, Lowell in the 1980s began to take the message of strategic defense before public audiences both receptive and hostile. In April 1984 he told a student audience in Berkeley that Star Wars research was necessary because the Soviets "have weapons in space. Their weapons work. We have no weapons in space." Later, at the Heritage Foundation in Washington, Lowell noted how Bethe had pronounced the nuclear X-ray laser a "splendid idea" and went on to wonder how the eminent physicist could still be against its use in a weapons system.

While the fortunes of Lowell and his friends rose during the early 1980s, Lowell's mentor, Teller, almost died. Teller, who Lowell had known for almost a quarter century, became seriously ill after a long history of heart problems. In March 1984, at the age of 76, he had a triple coronary bypass operation. Friends thought he would soon pass away. The tenacious physicist, defying expectations, recovered and continued to lead an active life. But the writing was on the wall. Sooner or later, Lowell would have to fend for himself.

It was late afternoon as I rambled around Windy Ridge, musing about Lowell and his unusual career. It was time to get back to the lab. A short drive later, I met briefly with Carl Haussmann, an Associate Director of the weapons lab who watched over the S-1 Project and had an office in Building 1877 that he visited occasionally. Carl was an old-time administrator. In his late 50s, he had a beefy, weathered face that had seen lots of sunshine and hard work.

I asked why Lowell was so dedicated to his group of young scientists.

"I think he gets sustenance or mental satisfaction from the whole routine," said Carl. "He is very much a science and technology pied piper to these youngsters. And I mean that constructively. He's very bright and he can talk. He's a renaissance mentality in the sense that he can talk on almost any subject. The problem is to stop him from talking interminably on all subjects, although this really gets the kids' attention.

"When you get to know him a little better, you see that he doesn't walk on water all the time. As a matter of fact, my interactions with him are to help out there. I've had a lot of experience running and building programs. And so I half volunteered and was half asked to help out on S-1.

"Lowell tends to get overly optimistic. This may attract the kids at first, but after they've been working on these projects for a year or two, I think they have a better idea than Lowell as to what's possible, at least better than he's willing to admit.

"I was talking to Teller the other day and said I was trying to control Lowell. Teller said, 'Let's be realistic. All you can do is moderate him.' And that's all we want to do."

I wandered back into the halls of 1877. Toward dinner time a group formed and debated the merits of various restaurants. It was to be the Jade Garden, a Chinese place forty miles away in the San Joaquin Valley.

A dozen of us piled into two cars, a new BMW and Lowell's old blue station wagon. The mood in the station wagon was light—jokes and laughter. Lowell noted with a chuckle that grass had once started to grow in the back of the car after a lot of dirt and rain had washed in through an open window.

There was much talk of Lowell's past—of group houses he had lived in with early members of O Group, of his love of technology, of a huge computer he had once bought and kept in a barn. The young scientists loved to needle Lowell about his eccentricities, and they liked to talk about the network of friendships in the group. There was a beautiful sunset as we drove through the central valley, the fields golden in the dying light. Finally we arrived at the Jade Garden Restaurant & Lounge on Main Street in Manteca.

The mood in the car had started out wry and turned sentimental, bolstered by talk of friendships past and present. Now, around the table, things turned gruesome, as they sometimes do among males out to impress each other. Rod started things off by noting that the

Soviets had probably quit the Olympics in Los Angeles because they were scared to death of the "Cal Techies" and the pranks they played on everyone. There was general agreement at the table. The tricksters at Caltech were notorious. Then a dispute arose over the suicide rate at Caltech. Larry proudly contended that his alma mater had the highest rate in the nation, about 15 students from his class of 200 taking their own lives. Hon Wah was doubtful. Even MIT, which was a much larger school, did not have that many suicides. The conversation then turned to the recent death of a pilot at the Livermore airport. His plane had stalled and fallen into a sewage plant. This tale prompted much laughter.

On our way back to the lab the station wagon broke down at the top of the Altamont pass. We played on the windmill, and then settled down to await the rescue party. Conversation in the car turned to a favorite topic—global extinction—not by the flash of nuclear weapons but by the explosive impact of passing comets in the earth's distant past.

In the cool darkness of the car, one of the young scientists drew an optimistic conclusion from this cycle of cataclysm. "It would probably accelerate evolution," he said, "because you'd constantly wipe out lower forms of life and give other things a chance."

Lowell quickly weighed in with a more pessimistic analysis. "Sure," he said, "but maybe it dumped comets on the earth so often that for a long time nothing had a chance to evolve. It took an awfully long time, after all, to get from bacteria to something more substantial. Living things probably got wiped out in a pretty thorough fashion every few million years—the same sort of thing that happens when you set the blade of a power mower too close to the ground." Laughter rippled through the car at the analogy.

Later than expected, we made it back to the lab. Some people went back to work while others sat around and ate ice cream from the group's freezer.

Long after midnight, Lowell and I headed back to his house. It was cool at Windy Ridge, a fog sweeping over the hill. There were no stars. We went inside. Lowell fixed Cokes and we sat down in the living room. It was filled with big, old couches, a mixed set, reminiscent of a fraternity house. A picture of Rod's starship hung near a half-finished fireplace. The house was cool so we kept on our coats.

I asked Lowell to tell me about his early childhood and how he had gotten interested in science.

"In those days anybody that did well in school was obviously going to go into science," he said. "My father was a businessman. My parents were uneducated in a technical way. They both thought rapidly. And they tended to think quantitatively. My father was always trying to reduce things to numbers.

"My parents put me into school early and I found myself skipping half-grades. Soon I was among kids who were quite a bit older. This was when I was eight or nine. The older kids knew how to do arithmetic. I didn't. The thing that was particularly galling was that I recognized that I thought faster on virtually every score than the people who were performing math much faster than I was. I found it exceedingly frustrating. As a matter of fact I think I actually cried over it at home, over the humiliation day after day. So my father took me and taught me how to be very quick with numbers. He just drilled me. And he made the drills progressively more difficult. The odd thing that happened was that everything else speeded up too—reading, talking, everything. I used to talk fairly slowly, slower than Rod. It got to where I would jabber. I've always been curious as to how much faster I could have been pushed—how fast anybody can be pushed during that age period.

"I've been playing games with Mark every once in a while when Tom has to go out of town. Sometimes he'll leave Mark with me for a few days. Kids his age tend to be amazingly plastic. They'll pick up things very rapidly. Mark will pick it up, hold it for a while, but a week or two later he tends to slide back to normal. The situation with me was that sliding back was just completely intolerable. It was much more fun to be ahead than behind. I kind of brutalized myself. I had to get out of this unendurable situation of having everybody look at me standing there alone trying to figure out what these sums and differences were, of having it late, of having it wrong."

The youthful war within Lowell over math led him not only to an undergraduate degree in mathematics but to a lifelong infatuation with computers and their ability to crunch numbers. During the ride to the Jade Garden, one of the young scientists had mentioned how Lowell had once purchased a huge old IBM supercomputer known as the Stretch and kept it in a converted barn where he and several members of the "proto" O Group lived in the early 1970s. It measured about five feet high, six feet wide, and sixty feet long. It was the first supercomputer ever built by IBM, having been especially constructed for the Los Alamos and Livermore weapons labs.

"The machine was delivered in about 1959 to Los Alamos and 1960 to Livermore," Lowell said. "I saw the first one at Los Alamos when I was a junior in college and it had been there for a bit over a year. It was supposed to be the start of a supercomputer line from IBM. The problem was that they packed so much into it that the machine got big and relatively slow. So it was not a prototype for an outstanding commercial success. I paid $2,100 for the Livermore one when the General Services Administration put it on the auction block. I was an assistant professor at Teller Tech in those days. Some people at the auction clearly wanted it for the gold in it. There were one or two people who wanted it for reasons I was thoroughly suspicious of. I wanted it for old times' sake. But the government offered to sell it either as a system or piece-wise. I bid both ways. All the people who had money bid for it as a system. It turned out, a day or two before the bids were opened, the National Science Foundation said it wanted the high-speed core memory. The rest of it got sold piecemeal, and I ended up getting it.

"I was immediately deluged by people who wanted to buy it, one guy saying there was $15,000 worth of gold in it. I decided I didn't want to see the thing melted down."

Lowell said there was also a pair of men who kept offering him more and more money for the machine, first saying they had a customer for it in the Philippines, then Hong Kong, then admitting that they didn't know where it would end up. But they had a customer. And their final offer was $100,000. Lowell suspected it would have eventually arrived in China or the Soviet Union.

Around this period Lowell was living in a barn that was just down the road from the weapons lab. He lived in the loft, and put the computer on the ground floor. "The lab management all came trekking out one afternoon to see if it was really there," he recalled.

"When Tom Weaver and his family decided that they wanted to come out to Livermore, I moved the computer out of the barn into the rabbit hutches. This was a high-class abandoned farm and the rabbit hutches were sturdy things. We reroofed them and poured a cement floor. And we moved the computer out there so Tom could have the ground floor of the barn. He proceeded to fix it up complete with ceiling and insulation. A total of eight to ten people lived on the property, which we rented."

I asked how many summer interns were expected this year in O Group.

"This is a summer which will be unusually high," he said. "I think there will be about seven, maybe eight. Back when I kind of ran the summer program for the whole lab, informally, I think we peaked one summer at 225. It went way down after that. I think the minimum number of interns the lab had was 60 or 70. Now I think it is around 90 to 110. The stipend is a little bit lower than a person with that amount of education would make. But they pay round-trip air fare and they'll ship some reasonable amount of luggage."

I was curious about the location of the Hertz Foundation and how it had been determined. According to tax returns, the foundation had started out in Chicago, the home of John Hertz, and later shifted to Los Angeles. Most recently, its address had become a post office box in the city of Livermore. The implication seemed to be that the weapons lab was somehow playing a greater role in its operations.

"It used to be in L.A. when the chairman of the foundation, Floyd B. Odlum, lived outside the city," Lowell said. "He invented the conglomerate. He was a very successful technological entrepreneur. He was most noted in his later years as founder and chairman of the Arthritis Foundation. He had a rather noted life before he retired. He died quite old."

According to my research, Odlum was also the financier behind the creation of the Atlas missile, the first to be able to drop nuclear warheads on Russia. When the government's financing of the missile's development was cut back in the 1950s, Odlum pumped funds from his Atlas Corporation into its development and research for three years until the government again gave it priority. It was a fact Lowell either did not know or had neglected to mention.

"Odlum retired as board chairman of Hertz several years before he died. The new board chairman was in New York and the new president of the foundation, Wilson Talley, was located in Berkeley and Livermore. And I was here at Livermore. And Edward was here. The foundation's activities centered on the fellowship program, and so it was eminently reasonable for the office to move here. The office of the foundation until very recently was a post office box. That's because the foundation doesn't have a full-time staff. It has people that get together once a year to operate the selection process. In our last meeting, we agreed to open an office where a secretary would sit and answer mail and so forth on a part-time basis. Right now the phone rings in the home of the foundation's assistant secretary, Kathryn Smith. She is retiring at the end of the academic year but she is essentially the nontechnical person who has made Teller Tech run for the last 22 years, or something like that. She was Talley's secretary and did this other stuff part-time."

It was getting late, and it seemed time to try to clear up some of the ambiguities about the defensive shield. Last night's session at Tom's house had left me confused. For a year I had watched the critics and Lowell spar over the pop-up proposal, and now suddenly it seemed to have disappeared, or at least to have lost some of its substance. Something else seemed to have taken its place. But I was not sure what it was. If the Soviets quickly developed a fast-burn booster, I asked, wasn't the proposal for a permanently orbiting battle station the only alternative? And wasn't this fraught with its own problems?

"A lot of people in the United States don't believe it is feasible to build fast-burn boosters for us or them," Lowell said. "The Soviet liquid-fuel ICBMs are very high-rising, slow-burning, cost-efficient sorts of beasts. The MX for various reasons burns faster, but it's still easy to pick it off with pop up. The question is whether the Soviets can build a version of MX that will work, that doesn't involve huge payload penalties, and that can finish burning while deep in the atmosphere so that a pop-up system can't get it. There are people in the aerospace industry who say, yes, you can. There are other people in the industry who say it isn't feasible, it would be an enormously difficult endeavor. The success of it in the United States, where we think we understand solid-fuel technology pretty well, is not at all assured on any time scale. For the Soviets, with their more primitive rocket technology, it would be a different issue entirely.

"If fast-burn boosters eventually do become available," Lowell continued, "pop-up systems will eventually be unable to cope with

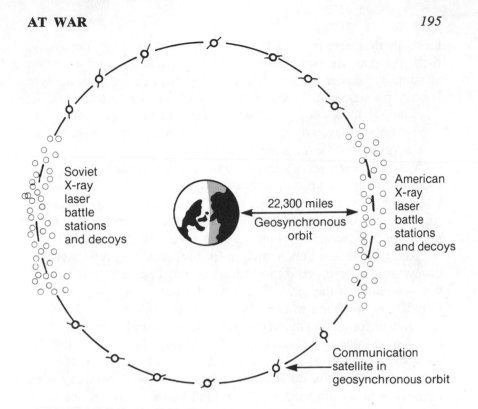

Soviet X-ray laser battle stations and decoys

22,300 miles
Geosynchronous orbit

American X-ray laser battle stations and decoys

Communication satellite in geosynchronous orbit

them. So the question then becomes what kind of orbital assets you deploy in order to reach those boosters before they burn out. The only way to do that with high efficiency is to put your assets in geosynchronous orbit. One of the political attractions of high orbits like that is that people couldn't say that your nuclear weapons were threatening to them, as they might be if they were in lower orbits—that you were going to drop weapons on their heads. Our thesis is that a nuclear weapon ceases to be a weapon of mass destruction if it can't get any energy to you in any reasonable period of time. It is not rational for you to feel threatened by it."

The assertion, of course, was debatable. In *Weapons and Hope* Dyson had specifically ruled out nuclear weapons for use in a shield because he said they always had the potential to be turned back into weapons of mass destruction. There were also treaties against their deployment in space.

Lowell pressed on. "The ideal system would be a few dozen X-ray laser platforms in synchronous orbit, completely autonomous, with locations that were essentially unknown, both to their owner and to their potential adversary. They would sit there and essentially shoot at multiple booster plumes. So that anytime they see two or more booster plumes in a three-minute time frame, you start shooting. They would allow one booster within their field of view at any time so you'd never have any problem with peaceful space launches—so nobody got their Venus mission shot down.

"We can't keep secrets in the United States and so you'd want these things to go up and wander around, to make it difficult to knock them out preemptively. You'd want them to be sufficiently small so that they are essentially undetectable, essentially invisible to any sensor technology unless you get very, very close to them.

"And there'd be a bunch of them for purposes of redundancy and decoys and so forth. And they'd have a so-called suppressed signature—'stealth' in the sense that they'd be nearly invisible not only to radar but anything working in the visible spectrum, in the infra-red, and so forth. Ideally, you'd want anybody and everybody who is concerned about such matters—the British, the French, the Soviets, the Chinese—to have some stations up there. They can't be countermanded. You don't know where they are. You don't even know how many are working. You don't know if any *are* working. But you put three dozen up there. The other guy puts five dozen up there. You put up 500 decoys. He puts up 1,500 decoys. You really don't know where yours are or where his are.

"You just know that every once in a while, you and he both conduct exercises—maybe jointly. And, sure enough, whenever you launch more than one missile at a time from anywhere on the planet, they are fired on. And you don't know whether there were three stations ready to fire or thirty or maybe a hundred. They carry different programs. They have different vulnerabilities and different strengths. Yours come in maybe seven different classes. He has maybe thirteen classes. They're programmed to different levels of sensitivity. Some will wait for a booster plume for a minute. Others will fire on a booster plume in thirty seconds. Others will insist on five booster plumes before firing. You have a wide variety of programs. And a wide variety of platform capabilities. And basically what you're interested in is making it very very difficult to ever conduct large-scale attacks by anybody on anybody else."

It was an awesome vision, one that with all its decoys and moving vehicles was similar to the racetrack mode for basing the MX missile, a scheme that was eventually abandoned. It had engendered a huge fight as experts wrangled over whether or not the Soviets would be able to figure out which silos were filled and which were empty.

"In this world," Lowell continued, "offensive systems have lost their political luster because their effectiveness is considered to be gravely in doubt. You don't have to demonstrate 100 percent ability to knock down every missile. You just have to raise very grave doubts about how the offense can stay alive against this kind of defense."

Why, I asked, would the battle stations be autonomous?

"So they couldn't be spoofed. So the other side can't take them over, saying, 'Hello, here's your new program.' "

This autonomy, though fraught with all the nightmares of computerized nuclear weapons pressing their own buttons, also seemed to open up intriguing possibilities.

Wouldn't autonomy build confidence in a way, I asked, since such battle stations would never be able to be used to brush aside a feeble retaliation? There would be no way for an aggressor to switch them off in order to carry out an attack with his offensive missiles.

"Sure," said Lowell, "so you couldn't play first strike. But who would believe you? You know you can't get away with it. But do they know you can't get away with it? Are they going to believe that you can't turn your satellites off if you decided to try a first strike?"

Again, the "weapons of life" seem to be open to much darker interpretations than were at first apparent.

Wasn't this a grave danger? I asked. There was no ambiguity about the present situation, about MAD. It was just guaranteed mutual suicide. By contrast, I said, all these defensive systems introduced an element of strategic ambiguity.

"There's *always* ambiguity," Lowell answered in a slow, deliberate fashion. "There are people in Washington who don't believe the current situation is based on mutual suicide, particularly these days. They say there's a distinct possibility that the Soviets could conduct a successful decapitation attack against us. And, by the way, if we got enough MXs and other things, then, under some circumstances—and I obviously can't discuss them at all—under some circumstances it's not clear that we couldn't decapitate them. Decapitation is much discussed these days. There's nothing about MAD that is unambiguous. Hard-target killers are seen as very interesting. The Soviets have them, we want them, and everybody knows what you can do with them. Decapitation wasn't a viable strategy six or seven years ago, but it's becoming a viable strategy now. The present situation is fraught with ambiguities, and I believe it is fraught with instabilities. The situation in which we are now looks to me like it is getting ever less stable because of the supershort time lines, if nothing else. Ignore the hard-target killers. Just consider their submarines off our coasts and our Pershings in Germany. Things can happen very quickly."

It seemed a good point. Yet in distinction to the inevitable worsening envisioned by Lowell, the critics said that the status quo had a chance of becoming more stable. Strategic forces could be structured in ways that were less threatening, they said, in ways that emphasized their use strictly for retaliation rather than offense. The MX missile was an ideal first-strike weapon because its ten very accurate warheads could take out a lot of military targets in the Soviet Union very quickly. For the same reason, it was also a very tempting target for the Soviets. Some strategic analysts thus argued that MX should be scrapped in favor of something like the Midgetman, a missile with a single warhead that would be mobile, less threatening as a first-strike weapon, and less tempting as a target. In addition, submarines were invulnerable to a first-strike attack. Finally, many critics argued, stability could best be enhanced by radical cuts in the nuclear arsenals of both superpowers.

For better or worse, Lowell said he would rather build geosynchronous X-ray laser battle stations. They had vulnerabilities that might be overcome with decoys, movement, and special materials, he said. They had ambiguities of usage that were no worse than the present situation, he argued.

If this was the case, I asked, then why had the debate centered on pop up for so long?

"It's because we're both afraid of discussing nuclear weapons in orbit. It's a political 'no no.' In addition, the critics don't like the fact that pop ups have obvious advantages—that they are relatively invulnerable, are very carefully controllable, have very high cost-efficiency, and cannot be threatened in advance in a credible fash-

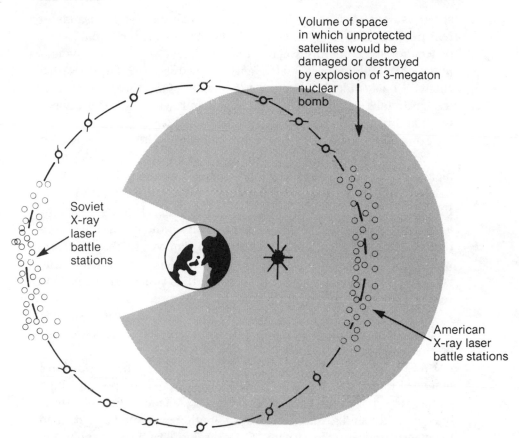

Volume of space in which unprotected satellites would be damaged or destroyed by explosion of 3-megaton nuclear bomb

Soviet X-ray laser battle stations

American X-ray laser battle stations

ion. The critics therefore fight very hard against the utility of pop up, saying it can be outwitted by fast boosters and so forth.

"In a Star Wars type of situation, it's difficult to make the case that a high-value target whose position in space is known will survive more than a few minutes. People who do war games on these things talk about a life expectancy of minutes for a platform in space. The types of probes that can be used are not just conventional antisatellite weapons, but all kinds of things which are based in or near the ground that could potentially do lethal amounts of damage to things in high orbits. I'm talking about things like ground-based lasers. How in the world do you defend yourself against a laser whose existence you don't even know of? But one laser anywhere in the Soviet Union or the United States can perhaps sweep the sky and do it very, very quickly. It can kill at the

speed of light. And it might be able to reach out for thousands or
tens of thousands of kilometers. Moreover, it's a nonverifiable sort
of technology in the arms-control sense. How do you know what's
under this building roof? Is it another warehouse? Or does that
roof roll back quickly to reveal a big laser? One that just reaches
out and stabs satellites like you reach out with an oxyacetylene
torch and bring down a moth?

"Somebody came by a few years ago and said, 'You guys are
crazy for talking about putting these things in orbit. There're technical hurdles and you're buying yourself an incredible pack of
trouble politically. Pop-up systems are going to be equally useful.
From a military standpoint, politicians and generals are going to be
a lot more confident if you have them down on the ground and continually monitor their performance. You can verify that they are
working. You have them under concrete, under your control. And
you only throw them up when you *know* that you need them. You
won't have to pay for anything that you don't use.' "

Despite the problems of orbital defense, I said, the critics seemed
to have demonstrated that pop up, too, was less attractive than
originally thought.

Lowell did not buy this at all. "The only thing the critics have
managed to say thus far is, 'Hey, you've got to get the pop ups high
enough to where they can see their targets.' That's the only thing
that anybody said. And so we say, 'Gentlemen, you have defined
the constraints on the system. Congratulations. The thought occurred to us a few years ago.' "

Despite my attempts to force Lowell into one position or another, he seemed intent on keeping his options open—both pop up
and orbiting battle stations.

Is defense inevitable? I asked.

"No," answered Lowell. "Both sides might decide that they're
not going to play this game because they're more comfortable with
an offense-dominated world. After all, we kind of understand offense. We've been setting here this way for fifteen or twenty years
and we know what it's like. It's not comfortable but we know how
to cope with it. We can do the things we want to do. We know how
to work with each other. We know how to contest with each other.
So let's not change it. It's not nice, but it's better than an uncertain
future. Everybody dislikes uncertainty."

Lowell had been rattling the ice in his empty glass, and he went back to the kitchen and got us both some more Coke. I needed the caffeine. It was past 3:00 A.M.

I felt I had a fair idea of what Lowell was proposing by way of a defensive shield. The week had been a kind of crash course in strategic defense, starting with a glimpse of the hardware and ending with Lowell's vision of how it all fit together. What still weighed on my mind was Peter and why he had worked on the nuclear X-ray laser despite what seemed to be strong reservations.

I asked why Peter did it.

"More than anything else," said Lowell, "it was competitiveness with George. The *Gulag* probably changed Peter's attitude more than any other single thing, but it took the Chapline challenge for this change to have real expression. Otherwise it would have stayed quite latent.

"Peter didn't like the fact that George sat down and scribbled on paper for a few hours and did his design by hand whereas Peter grubbed away for days and months and years trying to design the world's first X-ray laser. He basically thought that George was getting off too easy. And so he criticized George's schemes extensively. It was like what you see in *The Double Helix,* the competition between Watson and Crick on the one hand and Pauling on the other to discover the structure of the DNA molecule. Pauling was highly intuitive—that's the way George was—while Watson and Crick took an exceedingly systematic approach. The systematic folks in this world tend to win, which is kind of unfortunate because they're not the poets, not the intuitionists. They're the guys that sit down and work their heads off. And so Peter probably developed quite a few of his tools and concepts to hold George in check, quite frankly.

"And he was continually told by me that you can't beat something with nothing. You're not going to succeed in stopping George, because he's got the only game in town. I think if I had to guess—and all this is pure speculation—I'd say that the reason that Peter got interested in bomb-pumped X-ray lasers is that he finally accepted the assertion on my part that you can't beat something with nothing. He came up with a better idea. And he didn't say: 'I want to go out and try it.' He just said this scheme is better. It has these basic features that are just intrinsically better. And, sure enough, it looked like they were.

"George's test had already been scheduled. And he had planned a lot of reasonable things. But on the fringes there were things that looked like a low return on an investment. And so I went in to Roy [Woodruff] and said, 'Hey, this thing with George will probably work but why don't you take out some insurance. It looks like Peter's scheme will work too. It may not work as well as George's but it looks like it has lower technical risk. And, by the way, you get all sorts of advantages out of that. It's going to put George under a competitive whip and it will do the same for Peter.'

"He said fine. So I went and told Peter, 'Rejoice! You're in the experiment.' Peter looked like his favorite dog had just been run over. So he steadfastly ignored it. Nothing happened for a long time. Then the deadline loomed up. And Roy began to say, 'What are you guys going to do? The rest of this Juggernaut is moving. What's O Group doing?' I went and said to Tom, 'This is your section of the group. Peter is nominally in your area. How about taking some time and working with us and helping to make this happen? It's going to be very tough for me to do it by myself, working with a reluctant Peter.' And so Tom, much to my surprise, walked away from his fabulous program of astrophysics research and pitched in full time trying to design this experiment. These were extremely trying circumstances for Tom. When he works for long periods of time, arduously, he inevitably gets feverish and looks like he's about to die. And he had a young kid. And he had recently separated from his wife. So it was a mess for him. But he and Peter and I managed to get the design carried out. And then Tom, with his consummate mastery of just doing things right, put the experiment together with his own hands. And he came back after the thing had been sent down to the test site, brooded about it some more, and realized that a crucial blunder had been made. So he returned to the test site and supervised the corrections.

"Peter during that time was working and saying, 'Oh my, what have I gotten myself into? I don't want to have anything to do with this.' But I think among the other things that kept him at it, other than pride or whatever, was the thought that he wasn't going to back out of a competition with George. And so the experiment came off.

"Tom then buckled down again in an exceedingly workmanlike

fashion and analyzed the results. And it turned out to be a very difficult job of analysis, primarily because nobody had ever done anything like it before. I don't know whether you got this impression from talking with Tom or not, but he strikes me more like Hans Bethe than most anybody I know. He is extremely craftsman-like with everything he touches. Working with Tom is a real exercise in frustration for me because I tend to go too fast, to be too sloppy, or whatever. Tom moves at a decent pace and when he's passed over something, it is exceedingly unlikely that anyone will go back and find an error or a mistake. Peter was extremely fortunate to have somebody like Tom to work with, even though Peter probably didn't realize it.

"As it turned out, a lot of Peter's criticisms of George's work turned out to be apt. And Peter's proposals turned out to be at least as good as he claimed they would be, his suggestions as to the best way to approach X-ray lasers. Peter's idea just worked an awful lot better than George's.

"There was another side to the whole thing. Peter during his career had always been like a hot knife through warm butter. He whizzed through any challenge. With his Ph.D., for the first time in his life, he found it heavy going. He had set himself such insanely high goals. I suggested the basic problem to him and he sold himself on it—and nothing could tear him away. It was crazy. He worked like a fiend. He worked well beyond the capability of flesh and blood. He was determined to win. You've heard people joke about how he wouldn't go home to sleep—he'd just collapse on his desk. He had done this for four years at that time. And there was essentially no end in sight. It was not clear how in the world he was going to get a design for a laboratory X-ray laser which would be so compelling that people would go off and irradiate it with big fusion lasers.

"So we came along. And he saw this nuclear thing that we were talking about as diversionary in the worst sort of way. He was very, very uninterested in doing it. But he knew this experiment was going to be purely George's if he didn't pick up the option to participate. And while he didn't think that George was going to win, or win very big, the chances were very good that George would get signals out which would indicate X-ray lasing action—the world's first. I think that was what broke him loose from his Ph.D. research and caused him to sit down and work with Tom and me for whatever it was, six weeks or thereabouts, to grind out this design.

"The science that got done was rather acutely incidental to the human interactions between George and Peter. It was raw, unabashed competitiveness. It was amazing—even though I had seen it happen before, even though I'd read about it in *The Double Helix*. You kind of stand there and watch close up: the reason that things are advancing is that these two relatively young men are slugging it out for dominance in this particular technical arena. It says something about the way humans go about their business. I'm not sure it's terribly flattering, the way most science works. I would be very surprised if very many major scientific endeavors, maybe even minor ones, happen because a disinterested scientist coolly and dispassionately grinds away in his lab, devoid of thoughts about what this means in terms of competition, peer esteem, his wife and family, prizes and recognition. I'm afraid I'm sufficiently cynical to think that in excess of 90 percent of all science is done with those considerations in mind. Pushing back the frontiers of knowledge and advancing truth are distinctly secondary considerations."

I asked if the final design could have been done without Peter.

"It is exceedingly unlikely," Lowell replied. "The tools, the computer codes, were fashioned by him to be gripped only by his hands. Tom spent quite a bit of time trying to learn how to use his tools and spent even more time getting the bugs out. A single person, either Tom or me, in principle could have done those things, and done them without very much participation by Peter at all. It was possible in principle. But we almost certainly didn't have the time or the will power. The gates of the timetable were closing, slamming irrevocably, very rapidly. If it hadn't been a team effort, I don't think any one or even two of us could have sustained the required effort. It was an arduous experience from my standpoint, and I'm a fairly determined, fairly physically strong guy. It broke Tom's health to the point that I was afraid he was going to be hospitalized. It was very, very hard in the psychological sense on Peter, and it wore him very hard physically as well. So it could have been done in principle. I don't think it could have been done in practice without Peter, without Tom, probably without me. We divided up the design job into three roughly equal pieces. It was a matter where each one of us had to do our job or we would be letting down our teammates. It was a sufficiently small team that everybody worked within thirty feet of everyone else.

"Very frankly, those are the kinds of times you look back on for many years afterwards. They're some of the peaks of human experience—when you're working just as hard as you possibly can towards goals that look important, working with comrades of your own choice, and finally succeeding by the skin of your teeth. Those are some of the features of the outstanding experiences in life."

EPILOGUE

After President Reagan's call to arms, the government proposed, at a minimum, a $26 billion program of research over five years to investigate the feasibility of creating a defensive shield. A little less than 10 percent of the Star Wars budget goes for work on third-generation nuclear weapons. One beneficiary of this federal largess is Lowell Wood and the denizens of O Group. Their effort is small but pivotal for reasons of history, politics, science, and sheer enthusiasm. Like President Reagan's vision, the wizards of O Group have considerable appeal. After all, science has achieved so much in the twentieth century—the Manhattan project, the Apollo program, the computer revolution. Perhaps their efforts will result in one more miracle. Their raw enthusiasm, moreover, is so much more compelling than the cautionary talk of the critics. Warriors are intrinsically more interesting than worriers. The critics and kids are miles apart in this respect.

Will it work?

The answer from O Group, despite its aura of technological mastery, was "no," if the standard is the one implied by President

Reagan—a leakproof shield to stop every Soviet warhead. Larry expressed vague optimism that powerful weapons would eventually come along that were suited to that challenge. But like every good salesman, he seemed to be trying to convince himself. In general, the young scientists of O Group always tended to talk in terms of percentages when pressed for specifics of how well "it" might work. Andy went on about how a shield was a worthy goal "even if it's only 20 percent effective." Lowell, too, talked of fractions. "You don't have to demonstrate 100 percent ability to knock down every missile," he said. "You just have to raise very grave doubts about how the offense can stay alive against this kind of defense."

Of them all, Lowell was the most enthusiastic. In conversations after my visit he alluded to new "breakthroughs." He also said pop up had regained some life and that his plan for orbital deployment had lost its luster. "Teller beat me up until Rod and I came up with a better way to cope with fast-burn boosters," he said. Unfortunately, the nature of the breakthrough is classified, as is so often the case. Without slighting the remarkable prowess of American technology, it seems likely that the threat of Soviet countermeasures will keep the conversation focused in terms of percentages. And these are the harbingers of destruction. If only 1 percent of the eight thousand or so nuclear warheads in the Soviet strategic arsenal penetrated a shield and landed on urban targets in the United States, it would touch off one of the greatest disasters in recorded history. In terms of nation-wide protection, a leaky shield is just about as good as no shield at all. As Peter said, a shield "wouldn't keep cities from being obliterated."

However, O Group unambiguously said it would work if the standard was less rigorous than President Reagan's, and if one entered the deep and somewhat murky waters of strategy. Since a leaky shield will not protect cities, something else needs to be added to the recipe to make it appealing—missiles.

In almost every reference to strategic defense, the Livermore scientists pictured the retention of at least some part of the American land-based offensive arsenal. That way, they said, an aggressor could never be sure that he wouldn't suffer retaliation. In explaining why *limited* defense was a worthy goal, the young weapon makers at times expressed opinions similar to those in the news. For instance, Henry A. Kissinger, national security adviser to President Nixon, wrote in *The Los Angeles Times:* "Even granting—as

I do—that a perfect defense of the U.S. population is almost certainly unattainable, the existence of some defense means that the attacker must plan on saturating it. This massively complicates the attacker's calculations. Anything that magnifies doubt inspires hesitation and adds to deterrence."

Of course, critics argue that increasing an aggressor's "doubts" might paradoxically encourage him to push the button. And there is much debate as well over whether more "uncertainty" is needed in the first place—whether the American land-based arsenal is becoming vulnerable to attack by Soviet missiles, and, if so, whether it makes a difference. After all, there are always the submarines. Only 20 percent of the strategic nuclear weapons in the American arsenal are on land-based missiles. Moreover, even if the charge of vulnerability is correct and the situation viewed as threatening, there are many ways to deal with it other than space-based defense. The Scowcroft Commission made several recommendations for changes in the existing land-based nuclear arsenal. Another solution would be to deploy old-fashioned ground-based defenses around missile silos. Finally, there is always the possibility of negotiating deep cuts in the number of Soviet land-based missiles. In the case of orbiting battle stations and pop-up interceptors, the cure seems much too drastic (and expensive) for the purported disease.

Surprisingly, not just O Group but many federal officials and advisory committees express their hopes for Star Wars in terms of *limited* defense, although they still pay lip service to the President's more ambitious goal. According to R. Jeffrey Smith in *Science* magazine, reduced expectations were voiced by participants in the very first federal studies on the feasibility of Star Wars, the so-called Hoffman and Fletcher panels. This pragmatism eventually spread even to Keyworth, the ultimate true believer.

Nowhere is the limited approach summed up more succinctly than in a position paper issued by the White House in January 1985. Strategic defense, it said, "need not provide 100 percent protection in order to enhance deterrence significantly." It went on to emphasize that "providing a better, more stable basis for enhanced deterrence is the central purpose of the SDI program," referring to the Strategic Defense Initiative. The great change in all this is that deterrence is not being overthrown—as was the promise of the President's speech—but merely "enhanced." Offensive missiles are still the centerpiece of American policy. A paradox of this battle plan is that a firm yardstick for "feasibility" suddenly disappears. Is 50 percent protection of the land-based arsenal enough to enhance deterrence? Is 20 percent? Why not deploy a limited shield today and still talk about aiming for the elusive goal of perfect defense?

Andy talked about an additional alleged benefit of a leaky shield—that it would make MAD feasible with fewer missiles. This might be true if the Soviets had no shield. But if they did deploy one, the American military would undoubtedly want to dramatically increase its number of missiles, countermeasures, and antisatellite weapons in order to insure its ability to retaliate in the event of a Soviet first strike. For starters, the current American strategic arsenal, parts of which have stood ready for decades, would probably be scrapped in favor of a new generation of fast-burn boosters. To that expense would be added others. After all, Soviet defensive capabilities would evolve over the years, calling for an ever-changing array of expensive countermeasures in the American arsenal. According to Bill Keller in *The New York Times,* the Pentagon is already taking pains to insure that American missiles can crack any Soviet shield. Its secretive program on Advanced Strategic Missile Systems, which develops special shield-penetrating warheads, is scheduled to have its budget double this year to $174 million and to continue growing rapidly after that.

Moreover, even if space-based defense somehow meant that MAD could work with fewer missiles, it would always raise strategic instabilities as well. Former Secretary of Defense Harold Brown summed up the problem in *The New York Times:* "Each side would have to wonder whether its shrunken strategic offensive forces could survive a preemptive strike and still penetrate the other's defenses. Doubts could reinforce the temptation to launch a preemptive strike against either the defenses of the other side, its retaliatory capability, or both."

Is it a good thing?

Leaky shields inevitably lead to the dark side of the "weapons of life" argument. After all, offensive missiles are retained and might conceivably be used as first-strike weapons. According to some analysts, aiding offensive attacks is the main service a poor shield could effectively render. It would never withstand an enemy's uninhibited attack, only his ragged retaliation after the majority of his nuclear arsenal had been destroyed in a first strike. The implications are troubling. During a crisis the advantage would go to the side that fired its missiles first. It seems implausible that the United States would ever initiate such an attack. Yet space-based systems, including Soviet ones, would clearly have the potential to make such aggression less costly. Nuclear war would become more thinkable. Harold Brown hinted that a poor shield would be ideal for brushing aside a feeble retaliation. Andy said defense makes "your existing capability far more deadly." Even President Reagan alluded to the danger in his speech of March 1983: "I clearly recognize that defensive systems have limitations and raise certain problems and ambiguities," he said. "If paired with offensive systems, they can be viewed as fostering an aggressive policy, and no one wants that." The dark side of defense is unique to space-based systems, which try to protect whole nations, including both missiles and cities. By contrast, old-fashioned ground-based systems have little of this strategic ambiguity. They are mainly good for defending missiles, and if so used have no potential for making a first strike look more feasible.

President Reagan is perhaps sincere in saying, as he did in his speech, that the United States seeks neither military superiority nor political advantage from a space-based defense. The problem is that it lends itself exactly to this interpretation. Moreover, Reagan has aligned himself with those who clearly seek the upper hand. Just before he was elected President, the Republican Party in its platform called for "military and technological superiority over the Soviet Union." The search for a technical edge is echoed in Teller's advice to Reagan as well. In July 1983 he wrote the President to say advances in nuclear-drive weapons "by converting hydrogen bombs into hitherto unprecedented forms and then directing these in highly effective fashions against enemy targets would end the MAD era and commence a period of assured survival on terms favorable to the Western alliance."

The candor of the federal government, or lack of it, is an issue that pervades questions not only of military and political strategy but also of the arms it envisions to achieve its goals. Even though the nuclear X-ray laser helped get Star Wars off the ground, it has now fallen out of federal favor—at least in terms of public relations. Perhaps the paradox of making nuclear weapons "impotent and obsolete" by means of a new generation of nuclear weapons was too much for the government to bear.

Science advisor Keyworth, the first official to publicly hail the nuclear breakthroughs, set the stage for the reversal in a speech of October 1983. "I don't see a critical role in this defense initiative for nuclear weapons per se," he said. "First of all, I'm not sure that the uses proposed for nuclear weapons in space couldn't be performed with nonnuclear technologies. More important, the American people are not likely to enthusiastically support the placement of nuclear weapons in space."

In late 1984 both the President and Secretary of Defense Caspar W. Weinberger began to stress the "nonnuclear" approach. "We are searching for a weapon that might destroy nuclear weapons, *not be nuclear itself,* destroy weapons not people," the President said at a televised news conference in January 1985. [Emphasis added.] Though an appealing idea, this is pure fiction in terms of budgetary realities. The weapons labs are pushing ahead on third-generation nuclear weapons with fervor. R Program exists and is growing. So is Livermore, which expects its budget to top $1 billion before the end of the Reagan administration. And there is no doubt that the nuclear advances are slated for Star Wars. As the director of the Strategic Defense Initiative, Lieut. Gen. James A. Abrahamson, candidly told a group of Republican congressmen in August 1984: "Although funded separately [from the Pentagon's efforts], the Department of Energy program is integral to the overall Strategic Defense Initiative program." The point was made more forcibly in a memorandum signed both by Secretary of Defense Weinberger and by Secretary of Energy John S. Herrington in February 1985. Entitled "Policy for Nuclear Research in the Strategic Defense Initiative," it said the Star Wars program would investigate "new concepts which could, if proven feasible, convert nuclear energy in a carefully directed, controlled way so as to destroy attacking missiles, after they are launched, at a great distance."

Despite the record growth in the nation's nuclear-weapons program, some administration officials probably do have sincere doubts as to whether bomb-pumped weapons should play a role in the creation of a defensive shield. After all, numerous treaties forbid the deployment of nuclear weapons in orbit, and reliance on pop up for boost-phase intercepts calls for such rapid activation that humans would necessarily be eliminated from the nuclear chain of command. Perhaps President Reagan has recognized these limitations and is sincere in his search for a nonnuclear defense. If so, one of the few jobs left for the nuclear X-ray laser and its exotic cousins would be even more controversial—to attack Soviet satellites and battle stations. This, of course, would be a necessary task in the world of partial defense. If the American military is to have a retaliatory deterrent, it must be ready to try to outwit any Soviet shield.

All of which raises a dark question for which there seems to be no easy answer. Would computer errors and false alerts start an accidental war on an enemy's satellites and battle stations with X-ray lasers or other arms? And would an enemy suddenly deaf, blind, and dumb unleash its nuclear arsenal? As Teller pointed out, there would be only seconds to act in the hair-trigger world of strategic defense. And an enemy's satellites, crucial for trying to penetrate an American shield, might well be the first thing to go. By contrast, today's situation gives military officials plenty of time to cross-check sensors to see if an attack is real or the product of a faulty computer. The generals, moreover, have needed those precious minutes all too often. An investigation by Senators Gary Hart and Barry Goldwater once showed that computer and electrical breakdowns touch off false alerts two or three times a year, sometimes sending bomber crews racing for their planes.

Anything that brings the Soviets to the negotiating table cannot be altogether bad. The threat of Star Wars has perhaps started a dialogue that will bring about large reductions in the arsenals of both nuclear superpowers. But using it for anything other than a bargaining chip seems pure folly. A week of conversations at the lab convinced me that the assertions of the critics are generally correct: a move to defense would touch off an expensive new arms race that would make the world a more dangerous place in which to live. It would raise the risk of war.

Why do they work on it?

This question weighed on me in the months after my visit, the more as I concluded that strategic defense was not a good idea. Originally I had dismissed the critics. After all, they had a vested intellectual interest in the nuclear status quo, in many cases having helped create it. But a week of conversations turned me around. It was not a vision of scientific futility that gave me pause. Progress would doubtless continue to be made by O Group and the S-1 Project. Rather, it was learning something of the strategic instabilities and great expense associated with a move to partial defense.

After my visit I reasoned that the citizens of Lowell's group might also have doubts—doubts assuaged by factors other than defense ideology. This is not to suggest that the young scientists are insincere. Certainly many of them at one time or another have felt that the deployment of a defensive shield would be good for reasons of national security. But I went out to the lab naively thinking they *all* would be driven by a determination to fulfill the President's vision. I came back thinking they worked on nuclear weapons for at least fifteen reasons:

• America must never experience another Pearl Harbor or be taken by military surprise. And in an increasingly complex world, advanced technology is a possible aid in the preparation of sneak attacks. Almost every person I met at Livermore expressed support for the cause of military preparedness. In addition, part of the mandate of the weapons labs is to forestall the possibility of technical surprises by an enemy.

• There is money to be made in strategic defense and the technologies worked on by the young scientists. According to Kathleen Day in *The Los Angeles Times,* Livermore in January 1984 waived its commercial rights to the blue-green laser detector. Jack Marling then sold them to Helionetics, the company in which Teller holds stock. Such a move is perfectly legal. The government waives many rights to inventions at Livermore. But it illustrates the pecuniary angle at work. Indeed, Lowell was quite proud to go on at length about the number of millionaires that had grown out of his group. The founders of Valid Logic Systems have clearly achieved that status, at least in terms of stock, and perhaps other alumni have as well. Members of O Group and the S-1 Project work with some of the most advanced of the emerging technologies. In industry, their skills and ideas can bring a good price.

• The Hertz millions put Lowell in contact with some of the best science students in the nation and pay for the graduate education of many, including those who are recruited to work at the weapons lab. The poverty of many graduate students can help make this a powerful inducement. For the lab itself, the Hertz money stretches salaries. The whole Hertz connection raises questions. It would probably touch off a Congressional inquiry if the Unification Church of the Reverend Sun Myung Moon managed to get dozens of devotees employed at a nuclear weapons lab. Hertz probably seems benign to lab administrators because its interests seem identical to those of the United States government. But maybe they are not. Unfortunately, there is no way for the public to know. Though shrouded in secrecy, the lab is accountable ultimately to Congress and thus to the American public. Hertz is not. It is a private foundation that must file public income tax returns, but that is about all. Its agenda can be as private as it wants.

• Certainly there is a conviction among some of the young scientists that the era of offensive weaponry is at a dangerous impasse and that they are lending their talents to the creation of something new and better. For example, Andy specifically asked for a job related to the development of a defensive shield when he returned to the group. But in general, defense ideology does not seem to be a motive in their work. Carl Haussmann, the sage old administrator who keeps an eye on the S-1 Project, said the issue of strategic defense "wasn't required to make this an effective group at all. Some of the advanced concepts that these folks have been working on— the third-generation weapons—got started at this lab and were worked on by O Group before the Star Wars thing ever came along. And frankly, if SDI goes away tomorrow, some of those concepts will find other applications outside the SDI envelope. So I simply point out that SDI is an overlay which we all support—that is, more brain power studying the benefits of defensive systems. But there are technological paths opening up that will have a multitude of potential applications."

• The lab, as nowhere else on earth, gives Rod the opportunity to design big fusion engines to fulfill his dream of visiting the stars. In addition, Star Wars clearly promises the infusion of vast sums of money into the general development of space technologies. This is of great appeal to some science-fiction authors and fans, many of whom have stated that they plan to go into space on the back of the military. At a conference in November 1984, Rod and Lowell hinted at this confluence of interests in their presentation of a plan for a "laser railroad" that could put a million tons of shielding into space for the protection of orbital battle stations. An overview of their proposal was presented in the newsletter, *Military Space*. A cost-efficient "railroad" was needed, they said, because getting it up on the shuttle would cost "a few trillion dollars." They also said the laser railroad could loft sun reflectors into space for such jobs as nudging rainstorms over deserts. "We can thereby demonstrate our racial competence for terraforming other planets for human use by first bringing our own one to its full potential," they wrote.

• Larry went on at length about how defense could touch off economic competition with Russia, which would be good even if the Soviets put their money into producing offensive warheads. "I would like to see them try to escalate and spend their entire budget and see their country go to ruin," he said. In a similar way, the Reagan administration has long advocated such economic races as a means of trying to force economic reform in the Soviet Union. One danger of this approach is that economic and military issues can easily become confused. So what if a defensive shield doesn't work very well as long as it puts economic pressure on the Soviets? This kind of thinking might seem harmless, but only until buttons start getting pushed. If we really want to challenge the Russians economically, it might be safer to engage them in a race for world opinion by putting the possible trillion dollars for a space shield into economic aid for the Third World.

• Over dinner at the Danville Hotel, George was sincere in describing the intellectual drive behind his work on nuclear weapons. And Lowell mentioned it as well. This kind of nuclear curiosity is common among some physicists and is international in character. Both George and Lowell have been to Russia on several occasions, and their colleagues in Russia have been to the United States. Lowell's security slip came out at an international conference attended by Soviet scientists. Indeed, a cynic might view such genial professionalism as quiet collusion among the senior weapons scientists of East and West. After all, the arms race is in their best interest to the extent that it swells laboratory budgets and allows them to get on with the adventure of understanding the atom.

• Every engineer and scientist is delighted when they've got the right tools, and Livermore has the best. There are big lasers, supercomputers, electron microscopes, and whole laboratories devoted to the intricacies of micromanipulation. For Peter, the lab's supercomputers were the only way to run XRASER with any sort of efficiency. Livermore was also one of the few places on earth where he could hope to carry out an experimental program for the development of laboratory X-ray lasers. The Nova laser is a unique $176 million affair.

• As Lowell correctly pointed out, Peter sold himself on the nearly impossible goal of creating a laboratory X-ray laser. It was a pure scientific challenge. In a similar way, Larry is defying all his conservative peers by trying to singlehandedly create an optical computer. And where else but the S-1 Project can a graduate student get the chance to work on the construction of not just one but a whole series of supercomputers? Lowell prides himself on setting scientific goals that are virtually impossible to attain, a situation that sends some of the nation's most gifted graduate students into a frenzy of excitement.

• Larry, Andy, and Peter all emphasized the stimulation they gained from being with bright colleagues. It was fun. They worked together, ate together, played together, and lived together.

• The lab has many bright people who like to pit themselves against one another. This too is exciting. The competitive element in science is just as powerful as it is in sports or journalism, although it is usually downplayed in public arenas. Even with Peter, averse as he was to working on weapons, the competitive challenge from George seemed too much to resist.

• One result of fierce application can be notoriety. In November 1984, Peter was presented with the E. O. Lawrence Award of the Department of Energy, which carries a $10,000 prize. Peter was cited for "exceptional contributions to national security through his innovations and creativity in X-ray laser physics, including the prolific conception of X-ray laser schemes, the analysis of X-ray lasing phenomena, and the creation of extraordinary computational modeling tools." Peter is probably not driven by desire for prizes (except perhaps the Nobel). But their appearance after the fact is undoubtedly comforting.

• Tom seemed to suggest the possibility of diplomatic leverage that night over at his house. After talking about how the United States should show restraint in its "saber-rattling" for fear of the Soviets' launching a preemptive attack, he said: "If we're on the ball, we'll be able to extract across-the-board strategic arms reductions." Tom would never say so, but I got the impression that he views defense as a bargaining chip. Late that evening, in talking about the state of Soviet science, he said: "In the long run, I don't think we can count on any technological advantage." That kind of attitude does not lend itself to visions of American defensive battle stations able to outwit any kind of Soviet countermeasure.

• The aura of danger and risk associated with nuclear weapons and a defensive shield undoubtedly gives certain kinds of people a thrill, including some at the lab. I sensed this in a vague way during my visit, but the first time I heard it articulated was months later while talking with a former Hertz fellow who knew Lowell and the group. I asked why he thought they liked the weapons lab and mentioned their obvious excitement over access to good tools, friends, and ideas. "Sure," he said, "the lab has bright people and incredible resources, but so do a lot of universities. What makes them different is that theirs is also a power trip. What they're doing could save or destroy the world. They deal with that by enjoying it."

• What makes Lowell tick is difficult to determine. Perhaps a large part of his intensity derives from his relationship with Teller, who decades ago virtually adopted him as a son. It certainly has little to do with money, judging from his clothes, cars, and house. He does have careerist inclinations. When his climb up Livermore's bureaucratic ladder was frustrated, he made a remarkable come-back by throwing his energies into the development of the group of young scientists. And he obviously gets great joy out of being a bureaucratic catalyst. His comments on the race between Peter and George could only have been uttered by a man who enjoyed watch-ing the dash for the finish line. But it's more than that. Lowell as a young boy "brutalized" himself in order to learn math. He went on to take an undergraduate degree in mathematics. He is at war— with himself, the Soviets, the critics, and the world. But it's more than mere combativeness. He's on a nuclear crusade. As Herbert York, the first director of Livermore and later an advocate of arms control, remarked in *Race to Oblivion:* "The majority of the key individual promoters of the arms race derive a very large part of their self-esteem from their participation in what they believe to be an essential—even a holy—cause."

Such diverse motives are obviously not good or bad in them-selves. Many are found in any large group of scientists. But O Group is a key contestant in the arms race, and its members are telling us it's time to expand the scope of the competition. My only point is that there are many reasons beyond defense ideology or simple patriotism that keep the young scientists at work night after night in the seclusion of the Livermore valley.

To me, a large part of their enthusiasm stems from a desire to be at the forefront of science. O Group has no corner on such ambitions. There are many teams of young scientists around the country that burn with that kind of dedication. But Livermore does hold a special attraction because of its big tools—a situation that can produce curious diversions. Peter's story is clearly one of intellectual exploration that was forcibly diverted into weapons work. In the best of all possible worlds, Peter's kind of intensity and dedication would be harnessed to what I consider more productive ends. He would press a button, and money for challenging experiments would flow from the National Science Foundation. He would be a professor. He would share his enthusiasm with eager students. And society would benefit. Contrary to Peter's pessimism, laboratory X-ray lasers will find socially beneficial uses in the future. His sour outlook probably derives in part from compromises he made in the course of his work at Livermore. And despite his pessimism, he and his colleagues succeeded in creating the world's first laboratory X-ray laser. It took the efforts of Peter and a 40-member team from Livermore. The results, however, were less impressive than those of the first nuclear X-ray laser, which was said to have lased at the very short wavelength of 14 Angstroms. Working with the huge Novette laser at Livermore, the team was able to barely sneak into the X-ray region, reporting their optimal results to be at 155 Angstroms. At best, this point on the electromagnetic spectrum is considered a region of "soft" X-rays. The results were announced at a scientific meeting in Boston on October 29, 1984. Peter did not attend. In terms of elegance and achievement, his earlier accomplishment with the nuclear weapon in the Nevada desert stood unrivaled.

As long as the nuclear arms race exists, there have to be places like O Group to worry about the possibility of technological surprises. But there is an alternative. We and the Soviets and the other nuclear powers could negotiate a treaty that banned the testing of all nuclear weapons. More than any other step, this would help put a brake on the nuclear arms race.

For the moment, however, things are running unchecked. There is a big difference between keeping up your guard and mounting an all-out campaign. Under the auspices of the Strategic Defense

Initiative, billions of dollars are slated to flow into the development and testing of nuclear weapons. William W. Hoover, a retired Air Force Major-General and Assistant Secretary for Defense Programs at the Department of Energy, told me in an interview that the nation's weapon labs are now conducting tests of not only nuclear X-ray lasers but other third-generation weapons at the government's underground test site in Nevada. These might be EMP and microwave weapons. But maybe they are more exotic. The wizards of nuclear weaponry have other tricks up their sleeves—things like the brain bombs referred to by Nuckolls. Give the weapon makers enough money and they will transform heaven and earth.

Along with their labors go secrecy and all it implies for constricting the powers of the democratic process. This issue is seldom mentioned in the debate over Star Wars, yet it is vital to the future of the country. If the United States decides to go ahead and build a space-based defense, it will also be deciding to expand the hidden network of "skunk works" and secret laboratories, nuclear and otherwise, where young scientists will labor to try to produce the needed breakthroughs. O Groups will multiply. And contrary to comments by President Reagan, it is not likely that America will share its defense secrets with the Soviets. That would give them great leverage in outwitting an American shield.

Federal secrecy has already come into unusually wide play during the Reagan administration. According to a study by the General Accounting Office, in January 1983, just prior to the "Star Wars" speech, there were more than four *million* people in the United States holding security clearances. If a trillion-dollar program of space defense were to materialize, the number of clearances would soar. It would cause a fundamental shift in the character of American society. And secrecy is used not only to protect innovative ideas or system vulnerabilities but to mask bureaucratic error, turf expansion, and all the unsavory tactics that animate any large bureaucracy. It can hide correspondence that might prove embarrassing, as demonstrated by the American Presidents who sent classified letters to the lab. It can be a tool of manipulation, as shown by the government's selective declassification of secret material to "sell" controversial programs. It can also be the means of meting out punishment in policy disputes, as demonstrated by the Oppenheimer affair. Secrecy, even if sometimes necessary, is fundamentally at odds with democracy. Of course, in theory, our elected representatives are able to examine all that goes on in the dark corners of the government. But history shows that such supervision is often timid or missing altogether.

There are budgetary alternatives to pouring money into Star Wars. They are hackneyed and old but they need to be emphasized. We could expand the support of pure science. We could expand peaceful programs of space exploration and turn our enormous technological energies toward the stars. We could surprise the world and work with the Soviets on joint missions to the planets. We could support young scientists with federal grants and fellowships so they had alternatives to the Hertz Foundation.

During my stay at Livermore, I saw only a small and very selective part of what the lab had to offer. The vast majority of its citizens work behind closed doors and keep the results of their labors locked in safes. I got the razzle-dazzle tour and the heavy sales pitch on the possibilities for the creation of a nuclear shield. But most of it was abstractions and assertions. Only those with security clearances have an accurate idea of the actual state of nuclear research in the nation. And even they trade in abstractions. The young scientists have never seen the sky painted with the reds and oranges of a high-altitude nuclear explosion. They have never felt the flash of heat from a distant nuclear blast. They are creating a world of nuclear weapons they can know only through the sanitized flicker of electronic meters and the painstaking analysis of chart paper.

High-tech Gulags such as O Group are seductive. They push science and technology to the limit and impose none of the terrible physical privations of their Soviet counterparts. But in some respects they may be more insidious. The prisoners are there of their own accord, serving both science and war, creating in order to destroy, part of an elite yet pawns in a terrifying game.

ACKNOWLEDGMENTS

My thanks go first and foremost to members of O Group, S-1 Project, and R Program for their candor and hospitality. The book's conclusions are obviously my own, but I hope they find the reporting fair, accurate, and balanced, as promised. Most especially, thanks go to members of the group who facilitated my stay but who are not mentioned in the book, in particular Mike Farmwald, who kindly allowed me to turn his library into an office.

My gratitude also goes to the young scientists for their good judgment in a review we arranged of their remarks so they could catch any slips of classified information. Though journalistically unusual, the review was not unreasonable in light of their limited experience with reporters and the government's penalties for breaches of national security information. It follows that any federal secrets in the book are a result of my work and not theirs. For instance, the dates of particular nuclear X-ray laser experiments in Nevada are still secret although the existence of the device itself has been declassified. Some of the test dates were gleaned from *Aviation Week and Space Technology* or deduced from unclassified facts. Further, the young scientists provided no clues as to the correctness of my assertions in classified areas. In short, any federal secrets in the book come from previously published reports, my own deductions, or scientists outside the weapons lab.

Several individuals familiar with the workings of the atomic establishment gave generously of their time and expertise to help lay the foundations for this book and to review various drafts of the manuscript. Of necessity they remain anonymous. A heartfelt thanks to them for their assistance.

At the weapons lab, Mike Ross and Sue Stephenson of the public affairs department provided prompt and courteous assistance on numerous occasions over the months. Gloria Purpura, O Group's secretary, was the source of much help before, during, and after my visit. Outside Lowell's groups, many persons, too numerous to thank individually, kindly took time to be of assistance. In passing, some of them mentioned that they do not subscribe to all of Lowell's views. It goes without saying that Lowell's opinions are his own and do not necessarily reflect those of the federal government, the University of California, or the weapons lab.

In the city of Livermore, the Chamber of Commerce, the library, and the Heritage Guild were able providers of information. Barbara Bunshah of the Livermore History Center was especially helpful. Mike Nicholson, naturalist for the Livermore Area Recreation and Park District, kindly sent me material on the area's geology. Information on Simi Valley and the nearby rocket test facility was provided by Pat Havens of the Simi Valley Historical Society and Joyce Lincoln of the Rocketdyne Division of Rockwell International. Facts on the Hertz Foundation were gleaned from the exhaustive files of the Foundation Center of New York City.

For able assistance in the task of research, my gratitude belongs to Naomi J. Freundlich, Ryah Parker, and Lisa Peters.

For help and encouragement in preparation of the book, many thanks go to my family and to John T. Bosma, Paul Bracken, Joan Braderman, Jane E. Brody, Robert Ebisch, John and Karen Elliott, Richard Flaste, Linda J. Garmon, Jeff Gerth, Daniel Goleman, Constance Holden, Randi Hutter, Peter H. Lewis, William C. Maier, Carolyn Meinel, Henry Murphy, Holcomb B. Noble, John E. Pike, Wilmont Ragsdale, Michael Schrage, R. Jeffrey Smith, Josephine Stein, Marjorie Sun, Charles P. Vick, and Marsha Weiner.

At Simon and Schuster, Alice E. Mayhew, David Masello, and

Ann Godoff provided thoughtful comments and careful editing of the manuscript. My agent, Peter Matson, was the source of helpful suggestions and kind advice.

Last and far from least, my thanks go to Nicholas Wade, my co-author from another book, who provided the original idea for the week-in-the-life format, discerning comments on various drafts of the manuscript, and unfailing encouragement from start to finish.

William J. Broad
New York City
March 18, 1985

BIBLIOGRAPHY

Abrahamson, James A. "Statement on the Strategic Defense Initiative before the Republican Study Committee, House of Representatives, 98th Congress, Second Session," August 9, 1984.

Atkinson, Rick. "Underground Events Test Mettle of U.S. Atomic Arsenal," *The Washington Post,* May 29, 1984, section A, p. 1. An account of a DNA nuclear test in the Nevada desert.

Atomic Energy Commission. *In The Matter of J. Robert Oppenheimer: Transcript of Hearing before Personnel Security Board and Texts of Principal Documents and Letters* (MIT Press, Cambridge, 1970).

Aviation Week and Space Technology. "Technical Progress Dispels Skepticism on Laser Communications with Submarine," January 21, 1985, p. 121.

———. "Soviets Ready New Boosters at Tyuratam," August 27, 1984, p. 18.

———. "Laser Test," June 13, 1983, p. 15. Account of a nuclear X-ray laser experiment in Nevada.

———. "Livermore Laboratory to Boost Research on Nuclear Weapons," February 22, 1982, p. 56.

———. "Technology Eyed to Defend ICBMs, Spacecraft," July 28, 1980, p. 32. First hint of work on nuclear X-ray laser.

Berman, Robert P., and John C. Baker. *Soviet Strategic Forces* (The Brookings Institution, Washington, 1982).

Bernstein, Jeremy. *Hans Bethe: Prophet of Energy* (Basic Books, New York, 1980).

Bethe, Hans A., et al. *Space-Based Missile Defense* (Union of Concerned Scientists, Cambridge, March 1984). Expanded and reissued as *The Fallacy of Star Wars* (Vintage, New York, 1984).

———. "Reagan for the Defense," *Time,* April 4, 1983, p. 8. Contains Bethe's skeptical remark on strategic defense.

———. "Comments on The History of the H-Bomb," *Los Alamos Science,* Fall 1982, p. 43. Declassified text of 1954 article outlining Teller's mathematical errors.

Blumberg, Stanley A., and Gwinn Owens. *Energy and Conflict: The Life and Times of Edward Teller* (G. P. Putnam's Sons, New York, 1976).

Boatman, Bruce M. *Institutional Plan FY 83-88* (UCAR-10076-2, Lawrence Livermore National Laboratory, December 1982).

Boffey, Philip M. "Scientists Urged by Pope to Say No to War Research," *The New York Times,* November 13, 1983, section A, p. 1.

Bracken, Paul. *The Command and Control of Nuclear Forces* (Yale University Press, New Haven, 1983).

Broad, William J. "Reagan's Star Wars Bid: Many Ideas Converging," *The New York Times,* March 4, 1985, section A, p. 1. Review of Reagan's long interest in space-based defense and Teller's visits to the White House.

———. "Star Wars Research Forges Ahead," *The New York Times,* February 5, 1985, section C, p. 1. Contains General Hoover's remark that nuclear tests of third-generation weapons have expanded beyond X-ray laser.

———. "Reduced Goal Set On Reagan's Plan for Space Defense," *The New York Times,* December 23, 1984, section A, p. 1.

———. "The Young Physicists: Atoms and Patriotism Amid the Coke Bottles," *The New York Times,* January 31, 1984, section C, p. 1.

———. "Some Atomic Tests Being Kept Secret By Administration," *The New York Times,* January 29, 1984, section A, p. 1.

———. "X-ray Laser Weapon Gains Favor," *The New York Times,* November 15, 1983, section C, p. 1.

———. "The Chaos Factor," *Science 83,* January-February 1983, p. 40. Review of nuclear EMP effects.

———. "Rewriting the History of the H-Bomb," *Science,* November

19, 1982, p. 769. Background on Teller's mathematical errors and Bethe's 1954 paper.

Brown, Harold. "Reagan's Risky Approach," *The New York Times,* March 10, 1985, section E, p. 23.

Byrd, Lee. "Administration, Senators Clash Over Star Wars Plan," Associated Press, AA0665, April 25, 1984.

Carter, Ashton B. *Directed Energy Missile Defense in Space* (Office of Technology Assessment, Congress of the United States, Washington, April 1984).

————, and David N. Schwartz (Eds.). *Ballistic Missile Defense* (The Brookings Institution, Washington, 1984).

Chapline, George, and Lowell Wood. "X-ray lasers," *Physics Today,* June 1975, p. 40.

Citizens Advisory Council on National Space Policy. *America: A Spacefaring Nation* (L-5 Society, Tucson, 1983).

————. *Space: The Crucial Frontier* (L-5 Society, Tucson, 1981).

Cochran, Thomas B., William M. Arkin, and Milton M. Hoenig. *Nuclear Weapons Databook, Volume I: U.S. Nuclear Forces and Capabilities* (Ballinger, Cambridge, 1984).

D'Adamo, Amadeo F. "Wages of Star Wars Is a Plutonium Shroud," *The New York Times,* November 9, 1984, section A, p. 30.

Day, Kathleen. "Helionetics and Blue-Green Laser," *The Los Angeles Times,* May 13, 1984, section 5, p. 1.

DeLauer, Richard D. "People Protection Act," *Hearing on H. R. 3073* (U.S. Government Printing Office, Washington, 1983), pp. 17–31. Testimony given on November 10, 1983 before the Research and Development Subcommittee and Investigations Subcommittee of the Committee on Armed Services, House of Representatives, 98th Congress, First Session.

Department of Defense. *Soviet Military Power 1984* (U.S. Government Printing Office, Washington, 1984).

Department of Energy. *Announced United States Nuclear Tests July 1945 Through December 1983* (NVO-209 Rev. 4, Department of Energy, Las Vegas, January 1984).

De Volpi, A., et al. *Born Secret: The H-bomb, the Progressive Case and National Security* (Pergamon Press, New York, 1981). An overview of the issue of atomic secrecy.

Douglass, Joseph D., Jr., and Amoretta M. Hoeber. *Soviet Strategy for Nuclear War* (Hoover Institution, Stanford, 1979).

Drell, Sidney D., Philip J. Farley, and David Holloway. *The Reagan Strategic Defense Initiative: A Technical, Political, and Arms Control Assessment* (Center for International Security and Arms Control, Stanford University, July 1984). A 142-page critique of Star Wars.

Dyson, Freeman. *Weapons and Hope* (Harper & Row, New York, 1984).

Edson, Lee. "Scientific Man For All Seasons," *The New York Times Magazine,* March 10, 1968, p. 29. A profile of Hans Bethe.

Evans, Larry, and Ken Smith. *Chess World Championship 1972: Fischer vs. Spassky* (Simon and Schuster, New York, 1973).

Fiske, Edward B. *Selective Guide to Colleges 1984–85* (Times Books, New York, 1983).

Frey, Alton. "Strategic Myths Mislead Reagan," *The Washington Post,* October 2, 1983, section C, p. 5.

General Accounting Office. "Effect of National Security Decision Directive—84, Safeguarding National Security Information" (GAO/ NSIAD-84-26, B-206067, General Accounting Office, Congress of the United States, Washington, October 18, 1983).

Gerth, Jeff. "Reagan Advisors Received Stock in Laser Concern," *The New York Times,* April 28, 1983, section A, p. 1. Account of Teller's link to Helionetics.

Glasstone, Samuel, and Philip J. Dolan. *The Effects of Nuclear Weapons* (U.S. Government Printing Office, Washington, 1977).

Groueff, Stephane. *Manhattan Project* (Little, Brown & Co., Boston, 1967).

Hagelstein, Peter L., et al. "Exploding-Foil Technique for Achieving a Soft X-ray Laser," *Physical Review Letters,* January 14, 1985, p. 106. This and next reference report on success of laboratory X-ray laser.

———, et al. "Demonstration of a Soft X-Ray Amplifier," *Physical Review Letters,* January 14, 1985, p. 110.

———. "Laser-Heated Flashlamps: A Step toward a Soft X-ray Laser," (Lawrence Livermore National Laboratory) *Energy and Technology Review,* January 1983, p. 23. Review of Livermore work on laboratory X-ray lasers.

———. *Physics of Short Wavelength Laser Design* (UCRL-53100, Lawrence Livermore National Laboratory, 1981). His Ph.D. thesis.

Hart, Gary, and Barry Goldwater. "Recent False Alerts from the Nation's Missile Attack Warning System," *Report to the Senate Committee on Armed Services* (U.S. Government Printing Office, Washington, October 9, 1980).

Hecht, Jeff. *Beam Weapons: The Next Arms Race* (Plenum, New York, 1984). An introduction to laser physics and the nuclear X-ray laser.

Heppenheimer, T. A. *The Man-Made Sun* (Little, Brown & Co., Boston, 1984).

Hersey, John. *The Child Buyer* (Knopf, New York, 1960).

Hertz Foundation, Fannie and John. "Purpose" (Hertz Foundation, P.O. Box 2230, Livermore, California 94550). A six-page brochure on the fellowship program.

———. *Directory of Fannie and John Hertz Foundation Fellows 1983–84* (Hertz Foundation, 1983). A 463-page book listing former and current fellows, their backgrounds, and their employers.

Hyde, Roderick A. "Cosmic Bombardment" (UCID-20062, Lawrence Livermore National Laboratory, March 19, 1984). A proposal to move earth-threatening asteroids with nuclear weapons.

———. "A Laser Fusion Rocket For Interplanetary Propulsion" (UCRL-88857, Lawrence Livermore National Laboratory, September 27, 1983).

———. "Earthbreak: A Review of Earth-to-Space Transportation" (UCRL-89252, Lawrence Livermore National Laboratory, May 24, 1983).

Jungk, Robert. *Brighter than a Thousand Suns: A Personal History of the Atomic Scientists* (Harcourt Brace Jovanovich, New York, 1958). A history of the Manhattan Project and its aftermath.

Keller, Bill. "U.S. Seeks Missiles to Evade Defenses," *The New York Times,* February 11, 1985, section A, p. 1.

Keyworth, George A., II. "March 23—Six Months Later," October 13, 1983. Speech to the Washington Chapter of the Armed Forces Communications and Electronics Association.

Kissinger, Henry A. "Soviet Signals are Changing," *The Los Angeles Times*, September 23, 1984, section 4, p. 1.

Kucewicz, William. "The Science of Snake Venom," *The Wall Street Journal,* April 25, 1984, section 1, p. 30.

Lawrence Livermore National Laboratory. "State of the Laboratory," *Energy and Technology Review,* July 1984. An 86-page look at the lab's funding and programs.

———. "30 Years of Technical Excellence: 1952-1982." A 90-page overview.

———. "LLL: 25 years in pictures." A photo brochure commemorating the lab's silver anniversary.

LeMay, Curtis E., and Dale O. Smith. *America Is in Danger* (Funk & Wagnalls, New York, 1968).

Marling, Jack B., et al. "An Ultra-High Q, Isotropically Sensitive Optical Filter Employing Atomic Resonance Transitions" (UCRL-80910, Lawrence Livermore National Laboratory, January 1978).

———, et al. "Advanced Blue-Green Electro-Optics: Very Narrow Bandwidth, Wide Field-of-View Detectors" (UCID-17915, Lawrence Livermore National Laboratory, September 30, 1977).

Maust, R. L., G. W. Goodman, Jr., and C. E. McLain. *History of Stra-tegic Defense* (System Planning Corporation, Arlington, Virginia, 1981).

Military Space. "Livermore Scientists Propose Laser Railroad," December 10, 1984, p. 3.

Miller, Judith. "New Generation of Nuclear Arms with Controlled Effects Foreseen," *The New York Times,* October 29, 1982, section A, p. 1. An early account of third-generation weapons.

Niven, Larry. *Ringworld* (Ballantine, New York, 1981).

Norman, Colin. "Weapons Proposal Stirs Disquiet at Stanford," *Science,* February 25, 1983, p. 936.

————. "Science Adviser Post Has Nominee in View," *Science,* May 22, 1981, p. 903. Background on appointment of Keyworth as Reagan's science advisor.

Reagan, Ronald. "President's News Conference on Foreign and Domestic Issues," *The New York Times,* January 10, 1985, section B, p. 8.

————. "President's Speech on Military Spending and a New Defense," *The New York Times,* March 24, 1983, section A, p. 20. The "Star Wars" speech.

Robinson, Arthur L. "Soft X-ray Laser at Lawrence Livermore Lab," *Science,* November 16, 1984, p. 821. Account of Livermore's success with laboratory X-ray laser.

————. "X-ray Holography Experiment Planned," *Science,* January 29, 1982, p. 488. Account of Livermore proposal to make holograms of biological molecules with nuclear X-ray laser.

Robinson, Clarence A., Jr. "Study Urges Exploiting of Technologies," *Aviation Week and Space Technology,* October 24, 1983, p. 50. Details of the Fletcher report.

————. "Advance Made on High-Energy Laser," *Aviation Week and Space Technology,* February 23, 1981, p. 25. Account of first successful test of nuclear X-ray laser.

Rogers, Keith. "New Role Seen for Lab: President's Adviser Predicts Shift in Research," (Livermore, California) *Valley Times,* January 16, 1983, p. 1. An account of speech in which Keyworth hailed the nuclear X-ray laser.

Sakharov, Andrei. "The Danger of Thermonuclear War," *Foreign Affairs,* Summer 1983, p. 1001.

Satterthwaite, Bob. "Former Resident Wins Nuclear Award," (Simi Valley, California) *Enterprise Sun & News,* February 29, 1982.

Scowcroft, Brent. *Report of the President's Commission on Strategic Forces* (White House, Washington, April 1983).

Shanor, Donald R. *Behind the Lines: The Private War Against Soviet Censorship* (St. Martin's Press, New York, 1985).

Smith, R. Jeffrey. "Weapons Bureaucracy Spurns Star Wars Goal," *Science,* April 6, 1984, p. 32.

Solzhenitsyn, Aleksandr I. *The Gulag Archipelago* (Harper & Row, New York, 1973).

Stein, Josie. "Fellowship for Work on 'Human Problems' Linked to Livermore" (Massachusetts Institute of Technology), *Link,* November 3-16, 1980, p. 1.

Teller, Edward. "Third Generation Systems," *Hearings on H.R. 2287 Department of Defense Authorization of Appropriations For Fiscal Year 1984* (U.S. Government Printing Office, Washington, 1983), pp. 1353-1371. Testimony given on April 28, 1983 before Committee on Armed Services, House of Representatives, 98th Congress, First Session.

―――. "Of Laser Weapons and Dr. Teller's Stock," *The New York Times,* July 1, 1983, section A, p. 22. Letter of rebuttal to Gerth article.

―――. "Not Only Humane, but Truly Effective," *U.S. News & World Report,* May 26, 1969, p. 87. Interview in support of Safeguard.

―――, and Allen Brown. *The Legacy of Hiroshima* (Doubleday, New York, 1962).

Vick, Charles P. "The Soviet G-1-e Manned Lunar Landing Programme Booster," *Journal of the British Interplanetary Society*, Vol. 38 (1985), p. 11.

Wade, Nicholas. "Defense Scientists Differ on Nuclear Stockpile Testing," *Science,* September 22, 1978, p. 1105. An account of President Carter's attempt at a comprehensive ban on the testing of nuclear weapons.

―――. "Safeguard: Disputed Weapon Nears Readiness on Plains of North Dakota," *Science,* September 27, 1974, p. 1137.

Walbridge, Edward W. "Angle Constraint for Nuclear-Pumped X-ray Laser Weapons," *Nature,* July 19, 1984, p. 180.

Watson, James D. *The Double Helix* (Atheneum, New York, 1968).

Weaver, Thomas A. "The Evolution of Massive Stars and the Origin of the Elements," (Lawrence Livermore National Laboratory) *Energy and Technology Review,* February 1980, p. 1.

West, Karen. "Interest in Chemist's Lab Started Scientist's Career," (Simi Valley, California) *Enterprise Sun & News,* March 2, 1982.

White House. *The President's Strategic Defense Initiative,* January 1985. A 10-page overview of the program's objectives.

Wood, Lowell, and Willard F. Libby. "Geophysical Implications of Radiocarbon Date Discrepancies," Chapter 16 of *Isotopic and Cosmic Chemistry* (North Holland Publishing Co., New York, 1964).

Wooten, Frederick. "Department of Applied Science: An Experiment in Graduate Education," (Lawrence Livermore National Laboratory) *Energy and Technology Review,* July 1978, p. 19.

York, Herbert. *The Advisors: Oppenheimer, Teller, and the Superbomb* (W. H. Freeman, San Francisco, 1976).

———. *Race to Oblivion* (Simon & Schuster, New York, 1970).

Zuckerman, Edward. *The Day After World War III* (Viking, New York, 1984).

Zumwalt, Elmo R., Jr. *On Watch* (Quadrangle, New York, 1976).

INDEX

ABOUT THE AUTHOR

William J. Broad is one of the most widely read science news reporters for *The New York Times*. He writes on a variety of topics, including "Star Wars," the space shuttle, computers, nuclear and conventional weaponry, physics, and the history of science. Mr. Broad holds a master's degree in History of Science from the University of Wisconsin and has been a reporter for *Science* and *Science News*. In 1981 he won the prestigious Science-in-Society Journalism Award, given by the National Association of Science Writers. He is the coauthor of the well-received book *Betrayers of the Truth: Fraud and Deceit in the Halls of Science*.